Learning About Women

GENDER, POLITICS, AND POWER

Jill K. Conway, Susan C. Bourque,
and Joan W. Scott, Editors

The University of Michigan Press   Ann Arbor

First published by The University of Michigan Press 1989
Copyright © 1987 by the American Academy of Arts and Sciences
All rights reserved

ISBN 0-472-09398-3 (clothbound)
ISBN 0-472-06398-7 (paperback)
Library of Congress Catalog Card No. 88-40604
Published in the United States of America by
The University of Michigan Press
Manufactured in the United States of America

1992   1991   4   3

This volume was originally published as the Fall 1987 issue of
Daedalus, Volume 116, Number 4, of the *Proceedings of the American
Academy of Arts and Sciences*.

Contents

Preface

IT IS ALMOST A QUARTER OF A CENTURY since *Dædalus* published its Spring 1964 issue entitled "The Woman in America," including articles by Erik Erikson and David Riesman, Alice Rossi and Edna Rostow, Esther Peterson and Lotte Bailyn, Jill Conway and Joan Erikson.[1] Subsequent hardcover and paperback book editions, edited by Robert J. Lifton, also included essays by Diana Trilling and David McClelland.

"The Woman in America," emerging when it did, had an enormous resonance. As the subject of a retrospective article written for this issue by Carl N. Degler (who also wrote for the original *Dædalus* study), it describes a world both familiar and strange. Degler's observations in "On Rereading 'The Woman in America' " suggest how substantial the changes have been since 1964, and why an ideological revolution, which he himself did not predict, has been so influential. While substantial political, social, and economic transformations have certainly taken place in the period between 1964 and the present, it is possible to exaggerate their depth and to believe that they have eradicated all inequities. The truth, in fact, is more complex; while there have been major advances, there have also been significant setbacks. The American political and social environments have been hospitable to a concern with equal rights for some time now, and the condition of women in American society has improved substantially since 1964. But the criteria used for judging that condition have also changed, and this, in time, may be seen as the most significant development of the period.

This change is at least partly due to new scholarship and new thinking about women. That feminists and others who write about women today do not do so in the manner of the 1960s is clearly evident in this issue. The title "Learning About Women" is meant to be ambiguous. The word *learning,* both noun and verb, conveys a double meaning: there is, incontestably, a new scholarship; that scholarship, in the questions it poses about the past and the present, challenges accepted opinion. In subjecting certain stereotypes and myths to a kind of critical examination they have not traditionally received, but also in exploring wholly new domains and directing attention to new themes, this scholarship leads to new discovery and the possibility of new learning, new understanding.

The term *gender,* which figures so prominently in this issue, had no place at all in the index of either the hardcover or the paperback book edition of the 1964 *Dædalus* issue. While there were numerous references to careers, child care, educated women, equality of the sexes, father's role in the home, feminism, freedom for women, marriage, mother-child relations, motherhood, occupations, parenthood, professional women, sex differences, sexual freedom, wages, and working women, the word *gender* was conspicuous for its absence. One is reminded of what Raymond Williams wrote in his book, *Culture and Society, 1780–1950:*

In the last decades of the eighteenth century, and in the first half of the nineteenth century, a number of words, which are now of capital importance, came for the first time into common English use, or, where they had already been generally used in the language, acquired new and important meanings. There is in fact a general pattern of change in these words, and this can be used as a special kind of map by which it is possible to look again at those wider changes in life and thought to which the changes in language evidently refer.

Five words are the key points from which this map can be drawn. They are *industry, democracy, class, art* and *culture.* The importance of these words, in our modern structure of meanings, is obvious. The changes in their use, at this critical period, bear witness to a general change in our characteristic ways of thinking about our common life: about our social, political and economic institutions; about the purposes which these institutions are designed to embody; and about the relations to these institutions and purposes of our activities in learning, education and the arts.[2]

The lexical process that Williams describes continues into the present. *Gender,* a term much used in sociological literature, has taken on new meanings in recent decades as scholars have gained new insights into the social organization of the relations between the sexes. Implicit in the new definitions of *gender* is a rejection of the idea that "biology is destiny"—that there is some sort of biological determinism at work in the world and that this force derives principally from sexual difference. The new scholarship emphasizes the cultural, social, political, and economic forces that influence social behavior and create specific patterns in the relations between men and women. By definition, these forces and patterns are not immutable; they change over time. The current concern with gender, in its social, cultural, and political manifestations, originated in studies of women. But several of the authors in this *Dædalus* issue argue that if gender is to become an analytical category of major importance—comparable, for example, to concepts of class, race, or nation—it cannot remain so narrowly confined; discussions of gender must include women *and* men. Indeed, the issue "Learning About Women" should be read as part of an ongoing effort to remind a society that is overwhelmingly present-centered that many conditions—more than are normally considered—have deep historical roots, and that many of today's popular romantic jeremiads that extoll the more virtuous and moral past are pure inventions.

Because the idea of gender is central to this issue, the three guest editors, Jill K. Conway, Susan C. Bourque, and Joan W. Scott, have coauthored a brief explanatory introduction on the concept. Recalling how important were the sociological theories of Talcott Parsons in the 1960s, and how influential were the psychological views of Freud, which so dominated social scientific inquiry in the interwar years and the immediate post-World War II period, it is not surprising that Margaret Mead's theory (advanced in 1935) that concepts of gender are principally cultural, not biological, did not take hold. That idea has taken on new life only recently, in a highly transmuted form. Today there is interest in gender as a social category, as a device for understanding the hierarchical orders that exist in various societies, and as a key to the complex relationships between men and women that distinguish one society from another.

Gender boundaries shift and change over time, and historians who have analyzed these fluctuations have done much to illuminate the subject of gender. So also have political theorists, anthropologists, psychologists, economists, and many others whose principal preoccupations are art, literature, or religion. Recent scholarship on gender has greatly increased our awareness of complex social and cultural processes that were once largely ignored. It is not only the family that is seen in new perspective, but all sorts of other social, economic, and political institutions that are powerfully influenced by gender stereotypes. Gender studies, in challenging conventional views of male and female attributes (in which society is characterized by a division of labor based on the male's characteristic *instrumental* behavior pattern and the female's characteristic *expressive* behavior pattern), call into question many of the shibboleths of an earlier day. Such views are today seen to be historically and anthropologically false. Behavior once thought deviant because it departed from a commonly accepted gender norm is interpreted in new ways. Indeed, all sorts of binary constructs based on biological difference are being reconsidered, making it less legitimate to characterize certain activities as male, others as female. The whole issue of equality takes on a new dimension when gender, as a culturally-determined phenomenon, is considered a historical force. Established gender categories may have created a two-tiered labor market that is immensely resistant to change, but this neither legitimates that market nor guarantees its permanence. Conway, Bourque, and Scott, sharing a view of gender categories that owe a great deal to culture and history, see them as reflecting something other than a preordained natural binary system.

Because an examination of political participation is crucial to any study of gender in contemporary society, this issue includes an essay on citizenship. Mary G. Dietz, investigating the political situation in the United States, focuses on how liberals have traditionally defined citizenship and why many feminists have found liberal concepts unacceptable. Dietz tells us that the liberals' notion that individuals exist as discrete and abstract entities devoted to liberty and equality bears the unmistakable mark of its origins in early capitalist society. Liberalism's commitment to individual self-interest and the pursuit of profit is predicated on an image of the individual as an actor in an economic marketplace in which (to quote Adam Smith) "the race for wealth, and honors, and preferments" can safely be pursued. In liberalism's terms, Dietz writes, "citizenship becomes less a collective, political activity than an individual, economic activity—the right to pursue one's interests, without hindrance, in the marketplace." As for democracy, liberalism defines it principally as the citizen's right to vote rather than in terms of collective, participatory activities.

Such liberal values may hold only limited appeal for two groups of feminists discussed by Dietz. While these feminist critics of liberalism may be very willing to work for specific liberal political goals— extension of pregnancy leaves, more and better child-care facilities, improved health care benefits, and the like—this will not lead them to embrace the liberal system. Whether they are Marxists (who insist on the capitalist and patriarchal foundations of the liberal state, empha- size the oppression inherent in sexual division of labor, and view politics largely as a revolutionary struggle) or maternalists (who insist on the significance of women's experience as mothers and are hostile to the male individualist world view with its limited notion of citizenship), most are unsympathetic to prevailing liberal ideas. If Marxist feminist theories have not contributed greatly to the devel- opment of a new idea of citizenship, maternalist theories have; Carol Gilligan's distinction between a female "ethic of care" and a male "ethic of justice" implies that responsibility and relationships may be as important as rights; that compassion, so essential in the life of the family, may be the route to a new "mode of public discourse."

While Dietz criticizes the maternalist theories and their emphasis on a binary model that she rejects, she is not unaware of the contributions the maternalists have made to a new view of citizen- ship. Her own preference, however, is for a theory that is more radical, less tinged with the colors, however muted, of traditional liberalism. Disdaining representative government, she argues instead for "participatory engagement," a form of democracy that she believes will bring individuals together as citizens and compel them to be active—concerned not only with the social or economic grievances of specific interest groups or with single-issue politics, but committed to public discourse and to self-government in the best sense of the term. For such a new feminist theory of citizenship to succeed, there must be a denial of the maternalist presumption that women have a "superior democratic nature," a more mature political voice; indeed, the whole idea of gender opposition, of female superiority, must be set aside.

Because political engagement is such a crucial contemporary theme, central to any study of gender, it seemed useful to ask two prominent political figures—both women, one in the United Kingdom and one in the United States—to reflect on women and politics in democratic societies. "Women in the Political World: Observations" is the result of joining together in a single document material derived from separate discussions with Shirley Williams and Elizabeth Holtzman. The commentary of the two politicians serves to emphasize certain major congruities, yet at the same time reveals differences that cannot be attributed solely to two styles of politics, one North American, the other British. Whether the issue is, as Holtzman implies, that there is still a strong popular sentiment that political office is "man's work," that senior-level executive positions generally call for qualities that women are unlikely to possess, or whether, as Williams suggests, the problem is really one of image, of what a woman is expected to be, and how enormously difficult it is for a woman in politics to conform to that image, both see that women have not made the political strides that early advocates of universal suffrage anticipated. Williams suggests, however, that it may be easier for a woman to make a career of politics in Great Britain than in the United States, and that this phenomenon has deep historical roots. The tradition of women rulers—the institution of monarchy itself—contributes in important ways; so also, in Williams's view, does the fact that there is less ambiguity in Britain about the role of the career woman than there is in the United States. Holtzman, knowing that few women have ever served in Congress (either in the House or in the Senate), and knowing how relatively easy it is for elected incumbents to remain in office in the United States, suggests that the incumbency advantage makes any sudden intrusion of large numbers of women virtually impossible. Still, changes are occurring, particularly at the municipal and state levels of U.S. government; elected positions at those levels can serve as stepping-stones to higher office. In Britain, where membership in Parliament is *the* political career, and a most demanding one, the task of caring for a family while at the same time tending to the interests of constituents is almost too daunting. According to Williams, until there is a revolution in child care and in childrearing, only a small number of British women will opt for a career in politics. Holtzman speaks of the difficulties American women experience in securing adequate funds for their political campaigns. This does not appear to be a problem in Britain, where Williams says "you can still run for peanuts." How women comport themselves in office, what help they seek, what issues are paramount to them and why, all relate to a larger question: What is the "patronage" or "support" system that works for women, that they can use both to advance their careers and to satisfy the interests they seek to represent and serve?

To move from politics to war—from reflections of the active politician to the study of the commemorative architectural monuments erected to honor those who fell in battle—may seem a dramatic and almost incongruous leap. In fact, it is not. As Ken Inglis attests in writing about the war memorials erected in Australia after World War I, these monuments are immensely expressive "documents," quite telling in their symbolic representations of both feminine and masculine virtue, at least as Australian society chose to record them. Because women were excluded from the fighting fronts, except those who chose to serve in the traditional female role of nurse, they figured only rarely in the memorials erected after 1918. When women were part of these Australian monuments, they appeared as "mothers of the race" or symbolic representations of Victory or Peace, but seldom as emblems of Liberty. The heavily masculine celebrations and rituals regularly enacted around these monuments emphasized military valor; they were organized principally by ex-soldiers. Not until 1966 were these traditional ceremonies ever regarded as provocative, an affront to a new generation of Australian women who rejected the values that they expressed. A collection of war memorials that had served to commemorate valor—to equate the citizen and the soldier, to make military service seem more consequential than any other—was suddenly brought into question. The ordinary soldier, who had once symbolized the nation's highest ideals and values, was not literally removed from his pedestal, but the easy and almost automatic acceptance of him as hero and model citizen was fundamentally challenged. A new generation's rejection of the gender stereotypes and values of a preceding one was manifested in its own demonstrations and celebrations. The earlier memory was not eradicated; it was simply built upon. The contribution of contemporary scholarship is to show how this can have happened.

If the soldier in Australia is (or was) a hero, the "schoolmarm" in the United States, endowed by popular mythology and folklore with extraordinary attributes, enjoyed a somewhat more ambivalent status. In most European societies, teaching remained a predominantly male profession until well into the twentieth century. In the United States, however, public education became increasingly dependent on the recruitment of young women as teachers after the middle of the nineteenth century. Jill K. Conway, in explaining how the teaching profession came to be female-dominated and what the consequences of this were for teachers, children, and American society, sees it as something other than an "enlightened policy" created to provide opportunity for worthy and respectable young single women. America's teachers, we are told, were rarely well educated. Most came to their positions with only the most rudimentary education, and the normal schools many attended provided what might best be described as remedial instruction. Women teachers, paid about 60 percent of what their male colleagues earned, were "boarded out," lodged with the families of students. This boarding system made good economic sense because it reduced the costs of public education borne by the community. It also commended itself for moral reasons, ostensibly providing a system of protecting women against impropriety. In such a system, marriage spelled the end of a career; consequently, teacher turnover was heavy and frequent. Why, then, was the predominantly female teaching corps established and accepted?

According to Conway, the U.S. public education system (which began in the Jacksonian era) was not conceived as an agency for intellectual development; it was seen as a social service, an extension of the home and its predominantly maternal values, to be provided at minimal cost to the community. The gender stereotypes of the day made it seem only logical that women should be the teachers in such a system. Women were believed to be particularly adept at tending to the emotional needs of the young and influencing their behavior and character. For such ends, no rigorous educational training was deemed either necessary or useful; any good healthy woman could be expected to do the job well.

Women teachers of the late nineteenth century were not likely to succeed at challenging either the male political and economic elites that had created the public school system or the gender stereotypes that were largely responsible for the public's ambivalence about the value and importance of teaching. Gender-based assumptions about female temperament and motivation had an enormous influence upon how schools were organized, what was taught, and why public education in the United States never developed the intellectual ambitions that were common elsewhere. To study American education through the lens of gender is to see how a major social system was shaped by opinion, myth, and stereotype—how politics and economic considerations intervened to create a distinctively American institution that had a tremendous impact on the whole society. In the United States, perceived gender differences may have served to mask fundamental political tensions that the traditional American democratic rhetoric could never openly acknowledge.

If school teaching was predominantly a woman's profession in America, the same could not be said for university teaching. Joan W. Scott, in analyzing how women have been treated in the latter profession, is concerned not so much with the barriers established to impede their entry as with how those fared who managed to make their way in. Examining the situation in her own discipline, history, she recognizes that women, like blacks and others minorities, were once considered marginal; their place in the profession mirrored their place in the historical narratives that were written. White men dominated not only the historical profession, but also the histories that emerged, even when those histories purported to treat Universal Man, humankind. Women, in short, were rendered invisible. In the spirit of democracy, the American Historical Association (AHA), founded in 1884, explicitly included women as members; but it was taken for granted that the women historians would write "scientific history," the new, robust, "masculine" kind that avoided the romanticism, the "feminine" antiquarianism, of another day. Because female teachers predominated in women's academies and colleges, it was hoped that their admission into the profession might make them active proselytizers for the "new" history, which was largely a study of political progress toward democracy.

The prototypical historical figure of the late nineteenth century (and well beyond) was a white Anglo-Saxon Western man. It was not acknowledged that women might have a particular kind of historical experience worthy of investigation. Men were the activists; women helped as "devoted" and "faithful" subordinates whose "natural" endowments were praised. Because of these gender stereotypes, women never achieved leadership roles in the profession. While the number of women historians grew, as it did in the 1920s and 1930s, most were consigned to teaching in women's colleges or on undergraduate faculties. In 1943, however, through a coalition of "progressive" historians and organized feminists, a woman, Nellie Neilson, became president of the AHA. But as Scott explains, this did not mean that the battle for equality had been won. After World War II, American historians began again to dwell on the necessity of preserving national tradition, to expatiate on the progress of democracy, echoing the Cold War ideology of the day. In such an environment, a new kind of history could not flourish. Thus, after a brief opening, the doors were closed again to women, to be reopened only in the late 1960s.

The second door-opening was more important than the first because it implied that another kind of history could be written—that what had been so long considered marginal could in fact be made central. With the emergence of a feminism committed to the organization of women's caucuses, the publication of separate journals, and a commitment to write women's history, there was a real hazard that the documentation of a women's world would become an end in itself. "Women's history" would be set off in a separate compartment, separated from "mainstream" history. The challenge, according to Scott, is not to stop with the creation of new chairs in women's history, but to incorporate the story of women within a larger context that treats humanity as a diverse—not unitary—concept.

Miriam Slater and Penina Migdal Glazer, while taking into account all that has happened to open the professions in America to women—noting, for example, that women now constitute one-third of the entering class in medical schools and half of those who enter law schools—know that this is the second feminist wave in the twentieth century. The first, which made significant headway during the early years of the century, lost its momentum during the conservative 1920s and the Depression-ridden 1930s. It is important to consult this historical record because women today are experiencing analogous resistances, and are in fact compelled to respond with strategies that have good historical antecedents. For example, some women seek to prove themselves as superperformers, more able and committed than any of their male colleagues. There are certain difficulties involved in doing this. It is hard to be a superperformer in a country without an adequate national system of day care, where salary differentials persist, and where women still bear the major responsibility for child care and household management. An alternative strategy for women is what the authors call "voluntary subordination," or the willingness to accept a position beneath one's qualifications in order to minimize tensions. If the role of assistant carries fewer burdens and receives less recognition in rewards or status, it is also less threatening. Today, as yesterday, certain positions are still regarded as uniquely suited to women because they are thought to require such stereotypical female qualities as "nurturance, self-sacrifice, limited ambition, and a lack of concern with financial reward." The "helping professions" are still deemed particularly suited to women, and some in our society have no wish to see this change.

Yet another strategy, that of "innovation," leads women to enter professions in which they do not directly compete with men because the fields themselves are women's "creation." Like others, this strategy has historical antecedents, and the authors give particular attention to the career of Alice Hamilton and her contributions to the development of industrial medicine. When Harvard decided to make an appointment in that area after the First World War, Hamilton was chosen, mostly because there was no other qualified candidate available. This, however, did not make her especially welcome to male colleagues on the Harvard Medical School faculty, nor did it serve to encourage other appointments of women. Indeed, it did not even influence the admission of women students, which came in 1945, six years after Hamilton's retirement. Given such conditions, it is not surprising that many women, searching for sociability and colleagueship, chose to make their careers in female-led institutions. In the United States, women's colleges played a significant role as the continuous employers of professional women scholars. As a strategy, separatism went well beyond the colleges into a variety of organizations, from clubs to settlement houses. That all these strategies are still in use today suggests that advances, however substantial, have not resulted in a wholly new political or psychological environment. Nor can it be assumed that any recent progress will be maintained.

Because science and technology have traditionally been regarded as male enclaves, but also because both are crucial to modern society, it is not surprising that an issue of *Dædalus* that seeks to explain contemporary thought on the subject of gender should deal with both of these fields in an international historical context. Anne Fausto-Sterling, recognizing that terms like *truth, bias, objectivity,* and *prejudice* have been much bandied about in recent years, argues that while scientific theory has helped to create social concepts like gender, social concepts have been no less important in influencing scientific inquiry. Starting with a historical example, the author considers the fertilization experiments of the Abbé Lazzaro Spallanzani, an eighteenth-century scientist best known for his disproof of the idea of spontaneous generation. Spallanzani, whose experiments on semen were both careful and intelligent, drew the wrong conclusions because of his flawed theoretical framework based on ovism. Fausto-Sterling goes on to describe how, in a similar fashion, certain modern biologists who seek to explain the development of the sexes ultimately provide an account of male development only, having failed to consider the active role of female hormones such as estrogen and progesterone.

Fausto-Sterling argues that "broad cultural paradigms about the nature of male and female have had a considerable effect on biological theory," that they have channeled experimentation along certain lines, leaving large issues unexplored or unnoticed. Yet this is not the whole story, for scientists—biologists, for example—have also shaped cultural constructs. At a time when some argue that boys are more capable at mathematics than girls because of a supposed connection between testosterone, hemispheric specialization of the brain, and mathematical reasoning—that in girls there is a biologically-based intellectual incapacity—it is critical that such theories, cloaked in scientific terminology, be subjected to close and careful scrutiny. If their implications are accepted unquestioningly, many young women may be dissuaded from considering scientific careers. The prevalence and power of gender-influenced and gender-biased opinion cannot be discounted.

Gender stereotyping is also addressed by Evelyn Fox Keller, who sees it as a human creation, not part of the nature that scientists observe. She maintains that any view that ignores the universal aspirations of science, that becomes, however unwittingly, an expression of stereotyped male or female characteristics, is necessarily flawed. She hopes to stimulate discussion within the scientific community, which has given too little consideration to feminist criticism of science. Because this criticism comes at a time when women are entering scientific fields in unprecedented numbers and when new career opportunities are opening, it is easy to see that the earlier equation of scientific norms with masculine ideals is no longer relevant. Does it really matter that a founding member of the Royal Society, Henry Oldenburg, believed that the society existed "to raise a Masculine Philosophy," or that Francis Bacon insisted that the new science required a "virile" mind? Although such ideas are no longer common, Evelyn Fox Keller sees them as significant because they continue to influence contemporary scientific inquiry—the questions asked, the institutional structures created, the methodological preferences shown. Success in science today, she insists, depends on an acceptance of norms that are opposed to what society and culture habitually define as feminine. So long as this is so, the fact that more women are in science than ever before, or that their contributions are now more generally recognized, is secondary. If the cultural ideals of gender have had a major impact on the way that science has evolved and the way that it is presently pursued, this certainly merits study.

To be a scientist (man or woman) is not the same as to be a feminist critic of science. The author, who began her career as the former and only gradually became the latter, includes autobiographical details in her essay to show why she became dissatisfied with the realist world view of science and, more particularly, with certain methodological claims of the physical sciences. These personal vignettes illustrate how she became increasingly preoccupied with the issue of gender ideology, and how that preoccupation eventually led her to perceive that science is shaped by rarely acknowledged but immensely influential gender-based ideological constructs.

If it is no longer possible for us to accept the conventional notions of male and female nature, neither can we accept the idea, so congenial to certain psychoanalysts, of "women's vision and creativity." These are myths; the categories of male, female, mind, and nature need to be completely reconceived. The author emphasizes that if science does not simply mirror nature, this does not imply that it simply mirrors culture or prevailing interests. Nature and culture interact in influencing scientific knowledge; one element cannot be studied independently of the others.

The question of the nature of culture, which is touched on in so many of the essays in this issue of *Dædalus*, preoccupies Robert Fox and Anna Guagnini as they reflect on how often economic decline is linked to a presumed deficiency in scientific and technical education, and how this is related to the assumption that the "conservative" nature of certain cultures accounts for their relative technological backwardness or even decline. The authors believe that such simple characterizations are worthless. Using Great Britain and France as examples, surveying conditions in both nations in the nineteenth and twentieth centuries and comparing them with those of Germany in the same periods, the authors are not persuaded that the universities of one nation were substantially more resistant to change than those of the others, or that the confrontation between traditional and modern values was ever as explicit as some imagine it to have been. While there were indeed significant differences, the most striking similarity among the three countries was that higher scientific and technical education made its way in a cultural context that was favorable to mathematics and pure science but remarkably indifferent to the needs of industry. It is a fact, the authors argue, that enormous industrial progress occurred in societies that were not especially hospitable, at least in their universities, to technical education. This is not to say that there was no scientific or technical education whatsoever—only that it was not offered by the oldest and most prestigious universities, and that it never seriously challenged the humanistic basis of higher education. The genius of German industry was its capacity to absorb and use the country's graduates in its own dynamic and innovative ventures.

As for the education of women for scientific or technical careers, Fox and Guagnini, looking at England and France before the First World War, are struck by the fact that the relatively small number of women who attended the universities did not avoid the sciences, hard or soft. Echoing a pattern found also in the United States, most opted for careers in education rather than industry; they found education a more "protected" field, generally considered more appropriate than industry for women and thus more likely to employ them. After World War I, women were more likely to pursue careers in industry than before, learning only then how difficult it was to convert an academic scientific degree into an employment credential. For women educated in science, teaching remained the one occupational road that was relatively open.

From a consideration of these first industrial societies and how their economic evolution was conceived, it is only a short step to the essay by Susan C. Bourque and Kay B. Warren, which reflects on how the developing countries of this century have perceived their economic problems, and why the expectation that technology transfer would be relatively easy turned out to be a mistaken one. The study of gender relations has made many aware that technological change is not accomplished in the manner once thought possible or with the consequences once predicted. New scholarship focused on gender shows a marked deterioration in the status of women in many places—a loss of certain traditional rights without a compensating gain of greater access to new technology or educational opportunity. While the call for greater access has served to rekindle old debates about the desirability of the new technology, its more important effect may have been to raise other, more complex issues that involve the links that exist between the family, cultural values, and women's access to both the polity and the economy.

This essay reflects the enormous growth in "learning about women" that has occurred internationally. There is now abundant knowledge about women's lives in the developing world, and a new international community of scholars is at work on social change. Earlier models of change and development have been reassessed. Feminist scholarship, both in the West and in Third World countries, suggests that effective access to technology in the Third World does not necessarily follow from changes in design and scale linked to women's maternal functions or their purportedly different natures, nor does it happen through changes in ownership of the means of production, or even in efforts to redirect world flows of capital. More complex political, economic, and educational measures are required. In this essay the authors explain why recent research on the impact of development has generated a dramatic clash of gender-sensitive perspectives. The array of conflicting analyses accounts for the continuing debates over the meaning of development for women, as well as the elusiveness of solutions to persistent inequities.

To read all of these essays, and then to read Carl Degler's retrospective analysis of the world of the 1960s, of the conditions that then obtained with respect to women, of the scholarship that was then common, and of the debates that have occurred since, is to be aware of great and perhaps significant change. It is too early to know whether gender will prove to be as important an analytical category in the next century as social class (the invention of the nineteenth century) has been in our own. It is not too early, however, to suggest that the analysis of society has been significantly affected by the recently developed concept of gender. While the influence of scholarship in gender is certainly more conspicuous in some areas than in others, it would be hazardous to predict what the state of gender studies may be in 2010, or how they will have evolved by then. The more that serious and continuing dialogue can be opened up to involve men and women both inside and outside gender studies, the more the field's ample dimensions will be recognized, and the more its utility for illuminating the lives of both men and women, historically and in contemporary situations, will be perceived. To see all this in an international dimension, a comparative context that gives new meaning to the term *culture,* will be to add a scholarly concern absent in too many other fields.

Stephen R. Graubard
Editor of the American Academy of Arts and
Sciences and of *Daedalus*

ENDNOTES

[1]*Dædalus* 93 (2) (Spring 1964).
[2]Raymond Williams, *Culture and Society, 1780–1950* (New York: Columbia University Press, 1983), p. xi.

Introduction: The Concept of Gender

IN 1962, when the essays were being prepared for the Spring 1964 *Dædalus* issue, "The Woman in America," Talcott Parsons was the social theorist whose views on the family and the roles of men and women in modern societies shaped conventional discourse. Parsons's three essays in the volume *Family, Socialization, and Interaction Process,*[1] written in the early 1950s, rested on the then-current view of modernization, which assumed that gender roles were biologically based and that the process of modernization had brought about a rationalization in role allocation. What Parsons meant by rationalization was the definition of gender roles in terms of economic and sexual function. His theories implied that same-sex communities such as the celibate clergy or cloistered religious would eventually disappear as nonfunctional. Central to Parsons's thinking was a set of assumptions about the normative nature of pair bonding in modern society. In his picture of the modern world, marriage and the family created by marriage functioned on mutually supportive economic and affectional bonds in which the male's capacity for instrumental (or public, productive, and managerial) work was complemented by the female's ability to manage the expressive aspect of family life and the rearing of children. To be sure, there were variations in the patterning of gender roles by class, but in Parsons's description the basic division of male instrumental behavior and female expressive behavior transcended class and national cultures. The Parsonian view of gender took at face value the characterizations of normal sexual behavior and temperament drawn by social scientists in the 1930s and 1940s, treated observed variations from those patterns as deviant, and ignored a countertradition of social analysis that was exemplified in Margaret Mead's 1935 *Sex and Tempera-ment in Three Primitive Societies.*[2] Mead had raised the revolution-ary idea that concepts of gender were cultural, not biological, and that they could vary widely in different environments. But in the 1940s and 1950s biologically based views so dominated the study of male and female behavior that observations like those reported in *Sex and Temperament* were relegated to the status of an earlier and outmoded school of social science.

In the last twenty-five years many different strands of scholarly inquiry have converged to produce a more complex understanding of gender as a cultural phenomenon. The nuances and variations of this cultural category now appear to be much more subtle than the formulation suggested by Mead. Today we see the social boundaries established by gender patterns as varying historically and across cultures yet also serving as fundamental components of any social system. The fact of living in a world shared by two sexes may be interpreted in an infinite variety of ways; these interpretations and the patterns they create operate at both the social and individual levels.

The production of culturally appropriate forms of male and female behavior is a central function of social authority and is mediated by the complex interactions of a wide range of economic, social, political, and religious institutions. Just as economic institutions produce the forms of consciousness and behavior we associate with class mentalities, so also do the institutions that deal with reproduc-tion and sexuality. Sexual and economic institutions interact with one another. We know, for instance, that capitalist economies develop characteristic forms of postponement of gratification and of sexual divisions of labor at the workplace and in the household. The mentalities produced are the result of complex interactions within a given social system. The reasons for changes in prescribed social norms for sexual temperaments and conduct are equally complex, and the social types that result cannot be understood as simple binary divisions or reflections of biological sex differences.

Nor is there exact coincidence among institutions. Recent social history has led us to see that changes in the family in early-modern and modern Europe did not neatly coincide with changes in the forms of government, economic organization, or religious practice. Indeed, prevailing styles of family life and child rearing had important influences on emerging economic and political institutions. To complicate the picture, institutions do not always succeed in their task of inculcating culturally acceptable conduct or conventional behavior. Individuals do not seem to simply accept or reflect normative designations. Rather, their notions of their own gender identity and sexuality are manifested in their refusals, reinterpretations, or partial acceptances of the dominant themes.

Gender boundaries, like those of class, are drawn to serve a variety of political, economic, and social functions. These boundaries are often movable and negotiable. They operate not only in the material base of a culture but also in the imagined world of the creative artist. Norms of gender are not always explicitly stated; they are often implicitly conveyed through uses of language and other symbols. Just as gender-specific language influences the way things are thought or said, the archetypal narrative forms of the West that assume a male protagonist influence the way stories are told about women.

The investigation of gender stereotypes has been aided by the techniques of the social historian and stimulated by the questions of feminist scholars. Feminists have added an interest in research on women's experience to the traditional concern of social historians to understand the lives of those outside official power structures. Feminist research has sent social scientists and humanists to the records created by women and led them to assess those records as important documents in their own right, not merely as evidence to be considered of minor social or cultural significance. Feminist academics have moved far beyond the realm of social history to make use of the techniques and insights—and to reassess some of the theoretical assumptions—of anthropologists, philosophers, literary critics, and social scientists. Scholars in every discipline have provided crucial new insights into the ways women's experience has been shaped in relation to men's and how sexual hierarchy and unequal distributions of power have become established. Simultaneously, key elements of the disciplines have been reshaped, and once-standard theoretical formulations have been rethought.

Studies conducted over the past fifteen years have thrown light on the extent to which categories of gender vary over time, and with them the social and cultural territories assigned to women and men. The existence of a celibate clergy and its importance in medieval Europe, for example, calls simple functionalist views into question, as do portrayals of Jesus as "mother" of humanity. In many historical periods, popular perceptions of male and female temperaments have changed significantly; these changes have been accompanied by the redrawing of social boundaries. Such a redrawing occurred during early Western urbanization and industrialization: household and workplace were physically separated and the middle-class woman's function assumed a form later described as expressive (to use the term assigned it in Parsons's theory). In North America, another shifting of boundaries took place as a result of the development of higher education for women and the accompanying acceptance of paid work outside the home for middle-class women; boundaries were created to separate the new women's service professions (teaching, nursing, and social work) from the higher-status male professions of law, engineering, and research science. The history of the profession of medicine in the United States is an interesting example of the process of redefining social boundaries. Once considered more a service activity than one based on knowledge generated by laboratory science, medicine was originally a field open to women. The transformation of medicine into a professional field occurred in the late nineteenth century; as part of that process, women were excluded from training in research-based medicine, and accepted standards of female modesty were altered so that women could be examined and treated by male doctors. Such observed changes have prompted speculation about the social, political, and economic functions of gender systems and the ways in which redefinitions occurring in any of these areas are responsive to changes in the others.

Having established the variability of gender systems in different times and places, scholars have posed new questions for social scientists. The study of gender, for example, has raised three broad questions about political life. First, how did Western political culture develop so as to exclude women from formal political activity? Second, what have been the available styles of political action for women, and how do they compare to those of other disenfranchised groups? And since style itself shapes meaning, how have women leaders functioned in relation to their constituencies? Third, how should we understand the problem of equality in a world of biological sex differences? How has the principle of equality been defined and implemented in relation to those differences? Each of these questions requires that we know something specific about women—

how they were treated, what they thought, and how they behaved. But they also require a broader exploration of relationships between women and men and of general cultural attitudes and political practices.

In the nineteenth century, James Stephen and John Stuart Mill wrote persuasive essays on the question of equality that found a place in the canon of classic texts of political thought. Their essays help us understand the issue from the point of view of thinkers who either ignored women or expected women to be subsumed within the collective identity of men. Today the study of gender requires us to ask how women concerned with political life understood the question of equality and to see the discussion of the question as incomplete until their perspectives are considered. How did a woman like Harriet Taylor in England or Jane Addams in the United States understand her gender, and what role did that understanding play in her approach to politics? Addams's *Democracy and Social Ethics*[3] and Taylor's *Enfranchisement of Women*[4] tell us how each understood equality and the circumstances under which it might occur for both women and men. Their formulations are an important part of the continuing conversation about equality in Western thought, a conversation that has been both lively and heated in our own time.

The questions about politics are related to anthropological questions. If we discard the fixed assumptions about gender roles that Western anthropologists once brought to their observations of other cultures, how can we begin to interpret the male and female rituals of these societies or their unfamiliar patternings of gendered behavior? Are there societies in which gender is not a primary way of organizing social systems? If gender roles are not determined by biology, can we identify the social factors that create them? Is it possible to generalize about gender across ethnographic studies? Can we explain gender in any particular society without also writing its history? How should we think about Western politics if we discard the myth that only males bond with one another? What is the basis of female bonding? Are male and female bonding necessarily antagonistic? Are there ways in which the rituals and customs of separate social territories may be understood as complementing and reinforcing one another? These questions have received a wide range of answers from different groups across the political spectrum, from different schools of thought within the feminist movement, and from conservative and liberal scholars. One consequence of the study of gender systems in the last quarter century is that no group, whatever its politics, can afford to ignore such questions any longer.

For psychology, too, a new range of questions is opened up by the study of gender. The orthodox Freudian view of the Oedipal drama experienced by men has been adapted by some psychologists to include discussions of women. But if one goes further and questions Freud's assumption that the male parent is the primary focus of a daughter's psychic attention, a dazzling array of questions about female development immediately demands answers. There is now an important school of thought (largely associated with the object relations theory first articulated in England by D.W. Winnicott and Melanie Klein) that argues for an explict analysis of female psychological development, maintaining that girls never experience the sharp separation from their mothers that boys do. Proponents of this school of thought hold that the boundaries between self and others are more diffuse for females than for males; hence, in this interpretation, women are more related to others and better able to reason empathetically. Their work has inspired important debates about "maternalism": Can a single behavioral trait be said to characterize women as a group, and if so, what does such characterization portend for policy decisions about military service or political rights? Another school of psychoanalysis, associated with poststructuralism and the French theorist Jacques Lacan, offers the more radical view that gender identities are not fixed in early childhood and that the wholeness of any self is a fiction that must be constantly reasserted and redefined in different contexts. This theory has spurred investigations into the relationship between history and individual psyches, and into what might be called the politics of sexual identity. It suggests that sexual identities are not biologically rooted, but instead continually pursued, and that this pursuit—whether heterosexual or homosexual—is made possible in contexts at once political and personal. The new ideas offered by these different and by no means compatible approaches raise another question: If biology is not destiny, can we theorize about the psychological differences between women and men without also studying culture, society, and history? This question suggests that the contemporary study of gender calls for a critical reassessment of the traditional concepts of all scholarly disciplines.

In the realm of economics, the major questions raised by the study of gender concern how and why similar expenditures of human energy have historically received different levels of reward according to the sex of the worker. This is a fundamental theoretical question because such differentiation exists in most workplaces worldwide, regardless of the form of ownership or the means of production. It is as widespread in rural peasant economies as in urban industrial settings, and occurs in capitalist as well as socialist economies. Apparently, neither the incremental addition of women workers to specific occupations nor the more dramatic transition from an industrial economy to a service economy has a moderating effect on gender differentiation in the labor force. Certainly, research on the experience of women workers during industrialization in the West has debunked the myth that industrialization vastly improved the status of women workers; change was not synonymous with progress for women in the labor market.

The study of gender and work is currently focused on how and why gender systems shape men's and women's relationships to technology, and why a two-tiered labor market defined by gender is so resistant to change. Differential investment in education, or differing levels of workplace participation—once seen as explanations for differential wages—are no longer perceived as adequate reasons for a substantial segment of the persisting gap between the earnings of women and men with similar levels of education or training. Some of the problems of women's career mobility, and of their lower lifetime earnings compared with those of men who have the same qualifications, seem now to be linked to the gender assumptions built into the structures of large organizations and to the individual identities of the professionals who inhabit them. Today, whether we study hospitals and research centers, profit-making corporations, or government bureaucracies, we see not only standard Weberian bureaucratic social types but also patterns of gender that reinforce normative rules and behaviors. At the core of gender assumptions in the United States lies the belief that neither society nor the employer has any interest in the child-rearing responsibilities of the worker (responsibilities so neatly assigned by gender in the Parsonian version of the modern family).

Examples of how gender assumptions shape professional culture abound. In the West the strong identification of the professional engineer or research physicist with masculinity has attracted the attention of several generations of writers on the process of professionalization. One important result of the study of gender in the professions is the recognition that the gender basis of work identities is remarkably durable and not easily modified by the addition of more women or men to an occupational group. Thus the liberal model of creating incremental change by granting access to an excluded group fails to take into account the durability of gender-based definitions of occupations. The persistence of gender identities in modern societies appears to be as much a question of conceptualization as of economic bias (although the two are related).

In modern science the representation of the scientist is masculine while that of the natural world to be investigated and brought under scientific control is feminine (gender identifications established by the leaders of the seventeenth-century scientific revolution). Thus the participation of women in modern scientific activity has not necessarily transformed the assumed relationship between scientist and nature. Gender categorization is also present in representations of technology and in assumptions about who can use machines and tools: Western notions determined that African males should be trained to drive tractors, despite the fact that African women were the primary agriculturalists. Although Western depictions of technology may create the impression that it is gender-neutral, its gender biases become apparent when it is transferred to non-Western societies.

In the realm of religious symbolism the recognition that gender categories vary in response to political and economic factors has provided a fresh perspective on the transitions from the world of mystery cults and fertility worship to patriarchal Christianity. Freud celebrated this transition and identified it as the source of Western society's capacity for rational thought and the establishment of law. Research conducted during the past twenty-five years has made us aware that early Christian communities supported many traditions counter to the patriarchal. The Freudian picture of development, in which psychic bonds with the mother must be supplanted by ties with the father, thus reflects a political history rather than a natural evolution. Similarly, this new scholarship leads us to seek an explanation for the hatred of Mariolatry, which was such a passionate theme in the ideas of Protestant reformers like John Calvin and John Knox, and to ask what political and economic tensions necessitated the removal of female imagery from representations of the transcendent in sixteenth-century Europe.

Gender systems—regardless of historical time period—are binary systems that oppose male to female, masculine to feminine, usually not on an equal basis but in hierarchical order. While symbolic associations with each gender have varied enormously, they have included individualism versus nurturance, the instrumental or engineered versus the naturally procreative, reason versus intuition, science versus nature, the creation of new goods versus service, exploitation versus conservation, classical versus romantic, universal human characteristics versus biological specificity, political versus domestic, and public versus private. The interesting thing about these binary oppositions is that they obscure much more complex social and cultural processes in which differences between women and men are neither apparent nor clear-cut. Therein, of course, lie their power and significance. In studying gender systems we learn that they represent not the functional assignment of biologically prescribed social roles but a means of cultural conceptualization and social organization.

What makes the study of gender so challenging and potentially so fruitful is the insight it provides into social and cultural systems. The scholar who seeks to understand how the relative weight of each gender can shift in relation to opposed sets of cultural values and established social boundaries, prompting the reordering of all other social, political, and cultural categories, learns much about the ambiguity of gender roles and the complexity of society. Those who study gender may revise our concepts of humanity and nature, and enlarge our sense of the human predicament. From this perspective, learning about women involves also learning about men. The study of gender is a way of understanding women not as an isolated aspect of society but as an integral part of it.

Jill K. Conway
Susan C. Bourque
Joan W. Scott

ENDNOTES

[1]Talcott Parsons and Robert F. Bayles, in collaboration with James Olds, Morris Zelditch, Jr., and Philip E. Slater, *Family, Socialization, and Interaction Process* (Glencoe, IL: Free Press, 1955).

[2]Margaret Mead, *Sex and Temperament in Three Primitive Societies* (New York: Morrow, 1935).

[3]Jane Addams, *Democracy and Social Ethics* (1902; reprint, St. Clair Shores, MN: Scholarly Press).

[4]Harriet Taylor, "Enfranchisement of Women"(*Westminster Review,* 1851), reprinted in Alice Rossi, ed., *Essays on Sex Equality* (Chicago: University of Chicago Press, 1970).

Mary G. Dietz

Context Is All: Feminism and Theories of Citizenship

I N MARGARET ATWOOD'S POWERFUL NOVEL *The Handmaid's Tale*,[1] the heroine Offred, a member of a new class of "two-legged wombs" in a dystopian society, often thinks to herself, "Context is all." Offred reminds us of an important truth: at each moment of our lives our every thought, value, and act—from the most mundane to the most lofty—takes its meaning and purpose from the wider political and social reality that constitutes and conditions us. In her newly reduced circumstances, Offred comes to see that matters beyond one's immediate purview make a great deal of difference with respect to living a more or less free and fully human life. But her realization comes too late.

Unlike Offred, feminists have long recognized as imperative the task of seeking out, defining, and criticizing the complex reality that governs the ways we think, the values we hold, and the relationships we share, especially with regard to gender. If context is all, then feminism in its various guises is committed to uncovering what is all around us and to revealing the power relations that constitute the creatures we become. "The personal is the political" is the credo of this critical practice.

Mary G. Dietz is assistant professor of political science at the University of Minnesota. Her publications include "Citizenship with a Feminist Face: The Problem with Maternal Thinking" (1985), "Trapping the Prince: Machiavelli and the Politics of Deception" (1986), and Between the Human and the Divine: The Political Thought of Simone Weil *(forthcoming in 1988). Her primary areas of study are the history of ideas, democratic theory, and feminist theory. Professor Dietz is currently writing a book on patriotism and conceptual change.*

1

The political and ideological context that most deeply conditions the American experience is liberalism and its attendant set of values, beliefs, and practices. Without question, the liberal tradition can count many among its adherents, but it has its critics as well. Over the past decade in the United States, few critics of liberalism have been as persistent or as wide-ranging as the feminists. Certainly no others have been as committed to articulating alternatives to the liberal vision of gender, the family, the sexual division of labor, and the relationship between the public and the private realm.[2]

In this essay I shall focus on the aspect of the feminists' critique that concerns citizenship. First I will outline the dominant features of liberalism's conception of citizenship, and then I will introduce two current feminist challenges to that conception. What I ultimately want to argue, however, is that although both of these challenges offer important insights, neither of them leads to a suitable alternative to the liberal view or a sufficiently compelling feminist political vision. In the third section of the essay I will make a preliminary sketch of what such a feminist vision of citizenship might be. In part, I would have it reconfirm the idea that "equal access is not enough."

I

The terrain of liberalism is vast, and its historical basis has over the past century been extensively surveyed in social, political, and moral theory.[3] All I shall present here is the bare bones of the liberal conception of citizenship, but this skeletal construction may sufficiently set off the feminist critiques that follow. With this in mind and the caveat that all conceptions change through time, we can begin by considering the features that have more or less consistently distinguished the views of liberal political thinkers.

First, there is the notion that human beings are atomistic, rational agents whose existence and interests are ontologically prior to society.[4] In the liberal society one might say that context is not "all." It is nothing, for liberalism conceives of the needs and capacities of individuals as being independent of any immediate social or political condition.[5] What counts is that we understand human beings as rational individuals who have intrinsic worth.

A second tenet of liberal political thought is that society should ensure the freedom of all its members to realize their capabilities. This is the central ethical principle of the Western liberal tradition. Perhaps the classic formulation is John Stuart Mill's observation that "the only freedom which deserves the name, is that of pursuing our own good in our own way, so long as we do not attempt to deprive others of theirs, or impede their efforts to obtain it."[6]

Closely associated with the principle of individual liberty is a third feature—an emphasis on human equality. Liberal theorists may differ in their formulations of this principle but not on its centrality. Locke, for example, held that "reason is the common rule and measure that God has given to mankind" and therefore that all men must be considered created equal and thereby worthy of the same dignity and respect. Bentham argued (not always consistently) that the case for equality rests on the fact that all individuals have the same capacity for pleasure and hence that the happiness of society is maximized when everyone has the same amount of wealth or income. In his "Liberal Legislation and Freedom of Contract," T.H. Green proclaimed that "every one has an interest in securing to every one else the free use and enjoyment and disposal of his possessions, so long as that freedom on the part of one does not interfere with a like freedom on the part of others, because such freedom contributes to that equal development of the faculties of all which is the highest good of all."[7] Since liberal theories usually begin with some version of the presumption of perfect equality among individual men, it is a relatively small step from this to the related argument that societal justice entails equal suffrage, in which every single person should count, in Herbert Spencer's words, "for as much any other single individual in the community."[8] As Allison Jagger writes, "Liberalism's belief in the ultimate worth of the individual is expressed in political egalitarianism."[9]

This egalitarianism takes the form of what theorists call "negative liberty," which Sir Isaiah Berlin in his classic essay on freedom characterizes as "the area within which a man can act unobstructed by others."[10] It is the absence of obstacles to possible choices and activities. What is at stake in this liberal conception is neither the "right" choice nor the "good" action but simply the freedom of the individual to choose his own values or ends without interference from others and consistent with a similar liberty for others. At the core of negative liberty, then, is a fourth feature of liberalism that speaks to the individual in his political guise as citizen: the conception of the individual as the "bearer of formal rights" designed to protect him from the infringement or interference of others and to guarantee him the same opportunities or "equal access" as others.

The concept of rights is of fundamental importance to the liberal political vision. In *A Theory of Justice,* John Rawls offers this classic formulation of the liberal view: "Each person possesses an inviolability founded on justice that even the welfare of society as a whole cannot override. . . . The rights secured by justice are not subject to political bargaining or the calculus of social interests."[11]

Not only does the concept of rights reinforce the underlying liberal principles of individual freedom and formal equality; it also sets up the distinction between "private" and "public" that informs so much of the liberal perspective on family and social institutions. Individual rights correspond to the notion of a private realm of freedom, separate and distinct from that of the public. Although liberal theorists disagree about the nature and degree of state intervention in the public realm—and even about what counts as "public"—they nevertheless accept the idea that certain rights are inviolable and exist in a private realm where the state cannot legitimately interfere. For much of liberalism's past this private realm has subsumed, in Agnes Heller's phrase, "the household of the emotions"—marriage, family, housework, and child care. In short, the liberal notion of "the private" has included what has been called "woman's sphere" as "male property" and sought not only to preserve it from the interference of the public realm but also to keep those who "belong" in that realm—women—from the life of the public.[12]

Another feature of liberalism tied to all of the above is the idea of the free individual as competitor. To understand it, we might recall liberalism's own context, its distinctive history and origin.[13] Liberalism emerged amid the final disintegration of, in Karl Marx's words, those "motley feudal ties"—in the decline of aristocracy and the rise of a new order of merchants and entrepreneurs with a "natural propensity," as Adam Smith wrote, "to trade, truck, and barter." The life of liberalism, in other words, began in capitalist market societies, and as Marx argued, it can only be fully comprehended in terms of the social and economic institutions that shaped it. For Max Weber, liberal political thought inherited the great transformation wrought by Protestantism and a new ethic of self and work soon to replace privilege, prescription, and primacy of rank. As both Marx and Weber recognized, liberalism was the practical consciousness, or the theoretical legitimation, of the values and practices emanating from the newly emergent market society. Accordingly, liberalism lent support to the active pursuit of things beneficial to an economic system based on production for the sake of profit.

Among these "things beneficial" is the notion of the rational man as a competitive individual who tends naturally to pursue his own interest and maximize his own gain. Although it would be mistaken to suggest that all liberal theorists conceive of human nature as being egoistic, most do argue that people tend naturally in this direction and must work to develop moral capacities to counter their basic selfish, acquisitive inclinations.[14] Thus, we can at least generally conclude that, for liberals, the motive force of human action is not to be found in any noble desires to achieve "the good life" or "the morally virtuous society" but rather in the inclination toward individual advancement or (in capitalist terms) the pursuit of profit according to the rules of the market.[15] Taken in this light, then, the liberal individual might be understood as the competitive entrepreneur, his civil society as an economic marketplace, and his ideal as the equal opportunity to engage, as Adam Smith wrote, in "the race for wealth, and honors, and preferments."

Vital in this race is the very issue that concerns us in this issue of *Dædalus*—the equality of access to the race itself, to the market society. What liberty comes to mean in this context is a set of formal guarantees to the individual that he (and later she) may enjoy a fair start in Smith's "race." What citizenship comes to mean in this liberal guise is something like equal membership in an economic and social sphere, more or less regulated by government and more or less dedicated to the assumption that the "market maketh man."[16] To put this another way, under liberalism, citizenship becomes less a collective, political activity than an individual, economic activity— the right to pursue one's interests, without hindrance, in the marketplace. Likewise, democracy is tied more to representative government and the right to vote than to the idea of the collective, participatory activity of citizens in the public realm.

This vision of the citizen as the bearer of rights, democracy as the capitalist market society, and politics as representative government is precisely what makes liberalism, despite its admirable and vital insistence on the values of individual freedom and equality, seem so politically barren to so many of its critics, past and present, conservative and radical. As far as feminism is concerned, perhaps Mary Shanley best sums up the problem liberalism poses when she writes:

While liberal ideals have been efficacious in overturning restrictions on women as individuals, liberal theory does not provide the language or concepts to help us understand the various kinds of human interdependence which are part of the life of both families and polities, nor to articulate a feminist vision of 'the good life.' Feminists are thus in the awkward position of having to use rhetoric in dealing with the state that does not adequately describe their goals and that may undercut their efforts at establishing new modes of life.[17]

II

For good and obvious reasons, one might expect that a feminist critique of liberalism would best begin by uncovering the reality behind the idea of equal access. Not only is equal access a central tenet of liberal thought; it is also a driving part of our contemporary political discourse that is used both to attack and to defend special pleas for women's rights. Just such a critique is what this volume undertakes.

But a complementary approach may be in order as well. There is merit, I think, to the argument that to begin with the question of equal access is already to grant too much, to deal too many high cards to the liberal hand. Quite literally, "access is not enough," for once in the domain of "equal access talk," we are tied into a whole network of liberal concepts—rights, interests, contracts, individualism, representative government, negative liberty. These open up some avenues of discourse but at the same time block off others. As Shanley implies, for feminists to sign on to these concepts may be to obscure rather than to illuminate a vision of politics, citizenship, and "the good life" that is appropriate to feminist values and concerns.

By this I do not mean to suggest that feminists who proceed from the question of access are doing something unhelpful or unimportant. On the contrary, by using gender as a unit of analysis, feminist scholars have revealed the inegalitarianism behind the myth of equal opportunity and made us aware of how such presumptions deny the social reality of unequal treatment, sexual discrimination, cultural stereotypes, and women's subordination both at home and in the marketplace. To the extent that this sort of gender analysis leads to positive political programs—the extension of pregnancy leaves, affirmative action plans, child-care facilities, comparable-worth wages, sexual harassment laws, health care benefits—feminists give indispensable assistance to liberal practice.

However, we should not overlook the fact that this sort of analysis has boundaries that are determined by the concepts of liberalism and the questions they entail. So, for example, when power is perceived in terms of access to social, economic, or political institutions, other possibilities (including the radical one that power has nothing to do with access to institutions at all) are left out. Or to take another example, if one establishes the enjoyment of rights or the pursuit of free trade as the criterion of citizenship, alternative conceptions like civic activity and participatory self-government are overlooked. Liberalism tends toward both an understanding of power as access and a conception of citizenship as civil liberty. What I want to emphasize is that neither of these formulations is adequate in and of itself or appropriate for a feminist political theory.

Of course, few feminist theorists would find these remarks startling or new. Indeed, much of recent feminist thought (liberal feminism notwithstanding) has been directed toward revealing the problems a liberal political theory poses for a vision of women's liberation and human emancipation. A variety of arguments and approaches has been articulated. Some have focused on the epistemological and ontological roots of liberalism, others on its implications for an ethical understanding of personhood, still others on the assumptions that underlie its methodology.[18]

On the political side and with regard to the liberal theory of freedom, the role of the state, the public and the private, and capitalism and democracy, feminist critics seem to fall into two camps—the Marxists and what I will call the maternalists.[19] These two camps are of primary concern in this essay because they address issues of "the good life" and, more precisely, the nature of political community. A brief look at each should suffice to bring us up to date on the feminist alternatives to the liberal conception of the citizen— alternatives that are, as I shall go on to argue, not fully satisfactory counters to the liberal view, although they provide suggestive and thought-provoking contributions to the political debate.

First, the Marxists. Feminists working within the Marxist tradition seek to reveal the capitalist and patriarchal foundations of the liberal state as well as the oppression inherent in the sexual division of labor—or, as one thinker puts it, "the consequences of women's dual contribution to subsistence in capitalism."[20] At stake in this economic critique, as another theorist argues, is the notion of the "state's involvement in protecting patriarchy as a system of power, much in the same way it protects capitalism and racism. . . . "[21] Insofar as they believe that the state participates in the oppression of women, Marxist feminists hold that the idea of the rights of citizenship granted by the state is a sham, a convenient ideological fiction that serves to obscure the underlying reality of a dominant male ruling class. Accordingly, so these theorists contend, the liberation of women will be possible only when the liberal state is overthrown and its capitalist and patriarchal structure dismantled. What will emerge is an end to the sexual division of labor and "a feminist politics that moves beyond liberalism."[22] What most Marxist feminists seem to mean by these politics is the egalitarian reordering of productive and reproductive labor and the achievement of truly liberating human relations, a society of "propertyless producers of use values."[23]

The strengths of this critique should be obvious. Marxist feminists would have us recognize that a system of economics and gender rooted in capitalist, male-dominant structures underlies much of liberal ideology, from the notion of independent, rational man to the conception of separate private and public realms, from the value of individualism to the equation of freedom with free trade. As such, the Marxist-feminist analysis reveals numerous inadequacies in the liberal feminist position, particularly in its mainstream view of women's work and its reliance on the law, the state, interest groups, and state-instituted reforms as the source of social justice, individual equality, and "access." The advantage of the Marxist-feminist approach is not only its critique of capitalism, which reveals the exploitative and socially constructed nature of women's work, but also its political critique, which challenges the liberal assumption that representative government is the sole sanctuary for politics and the legitimate arbiter of social change.

Nevertheless, even though the Marxist-feminist critique has much to offer from the standpoint of historical materialism, it has little to say on the subject of citizenship. As Sheldon Wolin has noted, "Most Marxists are interested in the 'masses' or the workers, but they dismiss citizenship as a bourgeois conceit, formal and empty. . . . "[24] Unfortunately, Marxist feminists are no exception to this generalization. *Citizenship* hardly appears in their vocabulary, much less any of the rest of its family of concepts: participation, action, democracy, community, and political freedom.

To the extent that Marxist feminists discuss citizenship at all, they usually conflate it with labor, class struggle, and socialist revolution, and with the advent of social change and certain economic conditions. In their view, true citizenship is realized with the collective ownership of the means of production and the end of oppression in the relations of reproduction. They associate both of these ideas with revolutionary action and the disappearance of the patriarchal state. In their approach to citizenship, Marxist feminists tend to reduce politics to revolutionary struggle, women to the category of "reproducers," and freedom to the realization of economic and social equality and the overthrowing of natural necessity. Once freedom is achieved, they seem to say, politics ends or becomes little more than what Marx himself once termed "the administration of things."

Now no one would deny that economic equality and social justice empower people. A society that values and strives for them with both men and women in mind deserves admiration and respect. What I am suggesting is that because Marxist feminism stops here, its liberatory vision of how things will be "after the revolution" is incomplete, for what emerges is a picture of economic, not political, freedom and a society of autonomous and fulfilled social beings, not a polity of citizens. As a result, a whole complex of vital political questions is sidestepped or ignored: What is political freedom? What does it mean to be a citizen? What does an expressly feminist political consciousness require? Or, to put the matter more bluntly, is there more to feminist politics than revolutionary struggle against the state?

The second camp of feminist theorists, the maternalists, would answer this last question with a resounding yes. They would have us reconsider both the liberal and the Marxist views of citizenship[25] and become committed to a conception of female political consciousness that is grounded in the virtues of woman's private sphere, primarily in mothering. Unlike the Marxist feminists, the maternal feminists hold that, as important as social justice is, it is not a sufficient condition for a truly liberatory feminist politics. Women must be addressed as mothers, not as "reproducers," and as participants in the public realm, not just as members of the social and economic orders.

Like the Marxist feminists, however, the maternal feminists eschew the liberal notion of the citizen as an individual holder of rights protected by the state. For the maternalist, such a notion is at best morally empty and at worst morally subversive since it rests on a distinctly masculine conception of the person as an independent, self-interested, economic being. When one translates this notion into a broader conception of politics, the maternal feminist argues, one is left with a vision of citizens as competitive marketeers and jobholders for whom civic activity is, at most, membership in interest groups. Thus, the maternal feminist would deny precisely what the liberal would defend—an individualist, rights-based, contractual conception of citizenship and a view of the public realm as one of competition. As one maternalist puts it:

The problem—or one of the problems—with a politics that begins and ends with mobilizing resources, achieving maximum impacts, calculating prudentially, articulating interest group claims . . . and so on, is not only its utter lack of imagination but its inability to engage in the reflective allegiance and committed loyalty of citizens. Oversimply, no substantive sense of civic virtue, no vision of political community that might serve as the groundwork of a life in common, is possible within a political life dominated by a self-interested, predatory, individualism.[26]

Maternal feminism is expressly designed to counter what it thinks are the arid and unimaginative qualities of the prevailing liberal view and, more emphatically, to present an alternative sense of civic virtue and citizenship. As a first step, it wants to establish the moral primacy of the family. Although this may seem to some a strange start for a feminist politics, the maternalists would have us rethink the rigid, liberal distinction of public and private realms and consider instead the "private" as the locus for a possible public morality and as a model for the activity of citizenship itself. Or, to put this another way, maternal feminism criticizes "statist" politics and individualist persons, and offers in their place the only other alternative it sees—a politics informed by the virtues of the private realm, and a person-hood committed to relational capacities, love, and caring for others.

What makes this view expressly feminist (rather than, say, traditionally conservative) is its claim that women's experience as mothers in the private realm endows them with a special capacity and a "moral imperative" for countering both the male liberal individualist world view and its masculinist notion of citizenship. Jean Bethke Elshtain describes mothering as a "complicated, rich, ambivalent, vexing, joyous activity" that upholds the principle that "the reality of a single human child [must] be kept before the mind's eye."[27] For her, the implications mothering holds for citizenship are clear: "Were maternal thinking to be taken as the base for feminist consciousness, a wedge for examining an increasingly overcontrolled public world would open immediately."[28]

Not only would maternal thinking chasten the "arrogant" (i.e., male) public; it would also provide the basis for a whole new conception of power, citizenship, and the public realm. The citizen that emerges is a loving being who, in Elshtain's words, is "devoted to the protection of vulnerable human life" and seeks to make the virtues of mothering the "template" for a new, more humane public world.

Much of the maternalist argument takes its inspiration from, or finds support in, the psychoanalytic object-relations theory of Nancy Chodorow and the moral development theory of Carol Gilligan.[29] These scholars argue that striking contrasts exist between men and women and can be understood in terms of certain experiential differences in the early stages of their development. At the crux of Chodorow and Gilligan's findings is the implication that women's morality is tied to a more mature and humane set of moral values than men's.[30] Gilligan identifies a female "ethic of care" that differs from the male "ethic of justice." The ethic of care revolves more around responsibility and relationships than rights, and more around the needs of particular situations than the application of general rules of conduct. Maternal feminists seize upon this psychological "binary opposition" and, in effect, politicize it. In their work, "the male voice" is that of the liberal individualist who stands in opposition to the female, whose voice is that of the compassionate citizen as loving mother. For maternal feminists, as for feminist psychologists, there is no doubt about which side of the opposition is normatively superior and deserving of elevation, both as a basis for political consciousness and as an ethical way of being. The maternalists might say that the female morality of responsibility "must extend its imperative to men," but they nevertheless grant a pride of place to women and to "women's sphere"—the family—as the wellspring of this new "mode of public discourse."[31] They also maintain that public discourse and citizenship should be informed by the virtues of mothering—love, attentiveness, compassion, care, and "engrossment"—in short, by all the virtues the liberal, statist, public realm disdains.

What are we to make of this vision of feminist citizenship? There is, I think, much to be gained from the maternalist approach, especially if we consider it within the context of the liberal and Marxist-feminist views. First, the maternalists are almost alone among other "feminisms" in their concern with the meaning of citizenship and political consciousness. Although we may disagree with their formulations, they deserve appreciation for making citizenship a matter of concern in a movement that (at least on its academic side) is too often caught up in the psychological, the literary, and the social rather than in problems of political theory that feminists must face. Second, the maternalists remind us of the inadequacy and limitations of a rights-based conception of the individual and a view of social justice as equal access. They would have us understand the dimensions of political morality in other ways and politics itself as potentially virtuous. Third, in an era when politics has on all sides become something like a swear word, the maternal feminists would have us rehumanize the way we think about political participation and recognize how, as interrelated "selves," we can strive for a more humane, relational, and shared community than our current political circumstances allow.

Despite these contributions, however, much is troubling about the maternalists' conception of citizenship. It has the same problems as do all theories that hold one side of an opposition to be superior to the other. For the maternalists, women are more moral than men because they are, or can be, or are raised by, mothers and because mothering itself is necessarily and universally an affective, caring, loving activity. Leaving aside what should be the obvious and problematic logical and sociological character of these claims, suffice it to say that the maternalists stand in danger of committing precisely the same mistake they find in the liberal view. They threaten to turn historically distinctive women into ahistorical, universalized entities.[32]

Even more serious is the conviction of the maternalists that feminists must choose between two worlds—the masculinist, competitive, statist public and the maternal, loving, virtuous private. To choose the public world, they argue, is to fall prey to both a politics and an ethic that recapitulates the dehumanizing features of the liberal-capitalist state. To choose the private world, however, is not only to reassert the value of a "women's realm" but also to adopt a maternal ethic potentially appropriate for citizenship, a deeply moral alternative to the liberal, statist one.[33]

When we look to mothering for a vision of feminist citizenship, however, we look in the wrong place—or, in the language of the maternalists, to the wrong "world." At the center of the mothering activity is not the distinctive political bond among equal citizens but the intimate bond between mother and child. But the maternalist would offer us no choice in the matter: we must turn to the "intimate private" because the "statist public" is corrupt. This choice is a specious one, however. Indeed, by equating the public with statist politics and the private with the virtue of intimacy, maternalist feminism reveals itself to be closer to the liberal view than we might at first suppose. Thus it is open to much the same charge as liberalism: its conception of citizenship is informed by a flawed conception of politics as impersonal, representative government. That liberalism is content to maintain such a conception and that maternalist feminism wants to replace it with a set of prescriptions drawn from the private is not the real issue. The problem for a feminist conception is that neither of the above will do, because both leave us with a one-sided view of politics and therefore of citizenship. What we need is an entirely different conception. For the remainder of this essay, I will sketch out an alternative basis for a feminist political vision, with a view to developing a more detailed feminist vision in the future. I offer the following recommendations more as a programmatic outline than as a comprehensive theory.

III

My basic point is a straightforward one: for a vision of citizenship, feminists should turn to the virtues, relations, and practices that are expressly political and, more exactly, participatory and democratic. What this requires, among other things, is a willingness to perceive politics in a way neither liberals nor maternalists do: as a human activity that is not necessarily or historically reducible to representative government or "the arrogant, male, public realm." By accepting such judgments, the feminist stands in danger of missing a valuable alternative conception of politics that is historically concrete and very much a part of women's lives. That conception is perhaps best called the democratic one, and it takes politics to be the collective and participatory engagement of citizens in the determination of the affairs of their community. The community may be the neighborhood, the city, the state, the region, or the nation itself. What counts is that all matters relating to the community are undertaken as "the people's affair."[34]

From a slightly different angle, we might understand democracy as the form of politics that brings people together as citizens. Indeed, the power of democracy rests in its capacity to transform the individual as teacher, trader, corporate executive, child, sibling, worker, artist, friend, or mother into a special sort of political being, a citizen among other citizens. Thus, democracy offers us an identity that neither liberalism, with its propensity to view the citizen as an individual bearer of rights, nor maternalism, with its attentiveness to mothering, provides. Democracy gives us a conception of ourselves as "speakers of words and doers of deeds" mutually participating in the public realm. To put this another way, the democratic vision does not legitimize the pursuit of every separate, individual interest or the transformation of private into public virtues. Insofar as it derives its meaning from the collective and public engagement of peers, it sees citizens neither as wary strangers (as the liberal marketplace would have it) nor as "loving intimates" (as the maternalist family imagines).

To return to my earlier point, democratic citizenship is a practice unlike any other; it has a distinctive set of relations, virtues, and principles all its own. Its relation is that of civic peers; its guiding virtue is mutual respect; its primary principle is the "positive liberty" of democracy and self-government, not simply the "negative liberty" of noninterference. To assume, then, that the relations that accompany the capitalist marketplace or the virtues that emerge from the intimate experience of mothering are the models for the practice of citizenship is to misperceive the distinctive characteristics of democratic political life and to misconstrue its special relations, virtues, and principles.

The maternalists would have us believe that this democratic political condition would, in fact, flow from the "insertion" of women's virtues as mothers into the public world. There is no reason to think that mothering necessarily induces commitment to democratic practices. Nor are there good grounds for arguing that a principle like "care for vulnerable human life" (as noble as that principle is) by definition encompasses a defense of participatory citizenship. An enlightened despotism, a welfare-state, a single-party bureaucracy, and a democratic republic may all respect mothers, protect children's lives, and show compassion for the vulnerable.

The political issue for feminists must not be just whether children are protected (or any other desirable end achieved) but how and by whom those ends are determined. My point is this: as long as feminists focus only on questions of social and economic concern—questions about children, family, schools, work, wages, pornography, abortion, abuse—they will not articulate a truly political vision, nor will they address the problem of citizenship. Only when they stress that the pursuit of those social and economic concerns must be undertaken through active engagement as citizens in the public world and when they declare the activity of citizenship itself a value will feminists be able to claim a truly liberatory politics as their own.

I hope it is clear that what I am arguing for is the democratization of the polity, not interest-group or single-issue politics-as-usual. A feminist commitment to democratic citizenship should not be confused with either the liberal politics of pressure groups and representative government or the idea that after victory or defeat on an issue, the game is over and we can "go home." As one democratic theorist writes:

The radical democrat does not agree . . . that after solving [a] problem it will be safe to abandon the democratic struggle and disband the organizations. . . . The radical democrat does not believe that any institutional or social arrangement can give an automatic and permanent solution to the main question of political virtue, or can repeal what may be the only scientific law political science has ever produced: power corrupts.[35]

The key idea here is that citizenship must be conceived of as a continuous activity and a good in itself, not as a momentary engagement (or a socialist revolution) with an eye to a final goal or a societal arrangement. This does not mean, of course, that democratic citizens do not pursue specific social and economic ends. Politics is about such things, after all, and the debates and discussions of civic peers will necessarily center on issues of social, political, and economic concern to the community. But at the same time the democratic vision is, and feminist citizenship must be, more than this. Perhaps it is best to say that this is a vision fixed not on an end but rather inspired by a principle—freedom—and by a political activity—positive liberty. That activity is a demanding process that never ends, for it means engaging in public debate and sharing responsibility for self-government. What I am pressing for, in both theory and practice, is a feminist revitalization of this activity.

The reader who has followed me this far is perhaps now wondering whether I have not simply reduced feminist political consciousness to democratic consciousness, leaving nothing in this vision of feminist citizenship for feminism itself. In concluding these reflec- . tions, let me suggest why I think the revitalization of democratic citizenship is an especially appropriate task for feminists to undertake. Although the argument can be made more generally, I will direct my remarks to feminism in the United States.

Like Offred in *The Handmaid's Tale,* we Americans live in reduced circumstances, politically speaking. How we understand ourselves as citizens has little to do with the democratic norms and values I have just defended, and it is probably fair to say that most Americans do not think of citizenship in this way at all. We seem hypnotized by a liberal conception of citizenship as rights, an unremitting consumerism that we confuse with freedom, and a capitalist ethic that we take as our collective identity.[36] Sheldon Wolin has noted that in the American political tradition there exist two "bodies" within the historic "body of the people"—a collectivity informed by democratic practices on the one hand and a collectivity informed by an antidemocratic political economy on the other.[37] The latter is a "liberal-capitalist citizenship" that has emerged triumphant today. Truly democratic practices have nearly ceased to be a part of politics in the United States. They exist only on the margins. More disturbing still, I think, even the memory of these practices seems to elude our collective imagination. As Hannah Arendt puts it, citizenship is the "lost treasure" of American political life.

What I want to argue is that we may yet recover the treasure. We may be able to breathe new life into the peoples' other "body"—into our democratic "selves." This prospect brings us back to feminism, which I think is a potential source for our political resuscitation. Feminism has been more than a social cause; it has been a political movement with distinctive attributes. Throughout its second wave in America, the movement has been informed by democratic organization and practice—by spontaneous gatherings and marches, diverse and multitudinous action groups, face-to-face assemblies, consensus decision making, nonhierarchical power structures, open speech and debate.[38] That is, embodied within the immediate political past of feminism in this country are forms of freedom that are far more compatible with the "democratic body" of the American experience than with the liberal-capitalist one.[39] These particular feminist forms are, potentially at least, compatible with the idea of collective, democratic citizenship on a wider scale.

I say "potentially" because feminists must first transform their own democratic practices into a more comprehensive theory of citizenship before they can arrive at an alternative to the nondemocratic liberal theory. Feminist political practice will not in some automatic way become an inspiration for a new citizenship. Instead, feminists must become self-conscious political thinkers—defenders of democracy—in a land of liberalism. To be sure, this task is neither easy nor short-term, but it is possible for feminists to undertake it in earnest because the foundation is already set in the movement's own experiences, in its persistent attention to issues of power, structure, and democracy, and in the historical precedent of women acting as citizens in the United States.[40]

A warning is in order, however. What a feminist defense of democracy must at all costs avoid is the temptation of "womanism." To turn to "women of the republic" and to feminist organization for inspiration in articulating democratic values is one thing; it is quite another to conclude that therein lies evidence of women's "superior democratic nature" or of their "more mature" political voice. A truly democratic defense of citizenship cannot afford to launch its appeal from a position of gender opposition and women's superiority. Such a premise would posit as a starting point precisely what a democratic attitude must deny—that one group of citizens' voices is generally better, more deserving of attention, more worthy of emulation, more moral, than another's. A feminist democrat cannot give way to this sort of temptation, lest democracy itself lose its meaning, and citizenship its special nature. With this in mind, feminists would be well advised to secure the political defense of their theory of democratic citizenship not only in their own territory but also in the diversity of other democratic territories historical and contemporary, male and female. We might include the townships and councils of revolutionary America, the populist National Farmers Alliance, the sit-down strikes of the 1930s, the civil rights movement, the soviets of the Russian Revolution, the French political clubs of 1789, the Spanish anarchist affinity groups, the KOR (Workers' Defense Committee) in Poland, the "mothers of the disappeared ones" in Argentina, and so on. In short, the aim of this political feminism is to remember and bring to light the many examples of democratic practices already in existence and to use these examples as inspiration for a form of political life that would challenge the dominant liberal one.[41] What this aim requires is not only a feminist determination to avoid "womanism" while remaining attentive to women but also a commitment to the activity of citizenship, which includes and requires the participation of men.

I began these reflections by agreeing with Offred that "context is all." I end on what I hope is a complementary and not an overly optimistic note. We are indeed conditioned by the contexts in which we live, but we are also the creators of our political and social constructions and we can change them if we are so determined. The recent history of democratic politics in this country has not been an altogether happy one, despite spontaneous movements and periodic successes. Rather than occasion despair, however, perhaps this realization can work to strengthen and renew our sense of urgency concerning our present condition and what is to be done.

First, however, the urgency must be felt, and the spirit necessary for revitalizing citizenship must be enlivened in the public realm. Democracy, in other words, awaits its "prime movers." My aim here has been to argue that one such mover might be feminism and to suggest why I think feminism is well suited to this demanding and difficult task that would benefit us all.

ENDNOTES

[1] Margaret Atwood, *The Handmaid's Tale* (New York: Simon & Schuster, 1986).
[2] For some idea of the wide-ranging nature of the feminist critique of liberalism, see the following: Irene Diamond, ed., *Families, Politics, and Public Policy: A Feminist Dialogue on Women and the State* (New York: Longman, 1983); Zillah Einstein, *The Radical Future of Liberal Feminism* (New York: Longman, 1981); Jean Bethke Elshtain, *Public Man, Private Woman* (Princeton, NJ: Princeton University Press, 1981); Sandra Harding and Merrill Hintikka, *Discovering Reality: Feminist Perspectives on Epistemology, Metaphysics, Methodology, and the Philosophy of Science* (Dordrecht: Reidel, 1983); Allison Jagger, *Feminist Politics and Human Nature* (New York: Rowman and Allenheld, 1983); Juliet Mitchell and Ann Oakley, *The Rights and Wrongs of Women* (Harmondsworth: Penguin, 1976); Linda Nicholson, *Gender and History* (New York: Columbia University Press, 1986); and Susan Moller Okin, *Women in Western Political Thought* (Princeton, NJ: Princeton University Press, 1979). For a feminist critique of social contract theory, see Seyla Benhabib, "The Generalized and Concrete Other: The Kohlberg-Gilligan Controversy and Feminist Theory," *Praxis International* 5 (4) (1986), pp. 402–24; Christine Di Stephano, "Masculinity as Ideology in Political Theory: Hobbesian Man Considered," *Women's Studies International Forum* 6 (6) (1983); Carole Pateman, "Women and Consent," *Political Theory* 8 (2) (1980), pp. 149–68; Carole Pateman and Teresa Brennan, "Mere Auxiliaries to the Commonwealth: Women and the Origins of Liberalism," *Political Studies* 27 (2) (1979), pp. 183–200; and Mary Lyndon Shanley, "Marriage Contract and Social Contract in Seventeenth-Century English Political Thought," *Western Political Quarterly* 32 (1) (1979), pp. 79–91. For a critique of the "rational man," see Nancy Hartsock, *Money, Sex, and Power* (New York: Longman, 1983); Genevieve Lloyd, *Man of Reason* (Minneapolis: University of Minnesota Press, 1984); and Iris Marion Young, "Impartiality and the Civic Public: Some Implications of Feminist Critiques of Moral and Political Theory," *Praxis International* 5 (4) (1986), pp. 381–401. On Locke, see Melissa Butler, "Early Liberal Roots of Feminism: John Locke and the Attack on Patriarchy," *American Political Science Review* 72 (1) (1978), pp. 135–50; Lorenne M.G. Clark, "Women and Locke: Who Owns the Apples in the Garden of Eden?" in Clark and Lynda Lange, eds., *The Sexism of Social and Political Theory* (Toronto: University of Toronto Press, 1979); and Carole Pateman, "Sublimation and Reification: Locke, Wolin, and the Liberal Democratic Conception of the Political," *Politics and Society* 5 (1975), pp. 441–67. On Mill, see Julia Annas, "Mill and the Subjection of Women," *Philosophy* 52 (1977), p. 179–94; Richard W. Krouse, "Patriarchal Liberalism and Beyond: From John Stuart Mill to Harriet Taylor," in Jean Bethke Elshtain, ed., *The Family in Political Thought* (Amherst: University of Massachusetts Press, 1982); and Jennifer Ring, "Mill's *Subjection of Women:* The Methodological Limits of Liberal Feminism," *Review of Politics* 47 (1) (1985). On liberal moral theory, see Lawrence Blum, "Kant and Hegel's Moral Paternalism: A Feminist Response," *Canadian Journal of Philosophy* 12 (1982), pp. 287–302.
[3] For a sense of the historical and intellectual development of liberalism over the past three centuries, see the following (in chronological order): L.T. Hobhouse, *Liberalism* (London, 1911); Guido De Ruggiero, *The History of European Liberalism* (Oxford: Oxford University Press, 1927); Harold Laski, *The Rise of*

European Liberalism (London: Allen & Unwin, 1936); George H. Sabine, *A History of Political Theory* (New York: Holt, 1937); Charles Howard McIlwain, *Constitutionalism and the Changing World* (New York: Macmillan, 1939); John H. Hallowell, *The Decline of Liberalism as an Ideology* (Berkeley: University of California Press, 1943); Thomas Maitland Marshall, *Citizenship and Social Class* (Cambridge: Cambridge University Press, 1950); Michael Polanyi, *The Logic of Liberty* (Chicago: University of Chicago Press, 1951); Louis Hartz, *The Liberal Tradition in America* (New York: Harcourt Brace, 1955); R.D. Cumming, *Human Nature and History, A Study of the Development of Liberal Democracy,* 2 vols. (Chicago: University of Chicago Press, 1969); C.B. MacPherson, *The Life and Times of Liberal Democracy* (Oxford: Oxford University Press, 1977); Alan Macfarlane, *Origins of English Individualism* (Oxford: Oxford University Press, 1978); Steven Seidman, *Liberalism and the Origins of European Social Theory* (Berkeley: University of California Press, 1983); and John Gray, *Liberalism* (Minneapolis: University of Minnesota Press, 1986).

[4]Although Thomas Hobbes was not within the main (and broadly defined) tradition of liberal theory that includes but is not limited to Locke, Kant, Smith, Madison, Montesquieu, Bentham, Mill, T.H. Green, L.T. Hobhouse, Dewey, and, recently, Rawls, Dworkin, and Nozick, he set the stage for the view of man that came to distinguish much of liberal thought. In *De Cive*, Hobbes wrote, "let us ... consider men as if but even now sprung out of the earth, and suddenly, like mushrooms come to full maturity, without all kinds of engagement to each other." "Philosophical Rudiments Concerning Government and Society," in Sir W. Molesworth, ed., *The English Works of Thomas Hobbes* (London: Longman, 1966), p. 102. This invocation to view man as an autonomous "self" outside society is discernible, in varied forms, from Locke's state of nature to Rawls's "veil of ignorance." Contemporary critics of liberalism refer to this formulation as the "unencumbered self"; see Michael Sandel, "The Procedural Republic and the Unencumbered Self," *Political Theory,* 12 (1) (1984), pp. 81–96.

I will use the male referent in this discussion of liberalism for two reasons: first, it serves as a reminder of the exclusively male discourse used in traditional political theory, including that of the few theorists who are willing to concede that *he/him* means "all." Second, many feminist theorists have persuasively argued that the term *man* as used in liberal thought is not simply a linguistic device or a generic label but a symbol for a concept reflecting both masculine values and virtues and patriarchalist practices. See Brennan and Pateman, "Mere Auxiliaries to the Commonwealth."

[5]As Brennan and Pateman point out in "Mere Auxiliaries," the idea that the individual is by nature free—that is, outside the bonds of society, history, and tradition—was bequeathed to liberalism by social contract theorists. The emergence of this idea in the seventeenth century not only marked "a decisive break with the traditional view that people were 'naturally' bound together in a hierarchy of inequality and subordination" but also established a conception of "natural" individual freedom as the condition of individual isolation from others prior to the (artificial) creation of "civil society."

[6]John Stuart Mill, "On Liberty," in Max Lerner, ed., *The Essential Works of John Stuart Mill* (New York: Bantam, 1961), p. 266.

[7]T.H. Green, "Liberal Legislation and Freedom of Contract," in John R. Rodman, ed., *The Political Theory of T.H. Green* (New York: Crofts, 1964).

[8]Quoted in Sheldon Wolin, *Politics and Vision* (Boston: Little, Brown, 1963).

[9]Jagger, *Feminist Politics*, p. 33.

[10]Sir Isaiah Berlin, "Two Concepts of Liberty," in *Four Essays on Liberty* (Oxford: Oxford University Press, 1969), p. 122. Berlin goes on to note something that will be important to the argument I make in section III—that "freedom [as negative liberty] is not, at any rate logically, connected with democracy or self-government.... The answer to the question 'Who governs me?' is logically distinct from the question 'How far does government interfere with me?' " (pp. 129–30). The latter question, as we shall see, is the one that is of primary concern for the liberal citizen; the former must be of concern to the democratic citizen, and accordingly, to feminist political thought.

[11]John Rawls, *A Theory of Justice* (Cambridge, MA: Harvard University Press, 1971).

[12]The denial of citizenship to women is, of course, a historical but not a contemporary feature of liberalism. Nevertheless, it is worth noting that at least in early liberal thought, the ethical principles that distinguish liberalism—individual freedom and social equality—were not in practice (and often not in theory) extended to women, but solely to "rational men," whose "rationality" was linked to the ownership of property.

[13]Liberalism's context is actually a highly complex set of shifting social, political, and historical situations. We must not forget that in its earliest (seventeenth- and eighteenth-century) manifestations with the Levellers, the True Whigs, the Commonwealthmen, and revolutionary "patriots," the proclamation of individual rights and social equality were acts of rebellion against king and court. The domain of capitalist "possessive individualism" developed in a separate but related set of practices. Thus liberalism's legacy is a radical as well as a capitalist one.

[14]See Jagger, *Feminist Politics*, p. 31.

[15]As C.B. MacPherson rightly points out in *The Life and Times of Liberal Democracy*, p. 2, one of the prevailing difficulties of liberalism is that it has tried to combine the idea of individual freedom as "self-development" with the entrepreneurial notion of liberalism as the "right of the stronger to do down the weaker by following market rules." Despite attempts by J.S. Mill, Robert Nozick, and others to reconcile market freedom with self-development freedom, a successful resolution has not yet been achieved. MacPherson argues that the two freedoms are profoundly inconsistent, but he also asserts that the liberal position "need not be taken to depend forever on an acceptance of capitalist assumptions, although historically it has been so taken" (p. 2). That historical reality is the one I focus on here, and is what I think predominates in the liberal American view of citizenship. However, like MacPherson, I do not think liberalism is necessarily bound (conceptually or practically) to what he calls the "capitalist market envelope."

[16]Ibid., p. 1.

[17]Mary Lyndon Shanley, "Afterword: Feminism and Families in a Liberal Polity," in Diamond, *Families, Politics, and Public Policy*, p. 360.

[18]For example, see Jagger, *Feminist Politics;* Naomi Scheman, "Individualism and the Objects of Psychology," in Harding and Hintikka, *Discovering Reality;* Jean Grimshaw, *Philosophy and Feminist Thinking* (Minneapolis: University of Minnesota Press, 1986); Nicholson, *Gender and History;* and Young, "Impartiality and the Civic Public."

[19]I intentionally leave radical feminism out of this discussion, not because it is insignificant or unimportant, but because it has, to date, not arrived at a consistent political position on the questions that concern us here. For a helpful critique of radical feminism's theoretical failings, see Jagger, *Feminist Politics*, pp. 286–90, and Joan Cocks, "Wordless Emotions: Some Critical Reflections on Radical Feminism," *Politics and Society* 13 (1) (1984), pp. 27–57.

[20]By delineating this category I do not mean to blur or erase the very real distinctions between various kinds of Marxist feminists or to obscure the importance of the "patriarchy versus capitalism" debate. For a sense of the diversity of Marxist (or socialist) feminism, see: Mariarose DallaCosta and Selma James, *Women and the Subversion of Community: A Woman's Place* (Bristol: Falling Wall Press, 1981); Hartsock, *Money, Sex, and Power;* Zillah Eisenstein, *Capitalist Patriarchy and the Case for Socialist Feminism* (New York: Monthly Review Press, 1978); Catherine A. Mackinnon, "Feminism, Marxism, Method, and the State: An Agenda for Theory," in Nannerl O. Keohane, Michelle Rosaldo, and Barbara Gelpi, eds., *Feminist Theory: A Critique of Ideology* (Chicago: University of Chicago Press, 1981); Sheila Rowbotham, *Women, Resistance, and Revolution* (New York: Vintage, 1974); and Lydia Sargent, ed., *Women and Revolution* (Boston: South End Press, 1981). The quotations are from Hartsock, *Money Sex, and Power*, p. 235.

[21]Eisenstein, *The Radical Future of Liberal Politics*, p. 223.

[22]Ibid., p. 222.

[23]Hartsock, *Money, Sex, and Power*, p. 247.

[24]Sheldon Wolin, "Revolutionary Action Today," *Democracy* 2 (4) (1982), pp. 17–28.

[25]For various maternalist views see, among others, Jean Bethke Elshtain, "Antigone's Daughters," *Democracy* 2 (2) (1982), pp. 46–59; Elshtain, "Feminism, Family and Community," *Dissent* 29 (4) (1982), pp. 442–49; and Elshtain, "Feminist Discourse and Its Discontents: Language, Power, and Meaning," *Signs* 3 (7) (1982), pp. 603–21; also Sara Ruddick, "Maternal Thinking," *Feminist Studies* 6 (2) (1980), pp. 342–67; Ruddick, "Preservative Love and Military Destruction: Reflections on Mothering and Peace," in Joyce Treblicot, ed., *Mothering: Essays on Feminist Theory* (Totowa, NJ: Littlefield Adams, 1983); and Hartsock, *Money, Sex, and Power* (Hartsock incorporates both Marxist and maternalist perspectives in her "feminist standpoint" theory).

[26]Elshtain, "Feminist Discourse," p. 617.

[27]Elshtain, *Public Man, Private Woman*, p. 243, and Elshtain, "Antigone's Daughters," p. 59.

[28]Elshtain, "Antigone's Daughters," p. 58.

[29]See Nancy Chodorow, The Reproduction of Mothering: Psychoanalysis and the Sociology of Gender (Berkeley: University of California Press, 1978), and Carol Gilligan, *In a Different Voice: Psychological Theory and Women's Development* (Cambridge: Harvard University Press, 1982).

[30]I qualify this with "implication" because Gilligan is by no means consistent about whether the "different voice" is exclusive to women or open to men. For an interesting critique, see Joan Tronto, "Women's Morality: Beyond Gender Difference to a Theory of Care," in *Signs* 12 (4) (1987), pp. 644–63.

[31]Elshtain, "Feminist Discourse," p. 621.

[32]For a complementary and elegant critique of binary opposition arguments, see Joan Scott, "Gender: A Useful Category of Historical Analysis," *American Historical Review* 91 (2) (1986), pp. 1053–75.

[33]For a more detailed critique, see Dietz, "Citizenship with a Feminist Face: The Problem with Maternal Thinking," *Political Theory* 13 (1) (1985), pp. 19–35.

[34]The alternative conception introduced here—of politics as participatory and citizenship as the active engagement of peers in the public realm—has been of considerable interest to political theorists and historians over the past twenty years and has developed in detail as an alternative to the liberal view. Feminists now need to consider the significance of this perspective in regard to their own political theories. Perhaps the leading contemporary exponent of politics as the active life of citizens is Hannah Arendt, *The Human Condition* (Chicago: University of Chicago Press, 1958) and *On Revolution* (New York: Penguin, 1963). But alternatives to liberalism are also explored as "civic republicanism" in the work of J.G.A. Pocock, *The Machiavellian Moment: Florentine Political Thought and the Atlantic Republican Tradition* (Princeton, NJ: Princeton University Press, 1975), and in the recent "communitarian turn" articulated by Michael Sandel in his critique of the tradition of thinkers from Kant to Rawls, *Liberalism and the Limits of Justice* (Cambridge, England: Cambridge University Press, 1982). For other "democratic" critiques of liberalism, see Benjamin Barber, *Strong Democracy: Participatory Politics for a New Age* (Berkeley: University of California Press, 1984); Joshua Cohen and Joel Rogers, *On Democracy: Toward a Transformation of American Society* (New York: Penguin, 1983); Russell Hanson, *The Democratic Imagination in America* (Princeton, NJ: Princeton University Press, 1985); Lawrence Goodwyn, *Democratic Promise: The Populist Movement in America* (New York: Oxford University Press, 1976); Carole Pateman, *Participation and Democratic Theory* (Cambridge, England: Cambridge University Press, 1970); Michael Walzer, *Radical Principles* (New York: Basic Books, 1980); and Sheldon Wolin, *Politics and Vision* (Boston: Little, Brown, 1963). Also see the short-lived but useful journal *Democracy* (1981–1983).

[35]C. Douglas Lummis, "The Radicalization of Democracy," *Democracy* 2 (4) (1982), pp. 9–16.

[36]I would reiterate, however, that despite its historical propensity to collapse democracy into a capitalist economic ethic, liberalism is not without its own vital ethical principles (namely, individual freedom and equality) that democrats ignore to their peril. The task for "ethical liberals," as MacPherson puts it in *The Life and Times of Liberal Democracy,* is to detach these principles from the "market assumptions" of capitalism and integrate them into a truly democratic vision of participatory citizenship. By the same token, the task for participatory democrats is to preserve the principles of freedom and equality that are the special legacy of liberalism.

[37]Sheldon Wolin, "The Peoples' Two Bodies," *Democracy* 1 (1) (1981), pp. 9–24.

[38]I do not intend to imply that feminism is the only democratic movement that has emerged in the recent American past or that it is the only one from which we can draw examples. There are others—the civil rights movement, the populist resurgence, the collective political gatherings occasioned by the farm crises of the 1980s, gay liberation, and so on. But in its organization and decentralized practices, the feminist movement has been the most consistently democratic, its liberal, interest-group side (NOW) notwithstanding.

[39]The phrase "forms of freedom" comes from Jane Mansbridge, "Feminism and the Forms of Freedom," in Frank Fischer and Carmen Siriani, eds., *Critical Studies in Organization and Bureaucracy* (Philadelphia: Temple University Press, 1984), pp. 472–86.

[40]Some of the historical precedents I have in mind are developed in Linda Kerber's book, *Women of the Republic* (New York: Norton, 1980), especially in chapter 3, "The Meaning of Female Patriotism," in which she reconsiders the political activism of women in revolutionary America. Other activist precedents that contemporary feminists might recall and preserve are discussed in Sara M. Evans and Harry C. Boyte, *Free Spaces: The Sources of Democratic Change in America* (New York: Harper & Row, 1986); these include the abolitionist movement, the suffrage movement, the Women's Christian Temperance Union, the settlement house movement, and the National Women's Trade Union League, as well as contemporary forms of feminist organization and action.

[41]My point here is not that the soviets of 1917 or the Polish KOR of 1978 can serve as models for participatory citizenship in late twentieth-century America, but rather that an alternative to liberal citizenship can take root only if it is distilled into a framework of conceptual notions. The historical moments I mention (and others) provide the experiential and practical reality for such a conceptual framework and thus merit incorporation into feminist democratic politics. Or, as Arendt writes in *On Revolution,* "What saves the affairs of moral men from their inherent futility is nothing but the incessant talk about them, which in turn remains futile unless certain concepts, certain guideposts for future remembrance and even for sheer reference, arise out of it" (p. 20). The diverse practices mentioned above should be perceived as guideposts and references that might inspire a democratic spirit rather than as literal examples to be emulated in keeping with such a spirit.

Elizabeth Holtzman and Shirley Williams

Women in the Political World: Observations

E DITOR'S NOTE: When Max Weber spoke of politics as a vocation in 1918, he could, despite his own consistent support of the women's emancipation movement, represent politics as essentially a male profession; the qualities required for success in politics were rendered in terms that unmistakably expressed gender attributes common in that day. In the years since, in democratic societies particularly, women have increasingly entered politics, though never in the numbers anticipated by the early suffragettes. It seemed useful, for this issue, to inquire about the experience of politics for women in our time. Elizabeth Holtzman in New York and Shirley Williams in London consented to give their views.

*   *   *

Elizabeth Holtzman: Women's access to political office in America is hampered most seriously by the stereotyped belief that a woman cannot hold a difficult job. I was confronted with a blatant example of this attitude during my 1981 campaign for district attorney. My opponent had a radio commercial featuring a woman who said, "Liz Holtzman, she's a nice girl; maybe I'd like to have her as a daughter

---

Elizabeth Holtzman, born in 1941 in Brooklyn, New York, is district attorney of Kings County (Brooklyn), New York. She was a member of the House of Representatives (1973–1981) and served on the judiciary committee that considered President Nixon's impeachment.

Shirley Williams, born in 1930 in London, England, is in her third term as president of the Social Democratic Party, which she cofounded in 1981. Educated in England and the United States, Williams has held a number of elected political positions in England. She is the author of Politics Is for People *(1981) and* Job to Live *(1985).*

but not as a DA." The message to voters was subtle but strong: women should not attempt to venture outside their traditional roles into male territory.

And some voters were persuaded. I would meet people on the street who would tell me, "Liz, I voted for you for Congress, I voted for you for Senate, but DA, that's not a job for a woman. How can you cope with the pressure?" they asked. "How can you deal with so many men working under you? How can you stand up to criminals?" It was a tough race since my main opponent was not the other candidate but the public's image of a district attorney as a man.

Now that I am well into my second term as district attorney, whether a woman can be effective in that job is probably no longer an issue in New York City. But it can be an issue elsewhere, and opinion polls continue to find that the public is skeptical about women in high positions—particularly in executive positions. One study of senior-level women business executives found that they frequently encounter myths about a woman's ability to travel, take criticism, work with numbers, or work as a manager. As long as these prejudicial attitudes remain, women who seek political office will have to overcome the hurdle of convincing voters they can do the job.

Shirley Williams: I think one of the major problems of a woman politician in either Great Britain or the United States, where the image of woman is changing, is a certain conflict between what is seen by people to be the image of a politician and what is seen to be the image of a woman. Until very recently, because politics is in many ways a rather old-fashioned profession, those images tended to be somewhat dated. You must realize that the profession is composed mostly of middle-aged or elderly individuals, so you don't pick up many of the contemporary youth images.

The image with which many American woman have to contend—more than British women, I think—is the image of wife and mother. It seems to be quite difficult, though I notice things are indeed changing—that a woman politician would normally be expected, in the States, to also be a wife and mother. She would be expected to have a happy marriage and yet a masculine, probably dominant, husband. As for the fixed image of women married to politicians in the States, I've noticed they are almost Victorian: a perfectly turned out, perfectly groomed lady who admires all her husband's speeches and normally walks half a pace behind him, everywhere, all the time. He is always seen to be gallant, helping her down aircraft steps, assisting her through doors, standing up when she enters a room, and so on. In other words, the "Mrs. Reagan," even "Mrs. Carter," figure is in many ways an old-fashioned, fixed, conventional image.

Mrs. Carter tried to break out of that a bit and got punished for doing so, or at least that is my impression. A lot of people were very critical of the idea that Jimmy Carter actually spoke to his wife about serious matters like politics; that was thought inappropriate. There is a direct contradiction in all this that has never been resolved in the United States, at least in my view. A woman politician in her own right necessarily walks into these extremely complex and contradictory images. It's very hard for her to find the one that both suits her and fits her.

As for the modern kind of woman, the kind that has been coming forward in the last ten years, we are beginning to get women intent on pursuing their own careers. But then they run into the sort of dilemma that led reporters to ask, "Mrs. Ferraro, who does the washing up?" Such questions haunt American women politicians. It is linked to what I regard in some ways as the tragedy of Geraldine Ferraro; such questions would not have been asked her if she had been a man, and there was no way for her to answer them. The dilemma of the American woman politician is almost encapsulated in such frivolous concerns.

Holtzman: Women candidates are frequently held to higher standards than their male counterparts; the media and other institutions scrutinize a female candidate much more closely than a male. The disparate treatment of Geraldine Ferraro and Mario Cuomo on the abortion issue is a good example. Though both are Catholic Democrats holding similar positions on this question, Ferraro came under much more intense attack for her views on abortion than did Cuomo.

Williams: I'll tell you why I think it's easier in Great Britain for a woman politician than in the United States—not easy, but easier. There are two reasons, really. The first is that the tradition of the career woman is simply older in Britain. If you look back at the last two centuries, there seem to be many more familiar names like Florence Nightingale, Elizabeth Fry, George Eliot, and Jane Austen than in the history of the United States, despite the brilliance of Emily

Dickinson. The historical tradition of Joan of Arc or Eve Curie, the tradition of the woman in her own right pursuing her own career, does not really exist in America. Curiously enough, considering that in many ways women are more equal in the States, it is more common to find women in high places in Europe and Asia than in America. I think this is largely because women have enjoyed such power for a long time, for instance, in Britain ever since the time that they presided over religious communities as prioresses, having their own role, a role that entailed the right to command.

There is, however, another reason specific to many European countries: it's much easier because of the monarchy. Think of our queens, Elizabeth I, Anne, Victoria, and Elizabeth II. It is not seen to be "unmasculine" in Europe to accept a woman in a commanding position; it is a very old, honored, historical tradition that dates with us from Boadicea. There is no American tradition of that kind whatsoever, nor, for that matter, does it exist in any other country that started life as a colony.

It is also true that the consort role is a perfectly respectable role for a man in Britain. Nobody thinks that the Duke of Edinburgh is a wimp because he finds himself in a consort role. And no one thinks Dennis Thatcher is either. And absolutely nobody asks Dennis Thatcher who does the washing up. He is thought to have his own life, being answerable for his own business dealings. Nobody would think to put Mrs. Thatcher through the wringer in the way that they put Mrs. Ferraro through the wringer because of her husband. So again the gap is very wide.

There is a much clearer resolution in Britain than in the United States about what the role of the career woman is. Even so, in Britain's politics there is still the assumption in most cases that a man will have his wife to help him, so we run into the old dilemma again. Certain constituency associations don't care to appoint a woman as a candidate for Parliament because they think that if they appoint a man they get two for the price of one.

Holtzman: Of course, the public's difficulty in imagining a woman in public office reflects in part a historical truth: very few women have held such positions. Since 1789 over 10,000 men have served in the U.S. House of Representatives; only 107 women. Some 1,140 men have been senators as opposed to 15 women. More men are elected to Congress in a single year than all the women who have been elected in the nation's history.

One reason there are fewer women elected is that there are fewer women incumbents. The American political system gives a tremendous advantage to incumbents; in 1986, for example, 98.5 percent of incumbent candidates retained their seats in the House. Since women started from a point of zero incumbents, the "incumbency principle" ensures that their rate of entry into office will be exceedingly slow. Even where women do become governors or senators, their election nearly always follows years of service in lower offices. The resulting situation for women, as for other groups denied easy access to the political system, is something of a catch-22: it is almost impossible to win an office unless you already hold an office.

There has been one notable exception to this rule: women taking over the offices of their husbands or fathers. Offices that remain in the hands of families are traditional in certain parliamentary democracies. Even internationally, some women have been propelled into positions of power by continuing the work of their male relatives: one thinks of Indira Gandhi, Corazon Aquino, and Winnie Mandela.

In the early twentieth century, being a political widow was almost the only way for an American woman to gain access to high public office. In 1937 there were three women in the United States Senate—Hattie Caraway (Alaska), Dixie Bibb Graves (Alabama), and Rose McConnell Long (Louisiana)—all Democrats and all serving as successors to their husbands. In 1925 there were two women governors: Nellie Ross of Wyoming and Miriam "Ma" Ferguson of Texas, both succeeding their husbands.

While today more women are elected in their own right, women's access to political office remains sadly limited. There are actually fewer women in the Senate today than fifty years ago, and only one more woman governor than sixty years ago. While the number of women currently in the House of Representatives—twenty-three—is the highest ever, it is only five greater than the number a quarter of a century ago.

While this lack of progress is disturbing, there are indications to suggest that the situation will change in the near future. Women have made tremendous gains in elections to lower levels of government. In the past fifteen years, the number of women serving in state legislatures and municipal offices has more than tripled; women now hold about 15 percent of these positions. More than half of the states have elected women to statewide office. Women also occupy about 18 percent of state cabinet-level positions. As time goes by, women will be increasingly able to use these offices as springboards onto higher levels.

Williams: In the U.K., there are now 41 women out of a House of Commons of 630. This is the first big improvement since 1929. Why is this so? A good number of unmarried women filled such roles in the twenties and thirties. The casualties of the First World War, at least in Europe, meant a generation of unmarried women with no prospect of marriage; many were able to take on professional work, giving their whole time and attention to it. They were not distracted by having to run two lives, which is what has affected European women since. After the Second World War in Britain, where the losses were so much less, the results were very different. We are in any case now out of the period where European populations were massively affected by war. Most women today get married at least once, and most have children or at least are able to have them if they wish to. That means that we are looking at generations of women who are trying to do two things at once—hold a job, care for a family.

The great revolution that has not happened is a revolution in shared responsibilities for the family, in child care and in child rearing. Until those happen, you will not see more than a very small number of women, in my view, opting for a job as demanding as politics.

Holtzman: Today, because television advertising is crucial in campaigns for high office, a candidate must raise huge sums of money—often millions of dollars—in order to run a credible race. Many commentators have recognized that women find it much more difficult than their male counterparts to raise such campaign funds, particularly early in a race, when funds mean a great deal.

In my own case, I had great difficulty raising money for my 1972 bid for the House of Representatives. My opponent had held his seat for nearly fifty years, and I was a political unknown opposed by the powerful Democratic machine. I was able to raise just $32,000 for that race ($100,000 was supposed to be the bare minimum needed—and I was told "anyone" could raise that amount.) Although we couldn't afford any polls, any radio or TV, we used "shoe leather" and volunteers as a substitute. Amazingly, it worked then, but it is much harder, if not impossible, to win campaigns on a shoestring today.

There are many reasons why women have more trouble raising money. They generally do not have access to the financial networks that the more established of the male candidates regularly tap for funds. These networks may originate in businesses and corporations in which there are very few women and continue into clubs and associations where women are excluded. Furthermore, the vast majority of women candidates are challengers, whose races are generally more expensive than those of incumbents; a House challenger race is thought to be twice as expensive. In addition, many men simply refuse to give money to a female candidate. Finally, soliciting donations from other women is more difficult because their salaries are, on the average, one-third lower than those of men in comparable positions.

Williams: This is a handicap that you don't have to the same extent in Britain. Many women politicians in the United States have told me that they find the business of raising money very difficult. Yet you cannot really run in the States without a lot of money being raised for you. In Britain you can still run for peanuts. While the electoral timetable is worse here, the money issue, the raising of campaign funds, and the sheer image confusion is much more complicated in the States. Because it is so difficult, I don't think there will be, at least in this millenium, an American woman president. There may just possibly be an American woman vice-president. But when you think of the States as a country where the majority of all the shareholdings are in the hands of women, where the equality of women in the family is much more established than in Europe, it is odd that so few women in the States have managed to enter the front rank of politics.

Holtzman: While getting women into office is a clear priority, it is also crucial that women who hold office use their position to better the condition of other women. Some elected women, unfortunately, have not taken up the cause of helping women achieve full equality. Perhaps they are made to feel that such advocacy is illegitimate or that they cannot successfully confront the political and social structures that have discriminated against women for so long.

The evidence suggests otherwise. During the past two decades, many women legislators have been able to wield their power to attack gender discrimination and its consequences. Without female sponsors, it is doubtful that key legislation removing discriminatory barriers against women in such areas as insurance, pensions, education, health benefits, and federally funded employment would ever have passed Congress.

Despite such achievements, there remains a full agenda for women in public office, particularly in addressing the economic plight of the nation's women. A crucial step in improving women's economic standing is eliminating discrimination in the workplace. Women continue to be concentrated in lower-paying, sex-segregated occupations, and their earnings are roughly two-thirds those of men in comparable positions. This wage discrimination is largely to blame for the feminization of poverty, which has reached crisis proportions in the past decade. Businesswomen face what Betty Friedan has called the "glass ceiling"; they are able to get entry-level positions and middle-management positions but are promoted no higher. Working women at all levels confront sexual harassment and abysmally inadequate child care.

When I first took office as district attorney, there were no women attorneys as bureau chiefs or deputy bureau chiefs and no women on the executive staff. Even though more than 30 percent of the attorneys were women, they were routinely passed over for promotions, regardless of ability or seniority. I decided to show that a woman boss could help create equal opportunity. Today about half of the bureau chiefs and 33 percent of deputy bureau chiefs are women. And the changes I made apply not only to lawyers: I insisted on the assignment of a female bodyguard (over the protests of the captain of the police squad, who had appointed an all-male team) and created a career ladder that allows those in clerical positions to move up. Some with families now work on flexible schedules or have part-time jobs more suited to their needs.

No one told me to make these workplace changes, and no one in power would have complained had the old ways continued. If women are to make the political system address these same problems on the state and national levels, then it is crucial that they organize to do so. Women in office must lead the way, not only by highlighting the issues but also by making the most of their political power. The

Congressional Caucus for Women's Issues is a model for this type of organization, uniting women and sympathetic men of both parties to act effectively on women's issues. Many state legislatures lack such organizations; in New York, for example, there is still no women's organization for assembly and senate members to work with on women's issues.

Williams: In Britain, the political agenda for women today includes equality of wages, equality of working conditions, maternity benefits, a national and a just system of taxation, and the like, but there is no overwhelming set of feminist demands; there is no assumption that women as a special, unique, and separate part of humanity cry out to be heard. This is not, however, to say that women MPs are subject to precisely the same pressures as their male colleagues. Women MPs get about two or three times as many letters on the average as do the men in Parliament. The better-known women members receive even more. Many more people write to these women MPs, from both within and without the constituency, expecting that they will get more conscientious and more sympathetic treatment. And the writers include both men and women. So all women MPs stagger under a great load of personal letters from the public.

One other point needs to be made. In a sense, Franklin Roosevelt, in his generation, performed a role that Harold Wilson did in my generation in appointing women, in acting as the essential patron which all politics requires. Women politicians always suffer from a lack of patrons because there are no senior women above them—or have not been—and because very many men will be nervous about being seen to be patronizing younger women. They make themselves vulnerable if they take on this role; many choose to avoid the risk.

Ken Inglis

Men, Women, and War Memorials: Anzac Australia

J OAN WALLACH SCOTT, commending in 1979 an approach to the history of women that promised to expose "the often silent and hidden operations of gender which are nonetheless present and defining forces of politics and political life," declared that the approach must include the examination of "metaphoric and symbolic representations of feminine and masculine."[1]

Eric Hobsbawm had offered one such piece of analysis in 1978 by addressing the question of why artists first represented socialism in female form and then replaced the female figure by a male, the worker. His dazzling answer connected the transition with changes in the actual sexual division of labor under capitalism and with the decline of a preindustrial millennialism that had assigned prophetic roles to women. Critics fell upon Hobsbawm, illuminating regions of the past that had been dark until he sent up his fireworks.[2]

One clear lesson drawn from this debate is that when we study and attempt to interpret representations of men and women, or any other icons, we must exercise caution. Yet the most cogent of Hobsbawm's critics was Maurice Agulhon—who, through his sensitive investigation of "Marianne," symbol of the French Republic,[3] has shown that

Ken Inglis, born in 1929 in Melbourne, Australia, is professor of history at the Research School of Social Sciences, Australian National University, Canberra. His principal books include Churches and the Working Classes in Victorian England *(1963),* The Australian Colonists *(1974), and* This Is the ABC: The Australian Broadcasting Commission, 1932–1983 *(1983). Professor Inglis is an initiator and general editor of* Australians: A Historical Library *(1987–88), an eleven-volume series being published for the bicentennial of European settlement in Australia; he is a contributor to three of the volumes.*

much can be learned about political and social history by studying icons. Agulhon has yet to extend his study to the twentieth century, and thus to analyze those memorials to the dead of 1914–18, which, he observes, became the principal pillars of visual symbolism in France, their main images being the motherland/fatherland, the Gallic rooster, and the soldier.[4]

As in France, so in other countries where people had large cause to commemorate deaths in the Great War: the memorials are an underused resource for history. How is it possible, asks a French student, that we neglect so exceptional a demonstration of public art? "Thirty-thousand works conceived by municipal councils with the consent of the victims' families—the expression of the culture of the age. . . . "[5]

Great war memorials mean even more in Australia, 10,000 miles away from where the fighting took place, than they do in France. For World War I, the proportion of military participants from Australia was almost as high as that in any belligerent nation: about half of all males aged eighteen to forty-five enlisted in the Australian Imperial Force, and one in five was killed. They represented the first international venture of a new nation (the Commonwealth of Australia had been formed in 1901), and from the moment the first "Anzacs" (men of the Australian and New Zealand Army Corps) went ashore at Gallipoli on 25 April 1915, they were venerated at home for putting their country on the slate of history. Sixty thousand Australian soldiers died in the Great War—as many as were killed in the American Expeditionary Force, but from a population of only four million rather than 100 million. They were all buried close to where they died, so every monument in their homeland had to serve both as a statement about the soldiers and as a substitute for their graves—a cenotaph, an empty tomb. Monuments of this kind may well be proportionately more numerous in Australia and New Zealand than anywhere else. Each of France's 30,000 civic memorials represents about forty-five dead; each of Australia's 2,000 or more such monuments represents about thirty dead. Moreover, they occupy a landscape not settled by Europeans until 1788, and still nearly bare of monuments by 1914.

As symbolic representations of feminine and masculine, what do these memorials affirm? I begin with memorials on which women are named, collectively or individually; I proceed to those bearing female figures and then to those, far more numerous, embodying males; and I inspect the ceremonies created around these monuments.

The women whose names appear alongside men's on the tablets of Australian war memorials were nurses. Some 2,700 nurses served with 300,000 men during the war, nearly 2,300 of them overseas; twenty-three died. Many a local memorial lists one or more nurses with the soldiers, and thereby classifies them as equals. Elsewhere there are doubts about the classification. At Wallsend in New South Wales, a tablet with the names of five nurses was added to a memorial after it had been unveiled. At the separate unveiling of this tablet in 1920, the president of the Wallsend hospital made a point of declaring that "he had heard it said that the nurses were not soldiers, but he considered them part of the army, and it was pleasing to see that steps had been taken to show appreciation of them."[6]

To my knowledge, the only effigy of a nurse on a local monument is at Maryborough in Queensland, where a memorial has three servicemen accompanied by one nurse (Fig. 1). Inside Melbourne's vast Shrine of Remembrance, possibly the most massive 1914–18 monument in the world, you can find two nurses on relief panels inside the building if you look hard. Nurses are more readily visible on Sydney's state monument. The Anzac Memorial in Hyde Park has a nurse among sixteen stone figures sitting on buttresses, and a nursing matron as one of four figures standing high up at each corner of the building. Inside, a nurse is depicted on a relief panel honoring the Army Medical Corps. To solve the problem of how to classify nurses, the authors of the official description turned them into mothers: "Here is depicted one of the noblest phases of the war—weary and wounded men tended with loving care by the mothers of the race. . . . " Perceived in this way, the nurse is both more and less than "part of the army."

No woman doctor is honored on a 1914–18 war memorial, for none was allowed to join the Australian Army Medical Corps. Nor would the military authorities enlist women to release men for combatant duties, as proposed by the National Council of Women and by individual volunteers. Herbert Spencer, the English philosopher, had argued that women should not have the vote until they furnished contingents to the army and navy. The British statesman Herbert Asquith was converted to female suffrage by observing the voluntary work of women during the war. Australian women had

Fig. 1. Nurse, Maryborough, Queensland.

been entitled to vote since 1902, but the fact of their citizenship appears not to have weighed with either the military authorities or the politicians when women clamored to do more than perform the traditional female role of nursing.[7]

Two state capitals, Brisbane and Adelaide, have memorial tributes, in the name of the state's women, to the men who died. Brisbane's is a bas-relief of soldiers and horses, with a fountain; Adelaide's is a cross of sacrifice. Neither makes women part of the image. The largest cities, Melbourne and Sydney, have no women's memorial, though in Sydney a committee had planned one that would bear effigies of women, unlike those in Brisbane and Adelaide: in a monument designed by a woman sculptor, Theo Cowan, the "virile figure" of a soldier was to be accompanied by an angel representing

Immortality, a hooded woman (Destiny), a baby (Birth), a boy (Love), and a female (Death). But this piece did not appeal to prospective donors, who kept their money, or to the state's Public Monuments Advisory Board, set up in 1919 to censor war memorials in public places, which did not approve it. Sydney did get one modest memorial in the name of women, a fountain in the rock face at the inner-harbor neighborhood of Woolloomooloo, near gates at which thousands of women had surrendered men to war. But the Woolloomooloo fountain is no more emblematic of women than are the official women's memorials in other cities, unless the fountain itself (as textbooks of sculpture sometimes say) is symbolically feminine. The dominant theme of the few memorials built in the name of women beyond the capital cities—usually the work of bodies established during the war to rally women and girls behind the soldiers and their cause—is celebration of the soldier.

A number of individual women are named on memorials for laying foundation stones and for unveiling; others did those jobs without having their names recorded. Some were invited as wives of dignitaries such as governors, members of parliament, or shire presidents; some performed these duties as bereaved mothers or widows. Granny Riach, named as unveiler of the memorial at Thirroul, a small mining and railway town south of Sydney, was given the honor because she had collected most of the money for the monument. Australia during the second half of the Great War is usually depicted as a divided society, and the movement to commemorate the soldiers is generally interpreted as politically conservative. The Labor party certainly split during this time; the federal Labor government fell as a result of the dispute over whether conscription would be introduced to reinforce the expeditionary force, and industrial conflicts in 1917 and 1918 were surely connected with that controversy. But as all Thirroul knew, Granny Riach was a heroine of both returned soldiers and striking railway workers, and there were women like her in other small communities, enabled by ties of family and friendship to move comfortably between contesting causes. She simultaneously collected contributions for the war memorial and the strike fund. The strikers held a social evening to thank her, and the veterans dressed her in an army uniform and marched behind her down the main street for the unveiling in 1920. She pulled away the Union Jack that draped the memorial to reveal a stone soldier, a fountain, and an eight-sided

Fig. 2. Soldier, Thirroul, New SouthWales.

pedestal with marble tablets set on it (Fig. 2). The inscription of her name on the base reminded people that as principal maker of the memorial, Granny Riach had acted for the community. Two years later D.H. Lawrence, living in Thirroul and writing *Kangaroo*, contemplated this object: "A real township monument, bearing the names of everybody possible: the fallen, all those who donned khaki, the people who presented it, and Granny Rhys [*sic*]. Wonderfully in keeping with the place and its people. . . . "[8]

Some women were named "war workers," usually on tablets commissioned by local returned soldiers and placed inside or outside town halls. War workers were not women whom the war brought into the paid work force. Such women, especially those recruited to work in factories, became a problem when the men came back: they had to be discouraged from doing "men's work."[9] Nobody thought of honoring them. On the other hand, the women on the town hall tablets were helpmeets, hearth-tenders, who had undertaken voluntary work for the comfort of their menfolk as they waited, and who were rewarded by municipal acknowledgment. Some of the war workers had also contributed directly to the fighting forces by persuading men to enlist. They were mentioned in the *Official History of Australia in the War of 1914–1918,* though not by name, in two categories: "good women who . . . in their own mild way sent many a man to the recruiting stations" and "a shrieking sisterhood, who . . . made the air shudder with their demands upon all and sundry of the local young manhood."[10] Though these war workers were not honored on the memorials to soldiers, they might see themselves, if they chose, represented there in idealized figures of Motherhood or Womanhood.

Over the north portico of the Shrine of Remembrance in Melbourne, on a tympanum whose theme is the call to arms, a mother holds children. The municipal memorial at Malvern, a suburb of Melbourne, has a soldier and a young mother with infant in arms, each looking at a book of remembrance. Gatton, in Queensland, has a memorial with a mother who, unusually, is weeping. The South Australian War Memorial in Adelaide has a more generalized figure of Womanhood, said by the architects to symbolize woman's "tender maternal compassion, her sacrifice of son and lover, and her power of resistance under strain" (Fig. 3). This figure, winged, is a more or less close relative of the goddesses and quasi-goddesses of Graeco-Roman and Renaissance mythology who may be found on a number of monuments.

Winged Victories (strictly speaking, not goddesses, but messengers of the gods) were chosen for some communities. West Maitland in New South Wales has one, unveiled by the mayoress in 1923. Wellington in New South Wales has three female figures in bronze: Winged Victory holding her hero's sword, History recording his deeds, and Fame holding a laurel wreath. Redfern, an inner suburb of Sydney, has Fame or History seated below a soldier. Wollongong, just south of Granny Riach's territory in New South Wales, has a wingless Victory.

Fig. 3. Womanhood, Adelaide, South Australia.

That figure at West Maitland, officially Victory, was also said in the newspapers to be emblematic of Peace. Figures unambiguously named Peace are more numerous, I think, than Victories. Peace might stand alone, as in Leichhardt, Sydney, or in company, as in another Sydney suburb, Auburn, where Peace, with dove, is balanced by Justice, blindfolded, beneath a soldier with a draped flag. The Shrine of Remembrance in Melbourne has heroic female figures of Peace, Sacrifice, Justice, and Patriotism, not easily distinguishable from each other. There are other female abstractions, such as one in Mildura, Victoria, representing Grief (not weeping) surmounted by a cross (Fig. 4).

Most of these figures were made by professional sculptors who had learned to work in the classical tradition and were eager to do a

Fig. 4. Grief, Mildura, Victoria.

female statue. Their clients were not typically well versed in mythology, but they were not wholly passive: they were paying, they were commemorating, and they would say yes or no. They may have been uncertain about the orthodox accoutrements of Victory or Peace, but they knew that either was acceptable as a symbol. Apparently, no community wanted a statue of Bellona, Roman war goddess, though she was much to the taste of sculptors; when the most eminent of Australian-born practitioners, Bertram Mackennal, gave a bust of Bellona to the nation as a war memorial, she was moved from site to site like a vagrant and then put away. There is no Venus on a war memorial, for the obvious reason that the goddess of love and fertility is not perceived as fit for the purpose. Nor, as far as I know, is there any figure of Liberty, popular though she is in modern sculpture and commonly though she appears on French and American war memorials.

Liberty is a republican figure. She first appeared in France when the revolutionaries needed to replace the monarch as a symbolic personality for the nation. Liberty and Hercules competed for the job; Liberty won and was transformed into Marianne.[11] In the United States, Liberty evolved out of Columbia to be the female among contenders (including the rattlesnake, the eagle, Brother Jonathan, and Uncle Sam) to represent the American revolution and the newly declared republic. Of all the candidates, the Columbia/Liberty figure was evidently best suited to statuary: Liberty became France's centennial gift to the United States, icon of one republic translated to the other; as Columbia or Liberty she returned to France in the statuary of the American Battle Monuments Commission after 1918.[12]

Imperially loyal Australia had no call for statues of Liberty, either in war or in peace. Nor had artists created any other figure that satisfactorily symbolized Australia. Lacking the republican sentiment that had inspired Liberty and Marianne in France, and Liberty and Columbia in America, the Australians sometimes (but not often) made use of nondescript classical female figures; these were named Australia, or named for one of the six colonies (which became states after 1900), but were not taken to Australian hearts. Australians' sense of nationality was too mild, and too divided between the land they lived in and the imperial mother country, to be embodied in a sister of Marianne or Columbia.

The American cartoonist Livingston Hopkins, starting work for the Sydney *Bulletin* in 1883, fresh from a professional environment in which Thomas Nast and other newspaper artists had created a whole world of political allegory, was baffled as to how Australia or New South Wales should be represented. "In the early days," he later said, "whenever we had an occasion for a goddess or other personification of Australia, we found Minerva rather difficult to acclimatise. There was therefore in the *Bulletin* office a vacancy for some mythological figure to make itself generally useful." Hopkins was explaining how *Bulletin* artists came to invent the Little Boy from Manly, a child striding with innocent absurdity into the adult public world: a suitable symbol for comic cartoons, but lacking the solemnity and stature required of a symbolic figure for a national monument.[13]

Meanwhile, sculptors occasionally represented all or part of the nation with an insipid Minerva.

I know of only one war-memorial representation of Australia as a female: a monument at Mornington in Victoria represents Australia as a girl bending to put a laurel wreath on a fallen soldier. It is by the sculptor Dora Ohlfsen, who had worked as a nurse in an Italian hospital during the war; one reporter at the unveiling saw the figure not as the nation, but as a nurse.

For three of the nation's principal memorials, in Brisbane, Sydney, and Canberra, female Australias were designed by sculptors but not executed; for one reason or another, they did not seem right. For the Queensland state memorial in Brisbane, Bertram Mackennal planned an Australia juxtaposed with Britannia, but the design was rejected. For the New South Wales Anzac Memorial in Sydney, Rayner Hoff proposed another Britannia with female Australia as one of three groups of statuary, two of which were abandoned after a controversy. In Australia as elsewhere, war memorials often provoked conflict as people differed over just what sentiments should be affirmed by a monument and what was the right fit between meaning and symbol; the recent dispute over the Vietnam Veterans' Memorial in Washington, D.C., belongs to an unexplored tradition. The controversy over Sydney's principal monument to the Great War centered on its representation of women.

The architect Bruce Dellit imagined a sculptural group at the center of the memorial, composed of a hero "noble and glorious, in the Greek manner," dying after having killed a colossal bird of prey, and above, "a sorrowing woman nursing tenderly yet firmly an infant." The sculptor Rayner Hoff had another idea, which Dellit at once preferred to his own: the naked corpse of a soldier on a shield, supported by three females: wife (carrying baby), mother, and sister, in the classical form of caryatids. This group seemed to Dellit more masculine in effect, and therefore more appropriate, "for while women took part in the war, and female figures appear among Mr. Rayner Hoff's statuary, the conflict was mainly the concern of men."[14]

Hoff planned and modeled two other groups with strong feminine components. One was *Victory after Sacrifice*, 1918. This was his Australia-and-Britannia piece; the two female figures stood amid the dead who had made victory possible. The other group was *The*

Fig. 5. *The Crucifixion of Civilization*, proposed (and rejected) as the Anzac memorial in Sydney, New South Wales.

Crucifixion of Civilization, in which a naked, female Peace hung from a cross, surrounded by the armor, shield, and helmet of Mars, and with dead men and broken weapons at her feet (Fig. 5). Both of these groups were abandoned. So many objections were raised to them that it is difficult to determine which mattered most: they were too expensive, their modernism was out of place, the horrors at the feet of the female figures were distastefully vivid (Hoff himself had spent a year of the war in the trenches). The noisiest protests were ecclesiastical, and were directed not at Australia and Britannia, but at *The Crucifixion of Civilization* ("Nude Woman on Anzac Cross. RC Church Attack").[15] All Catholic priests who spoke up deplored it; Protestant clergymen were divided; but the alliance of Irish Catholic prudery and Anglo-Saxon puritanism was potent in the Sydney of

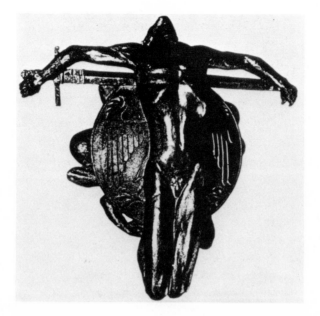

Fig. 6. *The Sacrifice*, Anzac memorial, Sydney (viewed from above).

1932. So the Anzac Memorial ended up featuring a matron and three men on the corners outside, a nurse and fifteen men lower down on the buttresses, a nurse inside on a relief panel, and at the center, in the Hall of Silence, a group called *The Sacrifice,* the naked hero borne aloft by his women (nude men evidently outraged no clergyman). Hoff wanted the group to embody sadness. If you look down on the group from the Well of Contemplation, as most visitors do—the space was designed to compel that downward gaze, as at the tombs of Napoleon and Grant—you see only one figure, the dead body (Fig. 6). Sword and shield show him to be a warrior, but he wears no uniform, and it is hard to imagine him a killer: he is passive, sacrificial, almost androgynous—not a giver of wounds but a receiver, like Saint Sebastian.[16] The side view of the Hall of Memory is less obligatory, but the upright, sustaining women and the baby are there to be seen by those who descend the steps (Fig. 7). Why the architect Dellit described the group as "more masculine" than his own projected figures is puzzling. The art historian Terry Smith, trying to render its complexities, writes: "The idea of achieving masculinity in its surrender to the feminine—i.e. achieving spiritual 'life' in the cessation of physical action, informs Hoff's astonishing

Fig. 7. Side view of *The Sacrifice*, Sydney.

sculpture. . . . "[17] Perhaps Dellit foresaw uneasiness on the part of the viewer and wanted to allay it. If the observer is baffled, the message set in the floor advises him or her not to search for words: LET SILENT CONTEMPLATION BE YOUR OFFERING.

No such ambiguity about gender is present in the national monument, the Australian War Memorial in Canberra; the makers took a long time, however, to settle on a thoroughly masculine symbol. The sculptor Leslie Bowles was commissioned to do an appropriate feature for the central space, a Hall of Memory. He proposed "a female figure, raised beyond a sarcophagus, symbolizing Australia proudly and courageously giving her all in the cause of freedom and honour."[18] But by the time she had become a plaster statuette, semidraped and classical, the sculptor decided (as had many before him) that such a figure was trite.

The national memorial took a long time to build. It was opened, but not finished, during World War II. On the day that war ended, the sculptor had a fresh vision for the Hall of Memory: a shaft composed of four figures, caryatid-like though of no identifiable sex, representing the four freedoms proclaimed as Allied war aims. That piece was vetoed by a conservative minister for the interior who hated modernism and who declared the work even worse than that of Jacob Epstein (known for his boldly modern, often harsh works). Bowles died before he could try again. What was finally installed, executed by the sculptor Raymond Ewers after the trustees had taken advice from senior officers in the army, navy, and air force, was a huge soldier, bare-armed, tin-helmeted, and remote, in a posture of theatrical defiance (Fig. 8). The figure emits one clear message to people visiting their nation's capital: this memorial belongs to men at war.

On local memorials the names of men appear far more often than those of women as layers of foundation stones and unveilers. The inaugural rituals were normally performed by men of large or small authority in public affairs: governors-general, governors, premiers and other ministers, local members, municipal office-bearers. If a statement is inscribed on the monument, its purpose is to honor the men of the community who fought and fell. Some monument inscriptions list only the dead; most include all who served, with the names of the dead listed separately or marked with an asterisk or a sword. The lists of names are the one universal element: the monuments are there to proclaim, sometimes in the very words from Ecclesiasticus that are carved in every cemetery of the Imperial War Graves Commission, that "their name liveth for evermore." The human figure that appears most often on the monuments is the private soldier, or "the digger," as he came to be called during the war. D.H. Lawrence spotted him unerringly at Thirroul: "a statue in pale, fawnish stone, of a Tommy standing at ease, wearing his puttees and his turned up felt hat . . . about life size, but standing just overhead on a tall pedestal . . . small and still and rather touching."

He is not the only masculine figure on memorials, but exceptions are few. There are knights, late expressions of that revived cult of chivalry that Mark Girouard observed in England.[19] Australia's two most patrician schools, Geelong Grammar and the King's School, have memorials featuring knights; some see the dead warrior in the

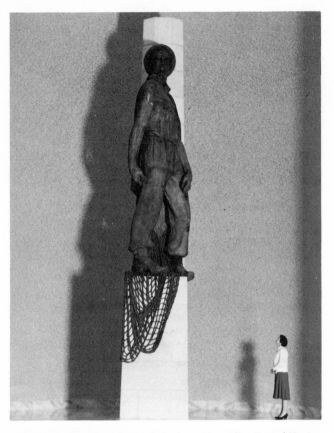

Fig. 8. Soldier, Australian War Memorial, Canberra, Australian Capital Territory. (Photograph courtesy of Australian War Memorial.)

crypt of Saint Mary's Catholic Cathedral in Sydney as knightly. But I have had to go inside, away from public ground, to find the knights. Angaston in South Australia has a unique monument, unveiled on Anzac Day 1921, with the archangel Michael in bronze, intended to represent the triumph of right over might.

There are not many figures of dying soldiers in Australian war memorials. France and Italy have many, often dying in the arms of a woman who symbolizes the motherland or Liberty. It has been proposed that such figures in France symbolize the Oedipal nation slaughtering its father; this Freudian interpretation seems dubious when one considers that so many of the dying figures, often named as *enfants* on the inscriptions, represent sons rather than fathers.[20] I wonder if those dying figures in Latin countries can be seen as secularized versions of the Pietà, a tradition not readily accessible to a mainly Protestant and civically nondenominational Australia.

Nor are there many pairs of soldiers, mate helping mate as in Australian legend. Aggressive figures are rare. This is partly a matter of material, technique, and cost: a belligerent lunge, putting the statue's center of gravity ahead of it, is easier for a sculptor to cast in bronze than for a mason to achieve in stone. But even vertical aggression in stone—an arm raised to throw a grenade or to call for action—is unusual. The Thirroul stance is far more common: solitary, passive, the soldier at rest, not on the way to kill; such figures stand on their pedestals in hundreds. The stone digger is what Australians most wanted before they were criticized by architects, sculptors, and advisory boards.

Forerunners of the stone digger appear in Australia and England on memorials to men who fought and died in South Africa between 1899 and 1902, and also on Civil War monuments in the United States. Connoisseurs of sculpture winced at these figures and tried to discourage communities from making similar choices to commemorate the men of 1914–18. The journal of the American Federation of Arts reproduced an advertising-circular illustration of a dumpy doughboy with a rifle—he could almost have fitted Lawrence's description of the figure at Thirroul—and captioned it "Forerunner of an invading army to be feared."[21] Custodians of high art in Australia, England, and America did their best to resist that invasion; they were more successful in England than in Australia, perhaps because mourners in the motherland were readier to take advice on such matters from people who were perceived as their cultural betters.

The digger is a plain and homely figure, created by artisans, not artists: "the [product] of the shop, not the studio," as the American Federation of Arts' journal put it.[22] He expresses both the craftsmanship of stonemasons and the wants of their clients, who commissioned a digger because they could afford him and he was to their taste. The editor of a journal in the building industry looked at the sculpture proposed for Sydney's Anzac Memorial and said, "the Australian Digger would [not] have appreciated anything so highflown as this in his memory. He would have preferred plain facts to flights of fancy."[23] But nobody actually protested the use of high sculpture in the grand civic monuments of Sydney, Melbourne, Adelaide, Brisbane, and Canberra. In the cathedrals of Anzac, elaboration, pomp, and artistry may have been appropriate; in the local monument, which was the equivalent of the parish church, Australian congregations of the 1920s were more comfortable with icons that were modest, domestic—belonging to the same world as the symbols in their cemeteries.

From the cemetery came the obelisk, which is the one symbol more common on Australian war memorials than the digger. Students of the obelisk have perceived it to be phallic. Should we therefore count obelisks as male when surveying representations of gender on war memorials, or would that be abandoning caution? Obelisks may be phallic, but they are also cheap, easily made by stonemasons, and have surfaces that readily take inscriptions of names and messages.

Digger and obelisk, Victory, Peace, column, clock tower, and arch: everywhere, after the survivors returned, the local memorials became sites for ceremonies enhancing that separateness of men which had long been noticed as a fact of Australian society. "The pub, the game, and the races," writes Jill Conway, "stood in constant tension with the family, and the emerging rituals of the culture gave a man a social territory away from women and children which was an important part of his identity."[24] Yes; and after 1918 add the clubrooms of the Returned Soldiers' League—which enrolled a higher proportion of veterans than any equivalent body in any other country—and the commemorative ceremonies of Anzac.

The returned men were encouraged to think of themselves as an aristocracy. The nation must honor them, said the *Sydney Morning Herald* on 25 April 1919, fourth anniversary of the landing at Gallipoli, by "the speedy and adequate use of their splendid manhood." Such rhetoric was common in the victorious countries. It was sharpened in Australia by the declaration that the soldiers had *made* the nation, had "lifted Australia from comparative obscurity," in the *Herald*'s words, and by the fact that the Australian Imperial Force, almost uniquely among the armies on either side, had been composed entirely of volunteers; having in that precise sense given themselves, they merited singular reward. The federal government gave them the world's most generous system of military pensions, and preference in public service employment. State governments passed laws requiring private employers also to give preference, as the

New South Wales Act of 1919 put it, "in any profession, business, or industry to a returned soldier or sailor who is capable of effectively performing the duties. . . . "[25] These measures were invoked against men who had not been to the war and, less commonly, against women, whose participation in the commercial, professional, and administrative sectors of the work force had increased when the men were away at war, and for the first time in the history of European Australia, the continent had been occupied by more females than males.[26]

Nobody thought of legislating preference for returned nurses, though at least one nurse, Annie Smith, was deemed eligible under Victoria's Discharged Soldiers Settlement Act for help to become a farmer. She struggled singlehandedly to run a dairy farm at Thorpdale in eastern Victoria and was forced to surrender it after a few years. "If a man had this place, who was capable of doing his work," said officials, "it would be good policy for the Board to allow him to proceed." The man who took over the farm was also soon forced to abandon it. The feminist historian who has documented Annie Smith's story notes that she was good at calming veterans who were raving victims of shell shock. She writes, "The war memorial that had been erected to commemorate the twelve Thorpdale boys who had made the 'supreme sacrifice' was no doubt a more comforting reminder of the recent war than the deranged cries of some who returned."[27]

The word *Anzac*, protected by law from profanation, was central to the rhetoric of those who spoke about returned soldiers and was regularly used by veterans themselves. An official war historian considered it a male word, a war cry "pitiless as a hurled spear. It conveys something savagely masculine, ruthless, resolute, clean driven home."[28] Saint Anzac, said an old digger, is Australia's patron saint, "a type of sacrificial manhood." Anzac Day, 25 April, became more sacred than any other day in the Australian calendar. The day itself, according to an official commemorative publication, "is like a great tall pillar standing on a vast plain that cannot help being seen, and as we look upon it we can only bow our heads."[29]

In other countries the war dead were remembered each year on 11 November, anniversary of the armistice. That day, shared with people in every country who had their dead to mourn, became the occasion for a celebration in France even more patriotic than Bastille

Day.[30] In the United States the war dead were mourned on Armistice Day and on Memorial Day, whose original name, Decoration Day, bespoke its origin in a time when women laid flowers on the graves of soldiers killed in the Civil War. A day of mourning, 11 November stood also for peace and reunion and the transformation of soldiers back into fathers, husbands, and sons. It encouraged a communal commemoration. Australians chose to remember their war dead not on the day fighting ended but on the day it began: 25 April stood for bloodshed, baptism by fire, the separation of soldiers from everybody else.

Many war memorials were designed and commissioned by broadly based committees. While women served on these committees in various capacities, the rituals enacted around the memorials on Anzac Day came to be controlled by organized returned soldiers. Granny Riach unveiled Thirroul's digger on Anzac Day in 1920, but no such woman could march in men's uniform or lead a contingent of veterans for long. The ceremonies became increasingly masculine. *Reveille,* organ of the Returned Soldiers League, reproached soldiers who had watched their fellow veterans go by during Sydney's Anzac Day march in 1928: "On such a day their place is in the march with their comrades—not on the sidewalks with their wives and families."[31] The men's job was to march, as they had marched away to war, and then to assemble at the memorial, remembering their dead. For women who attended ceremonies at memorials or Anzac Day services in churches, the ideal, as the son of one zealous returned soldier reflected, was Volumnia, mother of Shakespeare's Coriolanus (who, had she a dozen sons, "had rather had eleven die nobly for their Country, than one voluptuously surfeit out of action"). Graeme McInnes, recalling his boyhood in Melbourne in the 1920s, wrote that bereaved mothers, "as stern-faced as Volumnia, attended service standing erect and dry-eyed, their bosoms stitched with their dead sons' medals."[32]

Bands of women had formed during the war either to resist it, as did the Women's Peace Army, or to educate society against warfare, as did the Sisterhood of International Peace[33]—and to make common cause with like-minded women elsewhere. They attracted fewer supporters than did the imperially patriotic National Council of Women. Whether the peacemakers guessed it or not, a majority of Australian women voters supported conscription at referenda in

1916 and 1917 and a conservative, Win-the-War party victory in the federal election of 1917.[34] A modern analyst of the conscription referenda comments that "so far nothing in the electoral behaviour of Australian women justified the feminist hope that women would not vote to send men to war." Moreover, there were women who combined a love of peace with an attachment to Anzac symbolism and ceremony. Among Australia's most famous early feminists, Jessie Street thought Sydney's Anzac Memorial a fine monument, and Mary Gilmore was responsible for getting the town of Goulburn in New South Wales a more commanding war memorial than it would have had without her. Gilmore embraced both socialism and patriotism, somewhat to her own surprise and to the dismay of a later feminist, Carmel Shute, who includes her regretfully among prominent women who subscribed to the mystique of the male warrior by writing in terms that extolled the heroism and nobility of Australian soldiers. Shute argued in 1975 that the penetration of the myth of Anzac into the Australian psyche retarded the struggle for women's liberation for another fifty years.[35]

It was not until 1966 that any group of women used a war memorial for unprescribed ceremony on Anzac Day. That year in Melbourne, twenty women who opposed the sending of conscripts to Vietnam laid flowers on the World War II memorial beside the Shrine of Remembrance. Some wore hats or veils, some had war medals on their chests (Fig. 9). They might now be regarded as pioneers of a female countertradition. For some new-wave feminists, the war memorials and the rituals of Anzac Day are an affront, a provocation. Inspired by the American movement Women Against Rape, they have invented a tradition of rape in warfare and they have begun to stage demonstrations at or near war memorials (Fig. 10). Participants in these demonstrations have been tactically divided over whether to demand the right to join in Anzac Day ceremonies and lay their own partisan tributes on the memorial or to disrupt the traditional procession on its way to the monument. At the Australian War Memorial in Canberra on Anzac Day 1984, a group of women sang a song whose refrain ended: "though I come to lay this wreath/ I spit on your stone."

The war memorials once attracted only people who accepted what they affirmed. To this day, no Australian war memorial has been knocked down or blown up (as have monuments in such places as

Fig. 9. Women protesting, Anzac Day 1966.

Fig. 10. Women protesting, Anzac Day 1984.

France, Ireland, and the Soviet Union). Now the memorials gain attention from people, especially women, who reject their message or demand to change it. Three-quarters of a century after the first of these monuments was erected, they still have the power to arouse emotion.

ENDNOTES

Much of the information in this essay was collected by Jan Brazier and Judith McKay. The paper has benefited from help by Joy Damousi, Amirah Inglis, Marilyn Lake, Julian Thomas, and participants in the Gender, Technology, and Education conference held in September 1986 at Bellagio, Italy, from which this issue originated.

[1] Joan Wallach Scott, "Women in History: The Modern Period," *Past and Present* 101 (November 1983), p. 156.

[2] Eric Hobsbawm, "Man and Woman in Socialist Iconography," *History Workshop Journal* (6) (Autumn 1978), pp. 121–38. Critics in later issues said that Hobsbawm confused symbols of revolution with symbols of socialism; that he ignored representations of male workers earlier than fitted his argument; that in purporting to make amends to women he invoked an obsolete, prefeminist history of women's work; that his analysis of a particular female figure created by a nonsocialist pornographer betrayed sexual prurience; that he adopted a crudely reductionist model of the relations between art and social reality; and that he had engaged in premature internationalism, conflating several national stories that need first to be told apart before any common elements can usefully be assembled for analysis.

[3] Maurice Agulhon, *Marianne into Battle: Republican Imagery and Symbolism in France, 1789–1880* (Cambridge, England: Cambridge University Press, 1981). First published as *Marianne au combat: l'imagerie et la symbolique republicaines de 1789 à 1880* (Paris: Flammarion, 1979).

[4] Maurice Agulhon, "Politics, Images, and Symbols in Post-Revolutionary France," in *Rites of Power: Symbolism, Ritual and Politics Since the Middle Ages*, ed. Sean Walentz (Philadelphia: University of Pennsylvania Press, 1985), p. 196.

[5] Oliver Descamps, *Les monuments aux morts de la guerre 14–18: chefs-d'oeuvre d'art public* (Paris: Cahiers d'art public, 1978). The principal study so far is Antoine Prost, *Les anciens combattants et la société francaise 1914–1939* (Paris: Presses de la Fondation Nationale des Sciences Politiques, 1977), vol. 3. See also Michael Ignatieff, "Soviet War Memorials," *History Workshop Journal* (17) (Spring 1984), pp. 157–63, esp. on war memorials (not just in the U.S.S.R.) as "acts of collective amnesia."

[6] *Newcastle Morning Herald,* 9 February 1920.

[7] Jan Bassett, " 'Ready to Serve.' Australian Women and the Great War," *Journal of the Australian War Memorial* 2 (April 1983), pp. 8–16.

[8] D.H. Lawrence, *Kangaroo*, 1923, chapter X. Lawrence changes Riach to Rhys, and Thirroul to Mullumbimby. The making and unveiling of the memorial are reported in the *South Coast Times* and the *Illawarra Mercury*, and in E. Johnson, "Thirroul RSL 1920–77," a manuscript by the vice president of the Thirroul subbranch of the Returned Services League.

[9] Edna Ryan and Ann Conlon, *Gentle Invaders: Australian Women at Work, 1788–1974* (West Melbourne: Nelson, 1975), p. 98.

[10]Ernest Scott, *Australia During the War: The Official History of Australia in the War of 1914–1918*, vol. XI (Sydney: Angus and Robertson, 1938), p. 317.

[11]Lynn Hunt, "Hercules and the Radical Image in the French Revolution," *Representations* 1 (2) (Spring 1983), pp. 95–117, esp. p. 111.

[12]Alton Ketchum, *Uncle Sam: The Man and the Legend* (New York: Hill and Wang, 1959); Marvin Trachtenberg, *The Statue of Liberty* (London: Allen Lane, 1976).

[13]Dorothy J. Hopkins, *Hop of the Bulletin* (Sydney: Angus and Robertson, 1929), p. 136. On the Little Boy from Manly, see K.S. Inglis, *The Rehearsal: Australians at War in the Sudan, 1885* (Sydney: Rigby, 1985).

[14]Dellit's views on the Anzac Memorial sculpture and the controversy surrounding it are documented in Ken Scarlett, *Australian Sculptors* (West Melbourne: Nelson, 1980), pp. 265–72.

[15]Newspaper headline quoted in Scarlett, *Australian Sculptors*, pp. 266–67.

[16]The similarity to Saint Sebastian was remarked on by Michael Ignatieff in a discussion of Figure 6.

[17]Terry Smith, "Populism and Privilege in Australian Painting," *Australian Cultural History* 3 (1984), p. 40.

[18]K.S. Inglis, "A Sacred Place: The Making of the Australian War Memorial," *War and Society* 3 (2) (September 1985), pp. 116–22.

[19]Mark Girouard, *The Return to Camelot: Chivalry and the English Gentleman* (New Haven: Yale University Press, 1981).

[20]Descamps, *Les monuments aux morts.* In *Rites of Power,* ed. Walentz, Agulhon contrasts "very down-to-earth historians who accumulate important data about images, but who refuse to engage in symbolic speculations" with others who, "starting out with the cultural prestige that goes with studies of symbolism, hastily pick out a few examples from masses of information and then proceed to psychoanalyze France with a few strokes of the pen. The latter group is dazzling and fashionable, but the former group is more useful. Historians should try to reunite the two approaches." (p. 202.)

[21]*The American Magazine of Art* 10 (7) (May 1919), p. 270.

[22]Ibid. (March 1919), p. 180.

[23]George A. Taylor, in *Building* (Sydney: July 1930), p. 52.

[24]Jill Conway, "Gender in Australia," *Daedalus* 114 (1) (Winter 1985), pp. 350–51.

[25]Scott, *Australia During the War,* p. 185.

[26]On women in the work force, I draw upon the tentative judgment of W.A. Sinclair, "Women and Economic Change in Melbourne, 1871–1921," *Historical Studies* 20 (79) (October 1982), pp. 278–91.

[27]Marilyn Lake, "Annie Smith: 'Soldier Settler,' " in *Double Time—Women in Victoria,* ed. Marilyn Lake and Farley Kelley (Ringwood: Penguin Books, 1985), pp. 268–75.

[28]F. M. Cutlack, in *Anzac Day Sermons and Addresses* (Brisbane: Anzac Day Commemoration Committee, 1921), p. 27.

[29]*Anzac Day 1936* (Sydney: Anzac Day Commemoration Committee, 1936), p. iv.

[30]See Agulhon in *Rites of Power,* ed. Walentz, p. 197.

[31]*Reveille,* 30 April 1928.

[32]Graeme McInnes, *The Road to Gundagai* (London: Hamish Hamilton, 1965), p. 283.

[33]Darryn Kruse and Charles Sowerwine, "Feminism and Pacifism: 'Women's Sphere' in Peace and War," in *Australian Women: New Feminist Perspectives,* ed. Norma Grieve and Ailsa Burns (Melbourne: Oxford University Press, 1986), pp. 42–58.

[34]Glenn Withers, "The 1916–1917 Conscription Referenda: A Cliometric Reappraisal," *Historical Studies* 20 (78) (April 1982), pp. 36–47.

[35]Carmel Shute, "Heroines and Heroes: Sexual Mythology in Australia, 1914–1918," *Hecate* 1 (1) (January 1975), pp. 7–22.

Anne Fausto-Sterling

Society Writes Biology / Biology Constructs Gender

TRUTH, BIAS, OBJECTIVITY, PREJUDICE. In recent years both defenders and critics of the activities of the modern Western scientific community have used these words with a certain abandon as they engage in debate about the role of science and the scientist in our culture. Perhaps the best-known voice in this discussion is that of Thomas Kuhn, whose historical analyses of the "progress" of science threw into sharp relief the uneven nature of the development of scientific ideas.[1] In the past decade feminist analysts of science have joined the discussion. Historians, philosophers, anthropologists, and scientists who write from a feminist perspective have raised varied and complex questions about modern science.[2]

In this essay I propose to examine the interaction of two processes that have important consequences for our understanding of how science works. These are (1) the process by which cultural under-standings of gender become building blocks in supposedly objective understandings of nature, and (2) the process by which scientific theory helps to shape social concepts such as gender.

The two case studies presented in this essay (one historical, one contemporary) will illustrate how cultural understandings or beliefs, whether conscious or unconscious, influence the construction of scientific theory. Two current examples of the way scientific ideas are

Anne Fausto-Sterling, born in 1944 in New York, New York, is professor of medical sciences at Brown University. She is the author of Myths of Gender: Biological Theories About Women and Men *(1985) and numerous scientific articles on* Drosophila *development.*

used to define social norms will illustrate the role that scientific theory plays in the definition of social concepts.

SOCIAL CONSTRUCTION OF SCIENCE

The writings of a famous and highly imaginative Italian scientist, Abbé Lazzaro Spallanzani (1729–99), illustrate that the inner workings of the mind of a dedicated experimental scientist are complex and often under subconscious wraps.[3] Although Spallanzani is probably best known for his experimental disproof of the idea of spontaneous generation, he also made an important contribution to eighteenth-century thinking about fertilization and embryonic development. The presence of spermatozoa in the semen had been discovered in Spallanzani's time, but the role of these "vermicelli" (or "spermatozoan worms," as they were often called) remained a subject of considerable debate within the context of a long-lived controversy about the origin of the embryo. Ovists believed that it arose solely from the egg, while spermists maintained that the womb was a passive vessel that offered fertile ground for the growth and development of the semen.

The most famous of early biologists belonged to different camps. The frontispiece of William Harvey's *Concerning the Generation of Living Animals* depicts Zeus sitting on a throne and opening what looks like a bird's egg, out of which hop, fly, and crawl all manner of beasts, mythical and otherwise. On the egg is written *Ex ovo omnia.* On the other side we find Antony van Leeuwenhoek arguing that the animalcules in semen find their way to the womb, where they act as seed; he dismisses eggs as "emunctorys* . . . adhering to the bowels of animals."[4]

Spallanzani, an ovist, performed a series of experiments with mating frogs to disprove Carolus Linnaeus's claim that insemination must always be internal. In a classic demonstration of the scientific method, he observed that the male frog, grasping the female frog as she lays eggs, deposits semen on the eggs as they emerge from her uterus. To test the semen's function, he constructed little taffeta

---

*emunctory: *n, pl* -ries (NL *emunctorium,* fr. L *emunctus,* pp. of *emungere* to clean the nose, fr. *e-* + *-mungere* (akin to mucus): an organ (as a kidney) or part of the body (as the skin) that carries off body wastes. *(Webster's New Collegiate Dictionary)*

breeches for the male frogs (unwittingly presaging Kenneth Gra-
hame's *The Wind in the Willows*, in which toads wear clothes and
drive cars) and made the following observations:

The males, notwithstanding this incumbrance, seek the females with equal
eagerness and perform, as well as they can, the act of generation; but the
event is such as may be expected: the eggs are never prolific for want of
having been bedewed with semen, which sometimes may be seen in the
breeches in the form of drops. That these drops are real seed, appeared
clearly from the artificial fecondation that was obtained by means of them.[5]

In other words, Spallanzani showed not only that preventing semen
deposition prevented egg development, but also that when he spread
semen on the eggs, fertilization resulted. A model of good experimentation indeed.

But Spallanzani did not conclude from these or other experiments
that the vermicelli were necessary for the embryo to develop. Instead
he conducted a series of experiments in an attempt to find out how
much semen was needed to achieve fertilization. Observing that even
very tiny amounts were sufficient, he concluded that the important
factor was something he called the "seminal aura," which he thought
to be "nothing but the vapor of the seed exceedingly rarified."[6]
Believing that his results proved the ovists's theory, he proceeded to
perform a series of experiments on the seminal aura, all of which he
designed to disprove the role of the spermatozoan in fertilization. He
diluted semen samples until he could see no more sperm and found
the diluted fluid still capable of fertilization. He also filtered semen so
thoroughly that it could no longer induce development. The former
results he took as proof of the existence of a seminal aura; the latter
he ignored.[7]

In Spallanzani we have an example of a highly talented eighteenth-
century scientist doing careful experiments that prove, to our
modern-day eyes, the opposite of what he concluded. Because he
interpreted his investigations within a particular theoretical framework—that of ovism—his mind was closed to alternative conclusions
that seem obvious to those not so committed. Because Spallanzani
was a scientist of considerable authority and influence, his conclusions, rather than his experimental results, dominated biological
thought on fertilization. A correct account of the role of the sperm in
fertilization and development was not generally accepted for another

100 years. The point here is not that an incompetent scientist made a series of experimental errors, but that an extremely good scientist performed a series of beautifully controlled experiments but did not draw from them the correct conclusions. The process by which cultural categories shape perception and influence reasoning is little studied. The case of Spallanzani and his experiments on spermatozoa and their role in fertilization would be an excellent starting point for a cultural anthropologist who wished to analyze this process. That this phenomenon holds true for modern scientific activity can be seen in the next, more contemporary example.

During mammalian development all embryos (regardless of their potential sex) pass through a stage that embryologists have dubbed the "indifferent period." Examination of XX and XY embryos during this period shows no evidence of sex differences in either the embryonic gonad or sexually-related somatic structures such as the oviducts or the vas deferens. Present are a single gonad that will later take either a male or female path of development, and two sets of accessory structures known as the mesonephric and paramesonephric ducts. In female development the mesonephric ducts disintegrate while the paramesonephric ducts form the oviducts, uterus, and part of the vagina. In male development the paramesonephric ducts degenerate while the mesonephric ducts develop into the epididymal duct and the vas deferens. In general, then, mammals first develop a single pair of gonads, which subsequently takes either a male or a female direction, and both male and female accessory structures, only one set of which survives while the other degenerates. Baldly stated, up to a certain point all embryos are completely bisexual.

The choice of whether to follow a male or a female path of development is made through the intervention of the sex chromosomes and hormones present in utero. It is at this point in the story that a curious use of language that has set limits on the experimental questions asked about sexual development enters in. I will first recount the tale as it is told in text books, popular literature, and the vast majority of scientific papers, and then underline some of the story's peculiarities, showing how they have resulted in a supposedly general account of the development of the sexes that is in actuality only an account of male development. This example illustrates a case in which the meaning of *man* as a supposedly inclusive universal has slipped unnoticed into its meaning as an exclusive biological category. What biologists turn out to have provided as our account of the development of gender from a mechanistic point of view is really only an account of male differentiation.

The following excerpts come from an up-to-date and heavily used undergraduate embryology text written by Dr. Bruce M. Carlson. My intent is not to attack Carlson, who recounts an almost universally held set of beliefs, but merely to analyze the text to uncover some of the underlying structures of those beliefs. Carlson writes:

The sex-determining function of the Y chromosome is intimately bound with the activity of the H-Y antigen . . . its major function is to cause the organization of the primitive gonad into the testis. In the *absence* of the H-Y antigen the gonad later becomes transformed into the ovary. (Italics added.)

The account continues with a discussion of the formation of nongonadal (somatic) sex organs such as the uterus and vas deferens.

The early embryo develops a dual set of potential genital ducts [the mesonephric and paramesonephric ducts]. . . . Under the *influence of testosterone* secreted by the testes, the mesonephric ducts develop into the duct system through which spermatozoa are conveyed from the testes to the urethra. . . . The potentially female paramesonephric ducts regress *under the influence* of another secretion of the embryonic testes, the Mullerian Inhibitory Factor. (Italics added.)

In genetically female embryos neither testosterone nor Mullerian Inhibitory Factor is secreted by the gonads. In the *absence of testosterone* the mesonephric ducts regress and the *lack of Mullerian Inhibitory Factor* permits the paramesonephric ducts to develop into the oviducts, uterus and part of the vagina. The external genitalia also first take form in a morphologically indifferent condition and then develop either in the male direction *under the influence of testosterone* or in the female direction *if the influence of testosterone is lacking*. (Italics added.)[8]

Carlson also writes of "the natural tendency of the body to develop along female lines in the absence of other modifying influences."[9] The presence-or-absence-of-maleness concept is an old one. Simone de Beauvoir quoted Aristotle as saying that "the female is a female by virtue of a certain *lack* of qualities."[10] Psychologist Dr. John Money calls accounts of sexual development similar to Carlson's an example of "the Adam Principle" that something is *added* to an embryo to make it a male.[11] A well-known reproductive biologist, Dr. R.V.

Short, concludes an introductory account of sex determination differentiation by spelling out what he sees as the implications of that viewpoint:

In all systems that we have considered, maleness means mastery; the Y-chromosome over the X, the medulla [of the indifferent gonad] over the cortex, androgen over oestrogen. So physiologically speaking, there is no justification for believing in the equality of the sexes; *vive la différence!*[12]

The idea that the female represents some natural, fundamental "ground state" is also familiar. Strangely, although biologists emulate physicists by reducing organisms to smaller and smaller parts in order to investigate causes that precede causes ad infinitum, they are generally satisfied to accept the idea that a female direction of development occurs passively in the absence of instructions from so-called male sex hormones.* How does it happen? What are the mechanisms? Investigators ask these questions about male development (generically referred to as sexual differentiation), but only a few express interest in applying the same scrutiny to development of the female. This imbalance in levels of intellectual curiosity is reflected in the etymologies of the words that name sex hormones: *androgen* comes from the Greek *andros* and the Latin *generare* (to make a male), *estrogen* from the Latin *oestrus* (gadfly or frenzy). In fact, the word *gynogen*, which would be the etymologically and biologically correct counterpart to *androgen*, cannot be found in biological accounts of sexual development (or, for that matter, in any dictionary).

If we look carefully at the existing biological literature, we can see how we might construct a narrative that treats female sexual differentiation as requiring as much investigation and explanation as male sexual differentiation. We could begin by examining the many studies on hormonal control of sexual development in cold-blooded vertebrates. Some examples: the addition of estrogen to the water of certain XY (potentially male) fish causes them to develop as females rather than males; similarly, the addition of estrogen to the water of amphibian tadpoles before and during their metamorphosis to adults results in all exposed larvae becoming females.[13] Clearly, such

---

* In reality, both males and females produce estrogens and androgens, but in differing quantities.

research provides evidence that so-called female hormones actively induce female development; that is, they behave as gynogens. But the findings of studies on cold-blooded vertebrates are usually considered inapplicable to mammals. Only rarely does a publication on mammalian development include a consideration of the active role of female hormones.

Estrogen and progesterone (another female hormone) are not absent during female mammalian development. In addition to estrogen synthesis in the fetal ovary, all sexual development, both male and female, takes place in the presence of high concentrations of placentally-produced female hormones, especially the estrogens and progesterones.[14] That sexual development occurs in a sea of female placental hormones is recognized and viewed as a "problem" for male development. A variety of hypotheses have been proposed and experiments carried out to explain why the developing male embryo is not feminized by maternal hormones. Yet the scientist who is concerned about the potential feminizing effect of female hormones in male development is often the same one who writes that female development is not directed by hormones at all, but is an event that results from a lack of male hormones. This lopsided logic requires both attention and explanation.

What I've just written is, of course, an oversimplification. In some parts of the scientific literature the idea of a positive role for estrogen has begun to creep in. This is partly due to the discovery that testosterone may be converted into estrogen by certain cells in the body, and that what was long believed to be an effect of testosterone on male behavior in rodents is actually caused by the conversion of testosterone to estrogen by cells in the brain.[15] Nevertheless, the associations of male/presence/active and female/absence/passive still govern our concepts of human development and influence the language used to explain them in the current literature.

There is one other etymological/scientific issue to be teased out of the account of male and female development in vertebrates. It is the designation of the male gamete-transporting ducts as mesonephric (middle kidney) and the female's as paramesonephric (sitting next to the middle kidney). Three different types of kidneys have evolved during the evolution of vertebrates: the pronephros, the mesonephros, and the metanephros. In mammals the pronephros is vestigial in the embryo and completely absent in the adult. The mesonephros functions as a kidney in the embryos of some mammals, and its ducts become part of the adult postembryonic male gonadal duct system (this ancient connection between gamete transport and waste excretion is also seen in vertebrates such as those fish and amphibia whose kidney tubules are the means of transporting both sperm and urine to the outside.) The metanephros becomes the functional kidney at birth.

In female mammals there evolved a separate set of ducts (dubbed the paramesonephric ducts) having nothing to do with the kidneys, apparently designed only for the transport of ova. The prefix *para* has several meanings, including near, beside, adjacent to, closely resembling, almost, beyond, remotely or indirectly relating to, faulty or abnormal condition, and associated in an accessory capacity. The use of the prefix is common in the language of anatomy and certainly not restricted to structures related to sexual organs. The adrenal glands, for example, are sometimes referred to as the paranephros because of their location atop the kidneys, so the naming of the paramesonephric ducts for their positional relationship to ducts in the male (note that they have no separate name of their own as do the adrenals) could be nothing more than happenstance. It would be easier to sustain that argument, however, if the literature revealed further interest in both the embryonic and evolutionary origins of these ducts. Yet knowledge about them is lacking.

The changing function of an organ such as the embryonic kidney is a well-known evolutionary phenomenon. Front limbs, for example, have evolved into wings, arms, legs, and flippers. Bones that form parts of the jaw in reptiles have become the functional sound-receiving and -transferring bones of the inner ear in mammals. On the other hand, the appearance of a brand new structure is less common and presents a profoundly difficult explanatory problem for evolutionary biologists. Yet the evolutionary and embryological origins of the paramesonephric duct, which might be such a de novo structure, have been little studied; as one author writes, "The phylogenetic origin of paramesonephric ducts is again obscure."[16] As in the case of estrogen's role in governing female development, our lack of understanding of the origin and development of the paramesonephric duct represents a research path not taken. The reasons for this are probably multiple, but at least one of them must be that the road to understanding these ducts has been considered a side path, one lying next to or away from the main road that one must follow in order to understand male development.

Another example of how scientific language betrays a one-sided curiosity can be found in the literature on the study of male and female sexual differentiation of the rat brain, which until very recently has been framed around the idea that testosterone provides an "organizing effect" on the "intrinsic tendency to develop according to a female pattern of body structure and behavior."[17] (Does this phraseology imply that the female brain is disorganized?) Or consider the fact that mutations affecting androgen metabolism in humans and other mammals have been extensively studied and well-cataloged, but that none affecting estrogen metabolism have been isolated. Some authors have suggested that because implantation in the uterus is impossible without estrogen, an ovum affected by a mutation that interferes with estrogen metabolism would not survive. In other words, estrogen metabolism may be more poorly understood than androgen metabolism because it is essential for mammalian life. From this perspective, the focus on the role of androgens in sexual development, while not misplaced, certainly seems one-sided. Correcting the imbalance is not technically impossible; estrogen metabolism studies could be conducted with laboratory animals in ways that avoid the problem of lethality. It seems, though, that our considerable scientific and experimental ingenuity has not yet been directed toward solving this particular puzzle.

These cases from the biological literature strongly suggest that broad cultural paradigms about the nature of male and female have had a considerable effect on biological theory. The language used to describe "the facts" has channeled experimental thought along certain lanes, leaving others not only unexplored but unnoticed.

THE SCIENTIFIC CONSTRUCTION OF CULTURE

The idea that biologists can construct culture may be taken both literally and figuratively. Consider, for example, the current explosion of knowledge and technological capability that falls into the category of genetic technology. Growth hormone, produced during childhood and important for normal postnatal development, was available on only a very limited basis until recently because its only

source was purified human pituitary glands. Because of its unavailability and expense, its use in therapy was mandatorily restricted to
children who, because of growth hormone insufficiencies, would fail
to grow before puberty and would thus become adult dwarfs. Now,
however, the stretch of DNA that codes for growth hormone has
been cloned and inserted into a common bacterium that can easily be
grown in large quantities. As a result of such technical advances, large
quantities of relatively inexpensive growth hormone will become
commercially available in the very near future. What are the cultural
consequences of this "progress"?

In 1984 the National Institute of Child Health and Development
(NICHD) held a conference on the potential uses of a more easily
available growth hormone. Although a number of interesting issues
arose during the conference, I will focus on only one—what I call an
attempt to redefine normality—in this case, with regard to height. We
all know that humans come in many different heights. There are not
two classes, tall and short, but a continuous range, at the farthest
ends of which we have dwarfs and giants, people who are so far from
average height that few things in the world are designed to suit them.
Coat racks are too high or too low. Ditto water fountains. And
finding appropriate mass-produced clothing is out of the question.
There are several kinds of dwarfism and giantism, some of which
result from the body's production of too little or too much of certain
hormones. The question is, At what point do we consider such states
to be medically abnormal? At what point in the continuum of height
difference do we have a disease in need of a cure?

We could probably agree that three-foot-tall and eight-foot-tall
adults would have had an easier and better life if their condition had
been treated during childhood to bring them into a more "normal"
range. Instead of addressing this issue, however, the members of the
NICHD conference concentrated on defining a new disease, neither
dwarfism nor giantism, that they called "short stature." "The con-
ferees agreed . . . that the emotional suffering and lack of opportunity
for short persons to participate fully in society require more study
and *intervention*." They also reached the consensus that there is an
"urgent need for therapeutic trials to determine the effect of growth
hormone in short children *who do not have a growth hormone
deficiency*." (Italics added.)[18] As a result of the conference participants' definition of this new category of biological abnormality, there

will soon be a treatment available for short stature—a treatment that might otherwise have had a rather small market.

Such a redefinition of biological normality, especially when it involves increasing the potential market of a particular drug, is not new. For example, it is a little-known but reasonably widespread practice for private physicians to prescribe hormones for taller-than-average girls who express concern that they may grow "too tall for a woman." The hormone treatment brings them into puberty early, which causes them to stop growing and thus keeps them within the "normal" female height range. Here, social views about how tall a female should be lead to medical intervention with the growth process in order to keep a female's physical height within the socially prescribed norm. This norm is based in part on prior biological observation; it ignores the fact that the current well-fed Western European and North American populations are taller than generations past. The biological norm that has influenced the social norm is changing, while the social norm—at least for women—plays a role in an attempt to prevent further biological change.

Just as cultural values and beliefs shaped Spallanzani's observations and influenced scientists' perceptions of what was important to investigate in male/female development, so biological theory influences cultural norms. The far-reaching impact of such influences can be seen in the claim that men are biologically more competent at spatial visualization, and thus at mathematical skills, than women. In the United States, supposed sex differences in mathematical ability are often cited as an explanation for the relatively small percentage of women who work as mathematicians, engineers, physicists, and architects (not all European countries have the same skewed sex ratio of employment). The assertion that differences in mathematical ability are biologically based has had a well-documented effect on our entire educational system.[19] Rather than cover a large, complicated, and already well-reviewed literature on this topic, I will continue my case study approach by discussing the 1984 volume of *Progress in Brain Research*, a book entirely devoted to the topic of sex differences in the brain.[20]

The interspecific scope of the book is evident in its table of contents. An article on sex differences in testosterone metabolism in the Japanese quail sits side by side with articles on sex differences in the rat brain, in songbirds, in talapoin monkeys, in marmosets, and last but definitely not least, in humans. Some articles jump back and forth between species; for example, "Hormonal Organization of Sex Differences in Play Fighting and Spatial Behavior"[21] has two paragraphs on rhesus monkeys, followed by four on humans, one on humans and monkeys, one on monkeys and rats, and five on rats alone. The volume is characterized by the use of evidence drawn from studies of one species to formulate projections or applications for other species. Data drawn from many different species are used as though they apply to humans, with no acknowledgment of the theoretical issues involved in so doing. Thus theories based on studies of rats, postulating an organizing influence of testosterone on the brain, are either directly or by implication applied to humans as well. Yet any good comparative anatomist talking with a well-trained comparative ethologist would be quick to acknowledge the enormous differences in brain complexity and learning capacity—and in the relationships between hormone concentrations and particular behaviors—that exist across the phylogenetic spectrum.

The impact of the book and of such interspecific intermixing is difficult to evaluate because of the variable quality of the articles. In the same volume there are articles that disprove the organizational role of testosterone on the brain and articles that assume the truth of the organizer hypothesis. The scientific positivist would argue that this situation simply reflects the scientific process *en marche:* the pros and cons of a theory are openly debated, and the truth will out. At some levels the process of scientific debate does work in this volume. Yet in general what one sees is simply a mosaic of propositions. Differing perspectives on sex differences in the brain appear side by side, illustrating a broad pattern of views about the roles of male and female in our culture.

An article entitled "Sex Differences in Mathematical Abilities," for example, purports to provide a balanced account of biological and social theories on the origin of such differences, and concludes that a combination of both biological and social factors cause sex differences in mathematical ability. The authors are conducting a longitudinal study of young people who have been identified as having unusual mathematical talent. Their fairly substantial sample consists of about 40 percent girls. Their much-publicized finding is that among these youngsters, who are in the top 5 percent of their classes in terms of mathematical ability, more boys than girls score in the very high ranges (above 700) on college aptitude tests. Because most of these children have had the same number and kinds of math courses in school, the authors conclude that the observed differences in test performance may well be due to an innate biological difference, one they suggest is connected to different levels of prenatal exposure to testosterone in males and females.

In response to a question about the consequences of their work on math and science education for young women, the authors make the following ambiguous reply:

There are many more males than females who can reason extremely well mathematically. This is group data and . . . cannot be used to counsel any single person. Our data do, however, tell us that it is likely that many more boys than girls will be successful in their pursuit of degrees or careers in quantitatively oriented sciences.[22]

The logical jumps in this statement are problematic for a number of reasons, not the least of which is the authors' projection of potential success in college and business as if test scores were the sole determinants of one's professional progress. In this regard, the authors make much of their data showing higher male than female performance in high school on math aptitude tests, but let slip without discussion the fact that the same set of female students get higher *grades* in their math courses. Consideration of the quality of math and science education and its influence on the degree and career patterns of young men and women is peculiarly absent from the discussion, an absence, I argue, that stems from a reliance on "scientific data" of the sort presented in the volume—data that are removed from the social and political contexts in which the research has taken place. Disembodied scientific concepts are often used to make far-reaching social decisions about such things as the structure of our educational system.[23]

The views of the authors of the article on mathematical ability continue to receive widespread publicity. One recent example is a UPI story[24] about a paper delivered by Dr. Camilla Benbow at the national meetings of the American Association for the Advancement of Science. Newspapers and national television evening news reported her speculations of a connection between testosterone, hemispheric specialization of the brain, and the supposedly greater mathematical reasoning skills of males. The intellectual poverty of this viewpoint has been well-demonstrated in a variety of forums. A recently published study suggests the damaging effects on adolescent girls of such widespread publicity by showing that parents' confidence in their daughters' mathematical ability was significantly shaken by the implications of an earlier article by Benbow and Stanley, which received nationwide attention.[25] The suggestion of biologically based feminine intellectual incapacities can influence girls to limit their horizons. Not only must the door to mathematical study be open to females, but the path leading to it must be cleared of obstacles, some of which come in the form of gender-influenced and gender-biased scientific research.

In the 1984 volume of *Progress in Brain Research,* the intermingling of a wide range of animal studies (some of which are very well done, providing clear-cut results of experiments carried out under carefully controlled and defined laboratory conditions) with studies on humans (which are usually poorly done and taken out of social context) lends unwarranted scientific credence to the latter work. Ironically, the best aspects of the scientific process—the testing and reformulating of hypotheses—here lend a kind of moral support to the worst aspects—the unwarranted logical jumps in reasoning resting on data drawn from widely differing species, the nonconscious assimilation of cultural ideology into scientific theory, and the design and analysis of studies on human subjects without recognition of or regard to cultural frameworks and theory.

CONCLUSION

What should we conclude about the social function of science, and about science as an intellectual activity? Much recent writing about science has involved linear, unidirectional thinking: the social function of science is presented as either good or bad; science is held to be either totally objective or totally biased, a form of enquiry through which progressive knowledge may be gained or a form of enquiry shaped by the culture in which it has grown. Instead, the relationship between the activities of scientists, their cultural attitudes, the theories they devise, and their effects on human biology and social institutions are nonlinear and multidirectional. The same is true of reflections on the scientific process. The activities of scientists are self-deluding *and* self-correcting; they are at once potentially progressive and retrogressive. What we must do in writing about them is to shuttle back and forth along the strands of meaning in order to gain more complex and accurate understandings of the processes involved.

ENDNOTES

I would like to thank all the participants in the Conference on Gender, Technology, and Education at Bellagio, Italy, 7–11 October 1985, for their comments, support, and insights into the original draft of this paper. I am grateful to Sandra Harding, Evelyn Fox Keller, and Helen Longino for reading a draft of this paper and offering me their suggestions. I also thank Carol King for typing more than one version of the paper.

[1] Thomas W. Kuhn, *The Structure of Scientific Revolutions* (Chicago: University of Chicago Press, 1962).

[2] See, for example, Ruth Herschberger, *Adam's Rib* (New York: Pellegrini and Cudahy, 1984); Evelyn Fox Keller, *Reflections on Gender and Science* (New Haven, CT: Yale University Press, 1985); Anne Fausto-Sterling, *Myths of Gender* (New York: Basic Books, 1985); Ruth Bleier, *Science and Gender* (New York: Pergamon Press, 1984); Marian Lowe and Ruth Hubbard, *Woman's Nature* (New York: Pergamon Press, 1983); Carolyn Merchant, *The Death of Nature* (San Francisco: Harper & Row, 1980); Janet Sayers, *Biological Politics* (London: Tavistock, 1982); Sandra Harding, *The Science Question in Feminism* (Ithaca, NY: Cornell University Press, 1986).

[3] See also Evelyn Fox Keller, *A Feeling for the Organism* (San Francisco: Freeman, 1983), and June Goodfield, *An Imagined World* (New York: Harper & Row, 1981).

[4] Albert Tyler, "Comparative Gametology and Syngamy," in *Fertilization: Comparative Morphology, Biochemistry and Immunology*, vol. 1, ed. Charles B. Metz and Alberto Monroy (New York: Academic Press, 1967).

[5] Ibid.

[6] Ibid.

[7] Ibid.

[8] Bruce M. Carlson, *Patten's Foundations of Embryology* (New York: McGraw-Hill, 1981), pp. 459–61.

[9] Ibid.

[10] Simone De Beauvoir, *The Second Sex* (New York: Bantam, 1952), p. xvi.

[11] John Money, *Love and Lovesickness* (Baltimore: Johns Hopkins University Press, 1970), p. 5.

[12] R.V. Short, "Sex Determination and Differentiation," in *Embryonic and Fetal Development*, ed. C.R. Austin and R.V. Short (London: Cambridge University Press, 1972), p. 70.

[13] Ursula Mittwoch, *Genetics of Sex Differentiation* (New York: Academic Press, 1973).

[14] J.D. Wilson et al., "The Hormonal Control of Sexual Development," *Science* 211 (1981), pp. 1278–84.

[15]See Robert W. Goy and Bruce S. McEwen, eds., *Sexual Differentiation of the Brain* (Cambridge, MA: MIT Press, 1980); Bleier, *Science and Gender;* and *Progress in Brain Research* 61 (1984).

[16]M. Hildebrand, *Analysis of Vertebrate Structure* (New York: John Wiley & Sons, 1974).

[17]Goy and McEwen, *Sexual Differentiation,* p. 3.

[18]C. Gene Drafts, *Genewatch* 1 (5 & 6) (1985), p. 9.

[19]See Margaret Rossiter, *Women Scientists in America: Struggles and Strategies to 1940* (Baltimore: Johns Hopkins University Press, 1982); Sayers, *Biological Politics;* and Fausto-Sterling, *Myths of Gender.*

[20]*Progress in Brain Research* 61 (1984).

[21]William W. Beatty, "Hormonal Organization of Sex Differences in Play Fighting and Spatial Behavior," *Progress in Brain Research* 61 (1984), pp. 315–30.

[22]Camilla Persson Benbow and Robert M. Benbow, "Biological Correlates of High Mathematical Reasoning Ability," *Progress in Brain Research* 61, pp. 469–90.

[23]Rossiter, *Women Scientists in America;* Sayers, *Biological Politics;* and Fausto-Sterling, *Myths of Gender.*

[24]"In Math, Biology May Be Destiny," *Providence Journal,* 27 May 1986, p. A-9.

[25]J.W. Eccles and Janis E. Jacobs, "Social Forces Shape Math Attitudes and Performance," *Signs* 11, pp. 367–80.

Evelyn Fox Keller

Women Scientists and Feminist Critics of Science

H ISTORIANS, PHILOSOPHERS, AND SOCIOLOGISTS of science have, over the past twenty-five years, grown increasingly aware of the force of social and political factors in the production of scientific knowledge. Feminist scholars have recently added gender ideologies to the list of cultural variables affecting the observation of nature by scientists. Their analyses have thrown light on the role of gender ideals—first, in the historical development of science; second, in shaping the beliefs and behavior patterns we bring to the study of nature. Indirectly, the same analyses have also added to our current understanding of gender as a cultural rather than a biological construct. The introduction of this perspective has considerably enriched our understanding of the social dimensions of modern science, and in the process has helped to clarify rather than undermine the relation between science and nature. But many working scientists find the new perspectives generated by these insights incomprehensible. Perhaps largely because of the ease with which the social category of gender tends to be confused with biological sex, particularly acute misunderstanding has arisen between many women scientists and feminist critics of science. In this

Evelyn Fox Keller, born in 1936 in New York, New York, is professor of mathematics and humanities at Northeastern University and currently a fellow at the Institute for Advanced Study, Princeton, New Jersey. Her publications include A Feeling for the Organism: The Life and Work of Barbara McClintock *(1983),* Reflections on Gender and Science *(1985), and numerous articles in mathematical biology, molecular biology, and physics. More recently, Professor Keller has focused on the history, philosophy, and sociology of science. Her current work is on language and ideology in contemporary science.*

essay I will explore the differences in mind-sets responsible for such misunderstanding, using my own experience as a working scientist and feminist critic to guide me. My aim is an enlargement of world view, both for feminist critics and for working scientists—an enlargement I see as essential to the proper integration and development of the insights introduced by feminist critics of science.

INTRODUCTION

For centuries we have lived with the (conscious or unconscious) awareness of deep contradictions between our cultural ideals of "woman" and of "science." Today these contradictions are still deeply embedded in individual and collective consciousness, but they are no longer confined to the domain of implicit emotional and intuitive knowledge. They have been made explicit—brought into the domain of academic discourse, formally available to analysis and criticism. Over the past decade, feminist scholars have subjected these deep-rooted contradictions to serious historical, philosophical, and psychological inquiry. In so doing, they have offered radically new challenges to some of our most unexamined cultural assumptions.

Ironically, during the same decade, women have been going into scientific fields in unprecedented numbers. Of last year's entering class at MIT, 38 percent were women. In 1986 women constituted 31 percent of the scientific work force in America; even in physics, perhaps the most notoriously male stronghold of the sciences, the most recent data suggest that women are beginning to make their appearance, albeit slowly. What, today's women scientists are asking, are these feminists talking about? Prejudice, perhaps, but the very existence of women scientists seems to belie the notion of a contradiction between "woman" and "science."

While many questions can be usefully raised about how well today's women scientists will do, e.g., how many of them are getting tenure at the best universities, the issue I wish to focus on here is rather that of the difference in mind-set that lends such mutual incomprehensibility to the claims made by feminist critics of science and practicing scientists. If feminist scholars began writing out of the cultural breach between "woman" and "science," the breach we must contend with today divides women from women and working scientists from their feminist critics. It is a breach between radically different perceptions of science, truth, and knowledge.

THE NATURE OF THE PROBLEM

Feminist critics of science have argued that modern science evolved under the influence of a consciously chosen conjunction of scientific norms and masculine ideals. Henry Oldenburg, for example, a founding member and secretary of the Royal Society, declared that the intention of that society was "to raise a Masculine Philosophy . . . whereby the Mind of Man may be ennobled with the knowledge of Solid Truths."[1] Harking back to the rhetoric of Francis Bacon, the new science required a "virile" mind, properly cleansed of all traces of femininity. Only then would it be possible to establish Bacon's ideal of "a chaste and lawful marriage between Mind and Nature"— a sacred contract capable of "leading Nature with all her children to bind her to [man's] service and make her [his] slave."[2] This conjunction between scientific and masculine norms has been historically functional in guaranteeing a sexual division of emotional and intellectual labor that effectively excludes most women from scientific professions and simultaneously excludes all those values that have been traditionally regarded as "feminine" from the practice of science.

Today it may no longer be fashionable (or acceptable) to openly equate "scientific" with "masculine," but contemporary science nonetheless carries the history of that conjunction in the operative norms that guide its choice of questions, institutional structures, and methodological and explanatory preferences. Thus, the argument continues, although women may now find entrance to the world of science considerably easier than before, they still carry a residual handicap—if only by virtue of the fact that professional success requires conformation to norms that remain in opposition to what the culture—even today—labels "feminine." In the words of Nancy Hopkins, one of the more successful women scientists of our generation,

Obviously the intellectual processes involved in "real" science are as natural (or unnatural) to women as they are to men. But "professional" science was constructed by and for men (a certain type of man), and a woman who chooses to conquer this world at its higher echelons usually requires a major overhaul of self and world views.[3]

But residual handicaps for women scientists are not the only point of this argument. The issue of more general concern is the role that gender stereotypes have played within the actual workings of science. The exclusion of values culturally relegated to the female domain has led to an effective "masculinization" of science—to an unwitting alliance between scientific values and the ideals of masculinity embraced by our particular culture. The question that directly follows from this recognition is of utmost importance to all scientists, male or female: To what extent has such an alliance subverted our best hopes for science, our very aspirations to objectivity and universality?

Not surprisingly, this argument has attracted a great deal of attention far beyond the small community of feminist scholars. If correct, it has major implications for the history, philosophy, and sociology of science. At the very least, it suggests that cultural ideals of gender need to be considered major factors in the social and historical development of science. The argument also has implications for the practice of science. By calling into question the grounds on which some values have been judged "scientific" and others "unscientific," it invites all scientists, men and women alike, to reevaluate their own criteria for "good" science. A few scientists have begun to respond to this invitation. The vast majority, however, remain untouched.

Most scientists have not even encountered this argument. But to many of those who have, perhaps especially to women scientists, the argument itself is incomprehensible. Indeed, so incomprehensible is it that they rarely hear it as presented and instead unwittingly translate it into one of two closely related propositions that they do understand: (1) that women's nature is alien to science or (2) that women, again because of their nature, would do a different kind of science.[4]

These two restatements are propositions that, however repugnant (especially to women scientists), do make sense in that they are falsifiable. Indeed, they are readily falsified. With considerable relief, women scientists are able to refute the first proposition on empirical grounds (women are manifestly doing science), and the second, on logical grounds (by definition, there is only one science). And for those of us who might question such a definition of science, there are conspicuous political as well as empirical reasons for rejecting the premise that women would in fact do a different kind of science.

But the claim that has thus been so neatly refuted is not the one that the feminist critics of science have put forth. One central problem in the translation is the elimination of the distinction between sex and gender, missing from most scientific vocabulary but vitally important to contemporary feminism: sex is a biological category into which we are born as male or female infants, whereas gender is a cultural category specifying the characteristics of masculinity and feminity that shape our maturation into adult men and women. The very concept of "women's nature" is socially consti- tuted, belonging, finally, more to culture than to nature. We might think, therefore, that the reason for the misunderstanding between practicing scientists and feminist critics of science derives simply from a semantic gap in scientific vocabulary, one that ought to be readily rectifiable. But experience has shown that it is not so simple; despite repeated attempts at clarification, many scientists persist in conflating gender with sex and misreading the force that feminists attribute to gender ideology as a force attributable to the biological differences of sex. As a result, where others see a liberating potential in exhibiting the historical role of gender in science, pointing the way to a better science, these scientists see only a reactionary potential, fearing its use to support the exclusion of women from science.

The reasons for the disagreements between feminist critics and women scientists appear to be both deeper and more complex than mere semantics. Undoubtedly fueled by political concerns, these disagreements are not merely matters of vocabulary, logic, or empir- ical evidence. Rather, they are products of a fundamental difference in mind-set between feminist critics and women scientists. This gap is so great that to be a feminist scientist appears today to embody as much a contradiction as the possibility of being a woman scientist once seemed to do.[5]

For those who remain both scientists and feminists, the commit- ment to bridging this gap—to constructive communication between feminist critics and practicing scientists and to integrating feminist insights with the practice of science—is ontological. For others, the need to understand the nature of the difference between these two mind-sets is more intellectual than personal. My own scholarly purpose is both intellectual and personal. Recently I wrote on the intellectual and political factors that have prevented rapprochement between feminism and science. In this essay I will take a more unusual approach, attempting to reconstruct one particular trajectory from practicing scientist to feminist critic. The example I choose is the one I know best—my own. My reason is simple: I want to take advantage of the privileged access to the subjective dimensions of that trajectory provided to me, as an observer, by introspection. In other words, my purpose in this exercise is didactic rather than autobiographical. My hope is that a detailed reconstruction of my own route as a scientist to the current insights of feminist criticism might, despite its inevitable idiosyncrasies, nonetheless prove helpful in our attempt to understand the character of the differences in mind-set that divide us—helpful in the first place to me but I hope to others as well.

FROM WORKING SCIENTIST TO FEMINIST CRITIC: THREE CRITICAL POINTS IN A TRAJECTORY

1965. In my first years out of graduate school, I recall holding quite conventional beliefs about science. I believed not only in the possibility of clear and certain knowledge of the world but also in the uniquely privileged access to this knowledge provided by science in general and by physics in particular. I believed in the accessibility of an underlying (and unifying) "truth" about the world we live in, and I believed that the laws of physics give us the closest possible approximation of this truth. In short, I was well trained in both the traditional realist world views assumed by virtually all scientists and in the conventional epistemological ordering of the sciences. I had, after all, been trained first by theoretical physicists and later by molecular biologists. This is not to say that I lived my life according to the teachings of physics (or molecular biology), only that when it came to questions about what "really is," I knew where and how to look. Although I had serious conflicts about my own ability to contribute to and be part of this venture, I fully accepted science and scientists as arbiters of the truth. Physics (and physicists) were, of course, the highest arbiters.

Somewhere around this time, the proceedings of the first major conference held in the United States on women and the scientific professions[6] came to my attention. The proceedings argued for the necessity of having more women in science. Both Erik Erikson and Bruno Bettelheim pursued this point energetically, insisting on the invaluable contributions a "specifically female genius" could make to

science. Although Erikson and Bettelheim had, in their initial remarks, made a number of eminently reasonable observations and
recommendations, I flew to their concluding remarks as if I had been
waiting for them and indeed forgot everything else they had said.
From the vantage point I then occupied, my reaction was predictable:
I laughed. Laws of nature are universal. How could they possibly
depend on the sex of their discoverers? Obviously, I snickered, these
psychoanalysts know little enough about science (and, by implication,
about truth).[7]

1969. I was living in a suburban California house and found
myself with time to think seriously about my mounting conflict (as
well as that of virtually all my female colleagues) about being a
scientist. I had taken leave to accompany my husband on his
sabbatical and was remaining at home to care for our two small
children. Weekly, I would talk to the colleague I had left behind in
New York and listen to his growing enthusiasm about the spectacular
successes he was having in presenting our joint work. I tried to
understand why, despite the growing recognition of this work, my
own enthusiasm was diminishing. I found myself going to the library
in search of data about the fate of women scientists in general. More
truthfully, I was looking to document my growing disenchantment
with science as part of a more general phenomenon reflecting what I
had come to suspect was an underlying misfit between women and
science.

I wrote to Erik Erikson for comment on the alarming (yet
somehow satisfying) attrition data that I was collecting. Only a few
years after ridiculing his thoughts on the subject, here I was ready at
least to entertain, if not embrace, an argument about women being in
or out of science because of their "nature." Not once during that year
did it occur to me that at least part of my disenchantment might be
related to the fact that I was not sharing in the kudos my colleague
was reaping for our joint work.

1974. I had not dropped out of science, but I had moved into
interdisciplinary, undergraduate teaching. And I had just finished
teaching my first undergraduate women's studies course when I
received an invitation to give a series of "distinguished lectures" on
my work in mathematical biology at the University of Maryland.

This was a distinct honor, yet it presented a problem. In my women's studies course I had begun to talk openly about what it had been like as a woman to become a scientist. I had been persuaded to publicly air the exceedingly painful story of the struggle that had actually been—a story I had previously only talked about in private, if at all.[8] As a consequence, I began to see that it was not simply a private story. It had political as well as personal significance. The prospect of continuing to present myself as a disembodied scientist, of talking about my work as if it had been done in some abstract vacuum—as if my being a woman had been entirely irrelevant—had come to feel actually dishonest.

I resolved the conflict by deciding to present in my last lecture a demographic model of women in science—an excuse to devote the bulk of the lecture to a review of the barriers that worked against the survival of women as scientists and to a discussion of possible solutions. I concluded my review with the observation that perhaps the most important barrier to success for women in science derived from the pervasive belief in the intrinsic masculinity of scientific thought. Where, I asked, does such a belief come from? What is it doing in science, reputedly the most objective, neutral, and abstract endeavor we know? And what consequences does that belief have for the actual doing of science?

In 1974 "women in science" was not a proper subject for academic or scientific discussion; I was aware of violating professional protocol. Having given the lecture—having "carried it off"—I felt profoundly liberated. An essential milestone had been passed.

DISCUSSION

Although I did not know it then, this lecture marked the beginning of my work as a feminist critic of science. In it I raised three of the central questions that were to mark my research and writing over the next decade. I can now see that, with the concluding remarks of that lecture, I had also completed the basic shift in mind-set that made it possible to begin such a venture. Even though my views about gender, science, knowledge, and truth were to evolve considerably over the years to come, I had already made the two most essential steps: I had shifted my attention from the question of male and female nature to that of beliefs about male and female nature, i.e., to gender ideology. Also, I had admitted the possibility that such beliefs could affect science itself.

In hindsight, these two moves may seem simple enough, but when I reflect on my own history, as well as that of other women scientists, I can see that they were not. Indeed, from my earlier vantage point, they were unthinkable. In that mind-set, there was room neither for a distinction between sexual identity and beliefs about sexual identity (not even for the prior distinction between sex and gender upon which such a distinction depends) nor for the possibility that beliefs could affect science—a possibility that would itself require a clear distinction to be made between nature and science. If there was room in the earlier mind-set for a distinction between belief and reality, it was only to highlight "false" beliefs—illusions, prejudices. In that mind-set, beliefs per se were not seen as having a real force—neither the force to shape the development of men and women nor the force to shape the development of science. Although that frame of mind did mean acknowledging that some people may misperceive nature, human or otherwise, the nature of men and women is properly seen as given by male and female biology—just as science is simply a faithful reflection of nature. Gravity has force; DNA has force; beliefs do not. In other words, the locus of real force in the world was seen as physical, not mental.

It followed that any claim about differences between men and women could inevitably be read as a claim about male and female nature, a reading that Erikson and Bettelheim had themselves both taken for granted. And if science is further assumed to "mirror" nature, any claim of a disparity between women's creative vision and science as we know it immediately lends itself to being translated into the proposition that women cannot make good scientists. It is worth noting that although both Erikson and Bettelheim had clearly made the first move, neither had made the second. Indeed, they did not even claim that what they called "female genius" would lead to different "laws of Nature." What Erikson actually wrote was the following:

Is scientific inspiration really so impersonal and method-bound that personality plays no role in scientific creativity? And if we grant that a woman is never not a woman, even if and especially when she has become an excellent scientist and coworker beyond all special apologies and claims, then why deny so strenuously that there may be in science also . . . areas where the addition, to the male kind of creative vision, of women's vision and creativity may yet lead, not to new laws of verification, but to new areas of inquiry and to new applications? Such a possibility, I suggest, can be tested only if and when women are sufficiently represented in the sciences so that woman's mind may relax about the task and the role and apply itself to the unknown.[9]

Bettelheim had been even more equivocal:

I wish I knew more about physics and engineering, so that perhaps I could spell out for you how the specific female genius can find its realization in these particular fields of human endeavor. But I do know, for example, that the building of houses, of our homes, has been entrusted far too much to a masculine thinking about structure and material.[10]

In 1965, out of my own anxiety about the question of whether women could be good scientists, I not only looked for a statement of their argument in a form that I simultaneously feared *and* could repudiate (i.e., as a claim anticipating different "laws of nature"), but, as I can now see, read it where it was in fact not written. As a result, I could not even register the question they had actually asked. I could not imagine the possibility of any change in the accepted definition of science—not even in its applications or in its prevailing agenda of problems to investigate.

Any account of the circumstances that led to the change in mind-set that enabled me to pose the questions I later asked would be highly personal and idiosyncratic. But it seems to me that one motif in any such answer *would* have quite general applicability. In one way or another, science would have to come to be experientially dethroned as the uniquely privileged route to knowledge and truth. That is to say, one would have to personally experience alternative routes to knowledge sufficiently compelling to call the present epistemological hegemony of science into necessary question.

For me, that experience came from two sources: the women's movement and psychoanalysis. However different in kind, both were important factors in my life between 1964 and 1978. The signal ingredient that these two very different experiences had in common was the means to empower the subjective. Through its early consciousness-raising groups, the women's movement created the conditions for the lived realization that, as Catherine MacKinnon put it, "to know the politics of woman's situation is to know women's personal lives."[11] MacKinnon continued:

To feminism, the personal is epistemologically the political, and its epistemology is its politics. Feminism, on this level, is the theory of women's point
of view. . . . Consciousness raising is its quintessential expression. . . . Consciousness raising not only comes to know different things as politics; it
necessarily comes to know them in a different way.

It may surprise many to learn that psychoanalysis did something
quite similar for me. Through it, I came to reclaim a domain of
delegitimized knowledge as indeed legitimate. Whereas before I had
recognized only one kind of "real" knowledge, now I acquired,
through lived experience, access to another kind. It was not necessarily new knowledge, but rather newly acknowledged knowledge—
things I had known all along but didn't know that I knew. In other
words, I now understood that important kinds of knowledge about
the world could be acquired *through* internal experience rather than
merely by external experience.

Recognizing the personal as the political meant seeing the force of
politics in the personal realm as well as the force of the personal in the
political realm. One of the earliest insights to come out of such
analyses was an appreciation of the social constitution of gender—
distinguished from sex by a belief system with the power to realize
itself (more or less) in the bodies and minds of actual men and
women. It also became clear that a crucial part of the power of this
belief system derives from an ideology that denies the power of belief
by equating gender with sex, i.e., by defining gender as a given of
nature rather than as a set of cultural expectations.

Through psychoanalysis, I came to see the force of beliefs even
more directly. By paying attention to my own unwitting thoughts,
words, and actions (and in the process coming to see their internal
coherence), I became a direct witness of the force of beliefs—
particularly of beliefs that are not conscious. Psychoanalysis, of
course, harbors its own unwitting beliefs, and these remarks are not
offered as a defense either of Freudian doctrine or of the institution of
psychoanalysis as presently constituted. My point for now is simply
that psychoanalysis provided the opportunity for an internal (subjective) experience of the force of belief (and, of course, of feeling) so
sufficiently compelling as to enable me to ask questions that earlier I
had found unthinkable. No longer did I take natural science as the
necessary starting point for inquiry about the nature of the world
(including the human race). Once having seen the place and force of

beliefs and feelings in the constitution of even our most rational endeavors, it became possible to make the analysis of our own subjectivity a starting point for an inquiry into the nature of science. With the epistemological confidence thus acquired—in one way from the women's movement and in another from psychoanalysis—it became possible for me to embark on a feminist analysis of gender and science.

A third domain of experience also shaped my development over the decade in question. It was undoubtedly even more crucial than the two I have already mentioned. Before becoming a feminist or an analysand, I became a mother. The way the experience of motherhood interacted with the other two sets of experiences is not yet clear to me. I know, however, that it did. Two things are clear: (1) that it was motherhood (again, as socially more than as naturally constituted) that created the conditions that carried me from my position in the first vignette to that of the second, and (2) that I was at that time clearly not conscious of this fact.

The demands of motherhood, demands then assigned entirely to the biological mother, prevented me from reaping rewards that are a crucial stimulant to enthusiasm in science. But it was not simply the unavailability of a substitute caretaker for my children that led me to decline invitations to attend meetings or give seminars. It was also that I did not care to leave my children to do these things and was even relieved that I did not have to. From where I sat, the business of science—and scientific careers—simply did not seem that important.

If at the time I was willing to fall into the trap of pitting women's nature against conventional science, I did so because of an experience that had in some sense already dethroned conventional science. That I did not then see the connections between motherhood, scientific success, and enthusiasm—all so obvious now—reflected the fact that I did not then see how either motherhood or science could be made different. Nor did I recognize how our interests and enthusiasms are themselves dependent on the norms that are set for both these institutions. In that sense, turning to Erikson and Bettelheim may not have been so foolish after all. Although neither was asking how motherhood might be different, they were at least asking how science might be different.

In the end, I came to see that it was not possible to ask one question without also asking the other—indeed, without calling into question our very notions of "woman" and "man." The final part of my own journey from working scientist to feminist critic has required me to leave behind Erikson and Bettelheim's notions of male and female nature. Only then did it become possible to raise the questions in what I came to think of as their proper form—as questions not about the remaking of science from the perspective of "women's vision and creativity" but about the simultaneous remaking of our conceptions of men, women, and science. No one of these can be attempted without attending to the others. These projects of "remaking" cannot be separated from one another, because the development of individual men, women, and scientists depends so critically on the interlocking ideals of masculinity, femininity, and science that derive so much of their coherence, endurance, and force from the simultaneous acceptance of all three. As long as the qualities deemed responsible for the success of science remain defined largely in accord with so-called masculine virtues, in opposition to putative "feminine" virtues, it makes little sense to speak of the contribution of a "specific female genius" to science.[12] Nor does it make sense to think of augmenting conventional science with a different kind of science so long as those we presently call scientists remain the sole arbiters of what is scientific and what is not.[13] In the conclusion to my book *Reflections on Gender and Science,* I suggested that the emancipation of science from its "masculinist" heritage requires "not a juxtaposition or complementarity of male and female perspectives, nor . . . the substitution of one form of parochiality for another. Rather, it [requires] a transformation of the very categories of male and female, and, correspondingly, of mind and nature."[14]

CONCLUSION

As with all robust self-maintaining systems, changing our inherited system of gender and science is not likely to be easy. Still, change *is* possible and even beginning to happen. It can most effectively (and perhaps only) be brought about from within—from steadily chipping away at the system's many sustaining foci. Such an effort will depend crucially on a rapprochement between feminist critics of science and working scientists (be they women or men). So far, my discussion has been about the shift in mind-set from working scientist to feminist critic. A true rapprochement, however, requires that the shift be charted also in reverse. That is to say, feminist critics of science must at the very least reclaim access to the mind-set of the working scientist.

To do so, it is necessary to redress a glaring omission from much of our analyses to date, certainly one that would be most obvious to any working scientist. That omission, of course, is an adequate acknowledgment of the reliance of scientific knowledge on nature itself (i.e., on what is)—and, correlatively, of the remarkable record of technological success that science can claim. If we grant the force of belief, we must surely not neglect the even more dramatic force of scientific know-how. While beliefs, interests, and cultural norms surely can and do influence the definition of scientific goals as well as the criteria for success in meeting such goals, they cannot in themselves generate either epistemological or technological success. By themselves, without the cooperation of nature, beliefs cannot lead to the generation of useful knowledge. Our analysis began with the question of where and how the force of beliefs, interests, and cultural norms enters into the process by which effective knowledge is generated. The question that now remains is: Where and how does nature enter into that process? How do nature and culture interact in the production of scientific knowledge? I suggest that this last question, however difficult, is *the* question that feminist critics of science, along with other social critics of science, must now address. Until we do, our account of science not only will not, but also cannot, be recognizable to working scientists.

The question at issue, finally, has to do with the meaning of science. Although we may now see that science does not simply "mirror" nature, to say instead that it mirrors culture (or "interests") is to make a mockery of the commitment to the pursuit of the reliable knowledge that lies at the core of scientists' work. It is also to deny the manifest (at times even life-threatening) successes of science. Until we can articulate an adequate response to the question of how nature interacts with culture in the production of scientific knowledge, working scientists will continue to find their more traditional mind-sets more comfortable, more adequate. They will also persist in viewing the mind-set that grants force to beliefs and interests and not to nature as fundamentally mistaken—as incompatible, unintegrable, indeed laughable.

ENDNOTES

[1]Evelyn Fox Keller, *Reflections on Gender and Science* (New Haven, CT: Yale University Press, 1985), p. 52.

[2]Ibid., pp. 36–37. For further citations of Bacon's rhetoric, see Carolyn Merchant, *The Death of Nature* (New York: Harper & Row, 1981), and Sandra Harding, *The Science Question in Feminism* (Ithaca, NY: Cornell University Press, 1986).

[3]Nancy Hopkins, "The High Price of Success in Science," *Radcliffe Quarterly* 10, June 1976, pp. 16–18.

[4]Of course, women scientists are not the only ones who make such a translation; it is also made by many men, and even by some feminists who are not themselves scientists. It is routinely made by the popular press. The significant point here is that this mistranslation persists in the minds of most women scientists even after they are alerted to the distinction between sex and gender. The original argument is not getting through to them.

[5]Indeed, a striking number of feminist critics who began as working scientists have either changed their fields altogether or have felt obliged to at least temporarily interrupt their work as laboratory or "desk" scientists (I am thinking, for example, of Maggie Benston, Ruth Hubbard, Marian Lowe, Evelynn Hammonds, and myself).

[6]Jacquelyn A. Mattfield and Carol E. Van Aiken, eds., *Women and the Scientific Professions* (Cambridge, MA: MIT Press, 1965), pp. 3–19.

[7]I will later cite excerpts from these writings of Erikson and Bettelheim.

[8]This story was subsequently published in *Working It Out*, ed. Sara Ruddick and Pamela Daniels (New York: Pantheon, 1977).

[9]Erik H. Erikson, "Concluding Remarks," in Mattfield and Van Aiken, *Women and the Scientific Professions*, pp.232–46.

[10]Bruno Bettelheim, "The Commitment Required of a Woman Entering a Scientific Profession in Present-Day American Society," in Mattfield and Van Aiken, *Women and the Scientific Professions*, p. 18.

[11]Catherine MacKinnon, "Feminism, Marxism, Method, and the State: An Agenda for Theory," *Signs* 7, pp. 515–44.

[12]Furthermore, it does not even make sense to speak of the existence of a "specific female genius." Such a notion implies a degree of cultural homogeneity, adhering to a universal ideal of "masculinity" and "femininity." This is itself a myth—a myth belied by the observed variability in gender ideologies across categories of race, class, and ethnicity even within our own culture.

[13]As surely they will, and in a sense must, until a viable alternative becomes available.

[14]Keller, *Reflections on Gender and Science*, p. 178.

Joan W. Scott

History and Difference

H ISTORIES OF THE PROGRESS of democracy, of the expanding participation of individuals and groups in the social and political life of the United States, are often based on the notion of access. Emphasis usually goes to the physical connotation of this term. Thus, we metaphorically represent the gaining of access to resources, spaces, and institutions as passages through doors and gates, over obstacles, and around barriers and blockages; we measure accessibility quantitatively by noting the number of people or members of groups who gain entry.

While this emphasis has been useful for detecting discrimination or democratization, it has drawn attention away from important qualitative issues. How are those who cross the thresholds received? If they belong to a group different from the one already "inside," what are the terms of their incorporation? How do the new arrivals understand their relationship to the place they have entered? What are the terms of identity they establish?

These questions assume that entry alone does not solve the problems of discrimination, that organizations are hierarchically differentiated systems, and that physical access is not the end of the story. They are questions relevant generally to the study of social organization, but they have been posed most forcefully by those

Joan W. Scott, born in 1941 in Brooklyn, New York, is professor of social science at the Institute for Advanced Study in Princeton, New Jersey. She is the author of The Glassworkers of Carmaux *(1974) and coauthor, with Louise Tilly, of* Women, Work and Family *(1978, 1987). Her most recent work,* Gender and the Politics of History, *is forthcoming in 1988. Professor Scott was founding director of Brown University's Pembroke Center for Teaching and Research on Women.*

93

concerned about gender and race. That ought not to be surprising, since our culture has embodied difference in generative organs and skin color. The difficulties experienced by the bearers of these marks of difference indicate that access is more than a matter of "getting through the door."

The question of difference is often posed sociologically, but it is also conceptual. The social practices of the members of a craft or a profession are intimately related to the ways they interpret the meaning of their work. The knowledge said to be vested in a profession like medicine or history implies its structure, organization, and membership. Historians, for example, have until recently pictured their archetypal actor, the universal human agent, as a white male. Although they have assumed that Universal Man stands for all humankind, in fact this representation creates hierarchies and exclusions. Women, blacks, and various others have been either invisible as historical subjects or somehow depicted as less central, less important, than white men. As in written history, so in the organization of the historical profession: white men have predominated; women and minorities have occupied a secondary place.

Since the 1960s there have been changes both in written history and in the historical profession. Both developments involve what might be called the fall, or perhaps the particularization, of Universal Man. As it has become less possible to subsume historical subjects under the single category of "man," so women, blacks, and others have become visible and important, not only as subjects of history but also as professional historians.

Examination of the articulation of difference—the hierarchical and unequal relationships among different groups—reveals the interdependency of knowledge and organizational behavior. We understand the full meaning of occupational identities only when we see who is included in them, how differences among practitioners are dealt with, which differences matter, how they are understood, and whether they change over time. Difference, then, provides insight into what might be called the culture of a profession or the politics of a discipline.

My interest in this paper is in a particular kind of difference—gender, or sexual difference. I focus on women historians who, by virtue of holding doctorates in history, academic positions, and memberships in the American Historical Association (AHA), were recognized as members of the profession of history. Having accepted the discipline in its double sense—as a system of training and a system of rules—they qualified from the beginning as professionals. Their inclusion in an elite body of professionals, however, was not without complication. For while they assumed that access ought to give them full entitlement to professional identity, they regularly encountered reminders of their difference. Their perceptions of and reactions to how they were treated varied over time and in accordance with many factors, not the least of which were their understandings of history (their conception of the knowledge they professed) and their defini-tion of who was considered a historical subject. The experience of these women historians as they grappled with the problem of difference demonstrates how concepts of history that posit a unitary process experienced by a Universal Man pose an obstacle to equality.

I

When the American Historical Association was founded in 1884, women were included as members. The executive council resolved that "there is nothing in the Constitution . . . to prevent the admission of women into the Association upon the same qualifications as those required of men."[1] In the effort to organize the discipline, women were accepted as AHA members if they had some university training and used the scientific method considered so crucial to the new professional history. While holding advanced degrees granted women nominal membership in the tiny elite of scholars who constituted the AHA,[2] even those who did not hold Ph.D.'s were considered eligible, for the shared goal of founders such as J. Franklin Jameson and Herbert Baxter Adams was to disseminate history throughout the nation with the help of talented researchers and teachers. Despite this seemingly open policy, however, women faced discrimination once they were admitted to the association. The discrimination was sometimes subtle, sometimes quite explicit, and rested always on the assumption that, ultimately, sexual difference mattered.

Recruiting women to the AHA fit the larger democratic mission of the organization's founders. They were determined to wrest history from the gentlemen antiquarians whose practice, they felt, under-mined the tenets of science.[3] The founders promoted a new kind of professional history that opposed the more difficult study of institutions and politics to an older antiquarian focus on picturesque traditions and colorful incidents (what medieval historian Nellie Neilson referred to scornfully as "the praise of ladies dead and lovely knights").[4] And they attacked as elitist and somehow unscientific the notion that good historians must have classical training and literary sensibility. Jameson articulated the issue clearly in 1891:

Now it is the spread of thoroughly good second-class work ... that our science most needs at present; for it sorely needs the improvement in technical process, that superior finish of workmanship, which a large number of works of talent can do more to foster than a few works of literary genius.[5]

By including women in the AHA, the founders underscored their democratic, leveling impulse, their desire to "bring all the historical resources of the nation within the purview of [the] Association," and their belief that their science could be mastered by any intelligent person.[6] There was, in fact, an important point made by women's practice of scientific history: the power of objective investigation was such that it overcame any feminine predisposition to pursue quaint or esoteric topics. There was also a complicated symbolic dimension to the inclusion of women in the organization, and it relied on the oppositions of masculine/feminine and male/female. Whatever the sex of its practitioners, the old history was represented as feminine, the new as masculine. By enlisting women on the side of scientific history, its proponents demonstrated that they had vanquished whatever aristocratic and romantic tendencies remained in their newly organized discipline.

There were also quite straightforward reasons to bring women into the new association. Women represented an important institutional constituency for the creation of history departments and the implementation of standardized history curricula in the high schools, academies, and colleges of the nation. If the new history was to triumph, it had to be properly conveyed; the AHA founders approached their teaching with missionary zeal. In the 1880s and 1890s, women's colleges represented a significant component of the academic world, and (although headed by men) they were increasingly staffed by female teachers. Women who were members of the AHA could thus serve the useful function of bringing history to their strongholds—the women's academies and colleges. Nellie Neilson fulfilled that task at Mount Holyoke College; Lucy Maynard Salmon, whose field was American history, did the same at Vassar. When she was hired in 1887, President James Taylor wrote to Herbert Baxter Adams that the "inadequate provision" for history at his institution would soon be remedied. "The recent appointment of Miss Salmon . . . will doubtless result in the satisfactory reorganization of the entire department."[7]

AHA spokesmen insisted that the same history curriculum be taught to both women and men. They saw no irony in assigning students roles as members of the English House of Commons and having them debate issues of constitutional and legislative policy (a teaching method used in the 1880s and 1890s at Wellesley and Johns Hopkins),[8] despite the fact that women had no vote and no formal political role in either the United States or England. In addition, women were not excluded as objects of historical interest. Adams, for example, urging that history's scope go beyond a focus on great men, reminded his colleagues of

the unnumbered thousands, yea millions, of good men and true, and of faithful, devoted women . . . [who] support good leadership and carry humanity forward from generation to generation. It is often the biography of some plain man, like Abraham Lincoln, or some self-sacrificing woman, like Florence Nightingale, that affords the greatest encouragement and incentive to ordinary humanity. But we must remember that no man, no woman is worthy of biographical or historical record, unless in some way he or she has contributed to the welfare of society and the progress of the world.[9]

Despite some gestures in the direction of treating men and women equally, however, historians in the late nineteenth century treated them differently. This followed from the way history was conceptualized, from the assumption that processes of change were evolutionary, linear, and unitary. Welfare and progress were considered essentially political concepts, and progress was measured as movement toward democratic self-government. Adams advocated the study of "towns, plantations, parishes, and counties" as well as states and nations. Large and small, the units of analysis were polities and the conception of study was unitary and integrated.[10] The small units echoed the large; they provided ways of understanding how political organization worked and under what circumstances it progressed.[11]

The notion of history as the study of progress toward democracy embodied the assumption that the same linear process applied at different rates and in different forms to all people. The assumption of unity and universality made it possible to include all sorts of groups in history, but it also made specification of their difference unnecessary. A single, prototypical figure represented the historical subject: white (Anglo-Saxon), Western man. The study of history for Adams and his colleagues was the study of politics, and this meant the study of "man in organized society." The purpose of such study was self-knowledge, which "leads to self-determination and self-control." Beyond that, history's teaching had important political consequences, for it led to "self-government . . . the highest and best result of the experience of man in society."[12]

In pointing to these examples of man as the subject of history, I do not mean to say that historians like Adams excluded women from their conception of history; they did not. Rather, they subsumed women—included them in a generalized, unified conception that was represented in the idea of man but was always different from and subordinate to it. The feminine was but a particular instance, the masculine a universal signifier.

The consequences of such thinking were at once to deny and to recognize difference—to deny it by refusing to acknowledge that women (or blacks or Jews) might have a fundamentally different historical experience, and to recognize it by somehow disqualifying for equal treatment those different from the universal figure. This double effect was evident in the way history was written: middle-class white men were the typical subjects acting to make things happen, while women were represented (if at all) as "devoted" and "faithful" figures ensuring generational continuity through reproductive roles that were in a sense timeless and therefore outside history. It was also evident in institutional and organizational arrangements—in the leadership structure, for example, of the AHA. For despite the AHA's gestures of formal inclusiveness, it was simply taken for granted that the members who really mattered, as well as the leaders, were white men. The language of universality rested on and incorporated differentiations that resulted in unequal treatment of women in relation to men.

Adams worked hard to keep women as members of the organization, but it was always clear that they were women, special individuals differentiated not by achievement or training but by their presumed "natural" endowments and their association with women's colleges. The AHA, for example, held an annual "smoker" for the men of the association, while the women historians and wives of historians attended a "colonial dames' tea." Lucy Salmon wrote to protest these arrangements in 1905: "We do not care for afternoon teas where we meet society women, and deprecate entertainments that separate the members into two classes, men and women."[13] But women's objections to this segregatory practice were ignored.

The AHA never went beyond tokenism when it came to including women in leadership positions. Lucy Salmon was the only woman to serve on special committees (eventually including the executive council) in the early period, but when she urged Adams to include another woman on the Committee of Seven (the group concerned with the teaching of history), he wrote to a friend that he was "inclined to think that one woman is enough!"[14] In 1919, as a member of the council, Salmon lamented her inability to increase the number of women sharing power in the AHA:

I do not wish to seem to press the names of women for membership on any of these committees; and yet, as I think I have written more than once before, I can but feel that the Association has by self-denying ordinance been deprived of the services of a good many women.[15]

This situation continued well into the 1960s. Arthur Link (president of the AHA in 1984) has noted that for most of the association's history, "women were given short shrift in positions of leadership and governance." Only five women were included among the ninety-six members of the executive council before 1933, he says, and women were represented on committees in a ratio of about one to nine, an underrepresentation in relation to female membership in the association.[16]

Although there were high points for women in the AHA, these never resulted in a clear end to discriminatory treatment. The 1920s and 1930s, for example, saw a rise in the numbers of women who earned Ph.D.'s and were employed in history departments (especially in women's colleges). Yet as the prestige and power of research universities grew in this period, women were increasingly marginalized in their confinement to undergraduate faculties and female institutions.[17] By 1920 women constituted about 19 percent of the members of the AHA, but not even 5 percent of its leadership.[18] The prevailing tone was of an elite male club whose formal structure and informal social practices made women secondary members.

The patterns continued with little variation into the postwar period. Howard K. Beale, writing in 1953, noted that "discrimination against women is persistent," and part of a broad set of biases "against Negroes, Jews, Catholics, women, and persons not 'gentlemen' " that operated throughout the profession of history.[19] In 1970 a special AHA committee systematically documented the effects of these biases on women. The committee had been set up in response to the demands of women historians who argued that the recruitment of large numbers of women to the field of history, in process since the mid-1960s, would not itself guarantee equality; instead there had to be explicit attention to eradicating discrimination.[20] The committee's document, known as the Rose Report (for its chair, Willie Lee Rose), gave evidence of the long history of systematic underrepresentation of women within the AHA and the profession as a whole, and recommended the creation of a standing Committee on Women Historians (CWH) to provide advocacy and monitor statistics in an effort to "secure greater equity for women as prospective students and teachers of history."[21] By appointing this committee, the AHA formally acknowledged the persistence of gender differentiation and the need to attend to it as a long-term structural problem.

In the history of women in the AHA, one moment does stand out as a distinct exception to otherwise exclusionary practices at the leadership level: a woman became president of the association in 1943. Yet the election of Nellie Neilson was only a brief triumph of what seems to have been a coalition of progressive historians and organized feminists in the larger context of coalitions and popular-front mobilizations against fascism on the eve of America's entry into the Second World War. Neilson had been nominated for second vice-president (which automatically put her in line for the presidency) in 1940, a year that was particularly auspicious for its attention not only to women but to other previously neglected groups. Under Merle Curti's chairmanship the AHA program committee arranged several sessions on the theme of "the common man." Selig Perlman spoke on class in American labor history, W.E.B. DuBois chaired a panel on the Negro in the history of the United States, and Mildred Thompson presided over a session on women in history.[22]

The attention to women's history and the election of Neilson were the results of years of lobbying by women, some of them organized at the Berkshire Conference of Women Historians (founded in 1929), others simply acting out of deep feminist commitment. They were active enough in 1939 for the chair of the nominating committee to note in his report the existence of a feminist bloc.[23] Their pressure coincided with the determination of progressives like Curti and Beale to practice democracy within the association, to assert history's connection to the democratic processes it chronicled, at the very moment that constitutionalism and liberalism were under siege in Europe. The committee was explicit about its goal of including women, and wrote to all AHA members in May 1940 urging them to nominate and vote for "women of distinction" who "have not had sufficient recognition among the Association's officers."[24]

The election of Neilson did not, however, constitute or even initiate an evolution toward equality for women. The general pattern of underrepresentation persisted throughout her presidency, and as the war came to an end, that pattern was reinforced by a decline in the numbers of women receiving doctoral degrees and jobs in the field of history.[25] In addition, a new discourse emerged that emphasized the masculine qualities of the historian. It associated those qualities with the preservation of national traditions and democracy and with scholarly activities that renewed commitment to the kind of heroism that arose during the war effort. Calling for greater appreciation of businessmen's efforts to build America, Allan Nevins suggested in 1951, for example, that historians abandon "feminine idealism" and portray businessmen in "their true proportions as builders of an indispensable might."[26] The contrast between idealism and materialism, sentimentality and might, was presented as a contrast between femininity and masculinity; and although the contrast did not speak about women directly, it clearly implied an association of Cold War ideology with gender in depicting the traits and attitudes of the typical historian.

"I have seen in my generation the rise, and now the beginning, of the closing of doors to women," wrote Beatrice Hyslop, a historian of the French Revolution, as she contemplated retirement from Hunter

College in 1969.[27] Hyslop's comments referred to the 1950s and early 1960s and their contrast to the years of her doctoral work in the early 1930s. Ironically, she wrote just as a great transition began, but it would still be many years before women were regularly included in positions of power in the AHA, and it was not until 1987 that another woman, Natalie Zemon Davis, assumed the office of president.

II

While the AHA formally endorsed inclusiveness and spoke a language of universality, that language nonetheless implied difference, and the AHA still represented the typical historian and the typical historical actor as a white male. Women's likeness to this universal type was not taken for granted; it had to be demonstrated in the behavior of each woman. Thus, regardless of skills and training, women faced the challenge of repudiating the disabilities assumed to belong to their sex.

This was no easy task, whatever the strategy adopted. One could choose to ignore systems of differentiation and accept their limits so as to operate within them; but this, of course, left the systems in place and often put a great burden on the individual, who usually attributed the treatment she received to her own failings. One could consider specific instances of discrimination the result of the misogyny of particular persons and thus avoid making generalizations. One could acknowledge that there was systematic unequal treatment based on gender and condemn such injustices as violations of democratic principles. One could affirm the difference of women and elevate it to a position of complementarity or even superiority to men. Whether in the name of equality or difference, collective action by women could be extremely effective politically; but it held a potential for underscoring women's separate identity, of pointing up rather than playing down the contrast between male and female historians.

Since 1884 professional women historians have used all these strategies to combat discrimination, sometimes in combination. Examining these strategies gives us a way to grasp the operations of a profession as a differentiated system—to understand the effects of such a system on the persons perceived to be different and, in this case, to see how professional women historians formulated their critiques in relation to prevailing concepts of history.[28]

Lucy Salmon's strategy was to insist that women be included in the concept of humanity. As she made clear to the AHA, the practice of excluding women contradicted notions of universality and equality and resulted in a waste of available talent. She believed firmly in coeducation (she held bachelor's and master's degrees from the University of Michigan), though she always taught at a women's college. While she accepted the limits of available employment, she constantly battled President Taylor's attempts to regulate women faculty members' lives at Vassar.[29] Women, she believed, should be treated no differently from men; any other policy would be irrational or unjust.

The same conviction led Salmon to campaign for women's suffrage: she believed that the vote, once won, would guarantee the full and equal participation of women in a variety of political institutions (including, undoubtedly, professional associations). In fact, society would be the ultimate beneficiary, she asserted, because so many more talented and able people would be involved in the business of politics.

Salmon based her argument on the idea (shared with her professional colleagues and evident in all she wrote) that history meant progress toward democracy and equality. She saw prejudice against her sex as a matter of individual attitude or a reflection of insufficient experience, intelligence, or education—the relic of a less civilized past, destined eventually to disappear. Thus, she wrote of Woodrow Wilson, with whom she had studied for a Ph.D. at Bryn Mawr, that his life was governed by narrow and self-serving ambition. Furthermore, he did not like teaching, and

he was singularly ill-adapted to teaching women. He had apparently never had any of the normal relationships of life with women, he assumed that women were quite different from men, and he made, I felt, no effort to understand them. He always assumed that they were intellectually different from men and that, therefore, they would not interest him. I am quite sure that he never whole-heartedly believed in college education for women. He once said to me that a woman who had married an intellectual, educated man was often better educated than a woman who had had college training. All of this used to amuse me and I never presented any other side of the subject to him or stated my own views—it would have been useless to do so.

I felt that his opinions were simply derived from a limited educational and social experience and hoped he would some time learn better![30]

Like many of her contemporaries, Salmon participated in professional life assuming (even as she recognized or experienced discrimination) that equal treatment was her due. For her, "progress lay in the direction of obliterating rather than emphasizing the differences between men and women."[31] Salmon's biographer noted that she "distrusted any movement which recognized a special 'woman's sphere,'" and that she refused to acknowledge any such movement in her writing, her professional and political activities, or her personal deportment.[32] Such recognition would only perpetuate the false idea that biological differences between the sexes should be the basis for educational or professional distinctions. "Do not think," she wrote to a colleague, "that . . . I am not interested in the work that women are doing, I am intensely interested in all good work, but not specially because it is done by women." She conceded that women labored under many disabilities but insisted that these "must be removed . . . by women individually rather than collectively."[33]

Lucy Salmon succeeded in gaining professional prominence during her lifetime, and she individually removed obstacles to women. She increased the participation of women on AHA committees, and established an informal women's network to encourage and support women students who aspired to be historians. When she died, she was eulogized as an "original" thinker by Edward Cheney, who urged the publication of an unfinished manuscript of hers because "we ought not to allow anything she wrote to disappear."[34] Arguably, her work was more profound than that of many of her male associates, including Herbert Baxter Adams. Yet her name virtually disappeared from accounts of the history of the profession, including John Higham's *History,* a celebration of the discipline since its institutionalization in 1884 that was published in 1965. Higham's book demonstrates the workings of gender difference and the limits of individualized strategies to deal with it. Not only is Salmon's name absent from its pages on the leading historians in America but so are the names of virtually all women (and blacks). No works by women are included in any of the summaries of historiographic debates; Mary Beard appears in two footnotes as the author of a book about her husband and as coauthor with him of a book entirely credited to him in the text; and Nellie Neilson's presidency of the AHA is not even acknowledged in passing.[35] The invisibility of women in this book is not the result of their absence from the ranks of practicing historians and active AHA members; rather, it follows directly from the assumption that a universal white male figure can be used to typify the historical subject and that those different from him are insignificant because they are at once represented and excluded by him. To insist, as Salmon did, on the irrelevance of gender difference in the face of this kind of thinking was to attack the effects but not the source of differentiation, exclusion, and discrimination.

Another strategy was to reform the institutional policy of excluding women. This effort—sometimes by individuals, sometimes by collectively organized groups—emerged most forcefully in the 1920s and 1930s, a period of great ferment nationally and within the discipline of history.[36] Chairs for women were endowed at the research universities in attempts to rectify the virtual absence of women faculty from these male strongholds. George Herbert Palmer was probably following his wife's (Alice Freeman's) wishes when he left money to establish a full professorship for a woman in the University of Michigan history department. Similarly, Florence Porter Robinson, herself employed to teach home economics at Beloit College though she held a Ph.D. in history, left her estate to the University of Wisconsin to fund a chair in history for a woman. In both cases the donors stipulated that salaries and terms of employment be identical to men's.[37]

The issue of positions for women at universities was also taken up by the Berkshire Conference of Women Historians, an organization founded in 1929 by professors at East Coast women's colleges who wished that "we scattered women historians could get together oftener to exchange ideas." Returning on a train from an AHA meeting, a group of women discussed how they might generate a "greater sense of comradeship in our craft." According to Louise Loomis's recollection, the goal was to create an informal opportunity for discussion and "social contact" among themselves.[38] There was also resentment against a new practice among male historians to gather for informal conferences that explicitly excluded women. Although the members of the Berkshire Conference insisted they were not a "pressure group," they were an interest group and they exerted pressure on the AHA in the name of women.

From the first meeting on, they discussed ways to improve the situation of women historians. They planned a program of exchange professorships so that women could vary their experience outside the confines of their own institutions. This plan was never implemented, however, because of the impact of the Depression and of other more pressing concerns. Faced with informal discrimination, such as the preference for hiring men in women's colleges, and outright discriminatory laws against married women enacted by state and federal legislatures, the Berkshire Conference examined "the professional outlook for women" in the 1930s by comparing the hiring patterns, ranks, and salary scales for women and men.[39]

Emily Hickman of the New Jersey College for Women seems to have been the most outspoken and imaginative of the leaders. At one meeting she suggested that the American Association of University Women (AAUW) make a "statistical survey of the possibilities in academic life for women." She also thought that "biographies of eminent women" should be published "with a view to disproving rumors that none is suitable for a [college] presidency." Sending in nomination after nomination and urging sympathetic men to support the nominees, she turned the group's attention to the inclusion of women in positions of power in the AHA.[40]

The Berkshire Conference represented an organized effort to improve the situation of women historians, though it was confined to the East Coast. Acting with a sense of commitment to the feminist cause, women in other regions—sometimes clustered in women's colleges, sometimes isolated in coeducational institutions—also organized campaigns to place women in positions of power. An example is Mary Williams, a Latin American historian who received a Ph.D. from Stanford in 1914, taught briefly at Wellesley and then at Goucher College, and agitated for the nomination of Nellie Neilson to the presidency of the AHA in 1933[41]—the year Louise Phelps Kellogg, a member of one of several informal women's networks, served on the nominating committee.[42] The detailed story of these highly political efforts has yet to be written, but even a glance at them suggests a widespread and determined effort by women to challenge the inequities they suffered because of their sex.[43] Unlike Lucy Salmon, these women advocated and undertook collective action to challenge structures of differentiation within their profession.

The general ferment of the 1930s contributed to the kinds of action they took. Not only were interest groups a visible part of social and political life during the New Deal; they were increasingly the focus of historians' attention. John Higham has characterized the "new history" that came into full prominence in the 1930s as "progressive history." It focused on conflicts between sections and economic groups; "rather than unity, [it] emphasized diversity."[44] The story of the United States that progressive historians told was one of social protest, of the organization of movements that struggled in the name of the less privileged for improvement and change. The idea that a universal human subject existed did not disappear; indeed, the appeal for equality was made in the name of inalienable human rights. Neither was there change in the optimistic belief that history was a story of progress toward social as well as political democracy. The story was, however, increasingly complicated by the interplay of competing interest groups.

In this context, women identified themselves as an interest group. Their interest came not from some inherent need or sameness but from their experience of discrimination. They argued that irrelevant biological differences had been invoked to deny them jobs, leadership positions, and power; intellectual capacity and professional ability, they insisted, had nothing to do with sex. Yet if the disabling effects of differentiation were to be fought, collective action by women as women was necessary. The point was to include women in whatever was considered human, to insist on the androgyny, as it were, of Universal Man.

Not only did women press their interest as members of the profession of history; they also assembled archival sources and wrote histories of women. Their goal was to establish the fact that women were, as Mary Beard's book title put it, "a force in history."[45] Their focus was on women's positive contribution to the building of societies and cultures, a challenge to the presumed passivity and irrelevance of women and therefore to their invisibility in the historical record. Visibility was to confer humanity on women and to make self-evident the terms on which equality ought to be practiced.

Feminists of the 1920s and 1930s appealed to democratic principles and the belief in the universality of man to justify their right to full participation in the profession. They assumed that their interests were those of all historians; only prejudice prevented women's fulfillment of these interests. On one level, there was nothing in the masculine representation of the historical subject to prevent women's identification with it; they thought of themselves as viable actors capable of effecting change. Yet equality proved more difficult to procure than to demand because the symbol of man was less susceptible to pluralization than it seemed. The claim to man's universality rested on an implied contrast between difference and particularity; as long as man was universal, the mere existence of woman demonstrated her specificity. This proved repeatedly to be the case in the AHA, despite the articulate and forceful pressure feminists brought to bear. Beatrice Hyslop pondered the frustrations of the situation in these terms:

> Where a woman has the ability to be a prominent historian, why should there be discrimination just because she is a woman? A young man starting on a career wants an even chance to show his ability and to compete for rewards. Women historians ask for the same equality of opportunity. Too many times they are not even given a chance . . . Is there something about history . . . that excludes competence on the basis of sex?[46]

Hyslop thought not, but I suggest there was: differentiation on the basis of sex was implicit in the abstract but unmistakably gendered concept of man as the representative human subject. As long as historical actors and historians were represented as men, it would be difficult for women to put into effect the equality they believed was their due.

III

In the 1970s women historians used another kind of collective strategy. Committed to equalizing conditions for women and men, the new approach nonetheless emphasized difference in a way that some earlier feminists found discomforting, if not unacceptable. Attention to the interests of women as professionals, the organization of women's caucuses, the publication of separate journals, and the writing of women's history all ran the risk of validating, even if only inadvertently, the difference between women and men.

The new emphasis on difference took shape in a national context generated by government policies of affirmative action that established and legitimated movements of organized interest groups of women, blacks, and others. In 1961 President Kennedy's creation of national and state commissions on the status of women set in motion processes that resulted in the founding of the National Organization of Women (NOW) in 1966.[47] Within the AHA, the Coordinating Committee on Women in the Historical Profession (CCWHP) emerged in 1969 as the voice of women's interests.[48] Its pressure led to the formation of the AHA committee that issued the Rose Report in 1970.

That report opened a new era for women's participation in the AHA. After 1970 patterns of exclusion began to be reversed: women were appointed to key committees and elected to the council, and they gained increased impact on association policies (for example, they produced guidelines on fairness in hiring and tenure for departments of history).[49] The standing Committee on Women Historians (CWH), established in the wake of the Rose Report, was the force behind these changes. It designated women as a separate constituency requiring an advocacy of their own and gave them access to high-level policy deliberations.

The CWH was at once a symbol and an agent of change. No longer was it easy to use gender differences to categorize and thus to discriminate among historians. In furthering a separate collective identity for women historians, the CWH made them visible as a definably different group, and they won important concessions because of that visibility. Indeed, visibility made it possible to identify the negative aspects of differentiation and thus to counter discrimination; it also enabled positive political action by women as women historians.

The difficulty came in establishing the terms of identity. Should one simply reverse the valence and accept the differences already assigned to women but assess them positively? Should one substitute other unifying female traits, or define the common interest as a rejection of the terms of difference that others had imposed? If one rejected the terms of difference, in what name did one do so—humanity? Didn't that then return to issues of humanity's masculine representation and women's problematic relationship with that concept?

These questions (by no means yet answered) became even more acute with the emergence of women's history as a major field of scholarly inquiry in the 1970s. The organizational visibility of women coincided with their appearance as historical subjects in association with a reconceptualization of history that was evident by the early 1960s. This new vision of history was preoccupied, according to Higham, "with the tendency of stable structures to break down," with "the disastrous erosion of all institutional authority."[50] It turned away from formal politics to various areas of human experience, including work, family, and sexuality. It questioned the concept of history as linear progress toward democracy, and the convention of representing humankind in unitary terms. Historians wrote books about conflict and struggle, about changing modes of domination, about social hierarchy and resistance.

In the process they introduced a plurality of historical actors whose special points of view and varied stories had to be revealed because they were not the same as those of the "typical" white man. The archetypal figure became particularized. The Renaissance was not a "renaissance for women"; the discovery of America became, in part, a story of Indian removal; manifest destiny was exposed as an ideological justification for imperialist expansion; and slavery became not a "peculiar institution" but a chapter in the continuing story of American racism.[51] The different stories of women, blacks, the poor, and the colonized were not reducible to a single narrative line about the American man. But how could they be told?

For the most part, histories of these different groups were written as separate narratives alongside or in opposition to what was dubbed "mainstream history." Women's history became a subdiscipline within the field of history and generated a prodigious new scholarship on the lives and experiences of women. The new knowledge demonstrated what previous accounts had implicitly denied: women were agents of history, and their lives yielded insight into unstudied realms of human existence in addition to well-studied processes such as industrialization and urbanization.

The new women's history was often cast in terms that affirmed the separateness and difference of women in implicit contrast to the world of men already known to history: women had a separate culture, distinct notions of the meaning of work and family, identifiable artistic or literary signatures, and particular forms of political consciousness.[52] The documentation of this women's world became an end in itself; simply establishing its existence was considered a significant challenge to the mainstream. Historians assumed they knew all about the category "woman"; they ascribed its negative aspects to male dominance, or "patriarchy," its positive aspects to women's resistance, or "agency," without examining how the classification "woman" acquired social and political meaning in particular contexts.[53] This kind of women's history provided evidence for the existence of something that could be called a separate female sphere. Having made women visible, historians had also emphasized women's difference from men and had thus both challenged and confirmed the established narrative of American democracy: challenged it because they questioned the typicality of the traditional history, yet confirmed it because the stories about women were so different from the standard story as to seem parallel but not central—sometimes even trivial.

Both effects are evident in current professional practice. On the one hand, there are historians like Carl Degler who recognize the need for a new concept of history:

What is meant by history or the past will have to be changed before [women's history] becomes a part of it . . . since the conventional past was not only conceived (invented?) by men but includes, almost by definition, only those activities in which men have been engaged, while ignoring almost entirely the historical activities of women. . . . The challenge is now to rethink our conception of the past we teach and write about so that women . . . are included.[54]

On the other hand, most departments of history reject Degler's challenge and treat women's history as a separate field of study. For positions in nineteenth- or twentieth-century social history they hire people who have written about miners or railroad workers but reject those who have written about seamstresses or female textile workers as being "in the wrong field." The historians responsible for this kind of action commonly give the explanation that "we already have a women's historian." They consider the subject of women to be a special one that lies outside traditionally established fields. At bottom, they refuse to recognize the particularity and the specificity of men, the uselessness of the concept of Universal Man. In the face of this refusal, which evokes tradition, the legacy of civilization and the return of narrative on its behalf, integrating women into history is just as daunting a task as including women as equals with men in the concept of humanity.

The strategies of women historians have all foundered on the issue of difference as a conceptual and structural phenomenon. How to recognize and refuse terms of discrimination, how to act collectively on behalf of women without confirming the notion of a separate female sphere—these have been persistent dilemmas, never fully resolved. Indeed, debates about how to resolve them are at the center of current discussion among feminist historians. Women's history poses the same questions as women's collective action in the profession of history: Can the historical narrative—the great story of Western civilization or American democracy—sustain the pluralizing of its subject? Can we conceive of humanity in terms that are not gendered? Can we think about difference without reference to a norm, without establishment of a hierarchical ordering? Not easily— or at least not yet.

The continuing inequality of various groups challenges the ideal of democracy as the extension of access to ever-greater numbers of people. To adopt this simple notion of pluralism as a theory of democratic inclusion is to ignore the ways in which difference establishes and institutionalizes the various meanings of power. It has been impossible to demand equality without somehow recognizing difference, but too much insistence on difference (as Lucy Salmon pointed out) undercuts claims for equality. This conundrum exists not because of faulty strategy on the part of those who seek equal treatment but because of the inability of certain theories of liberalism to take difference, even as it defines equality, into account.

To resolve the equality–difference dilemma, we must critically analyze the categories we most often take for granted: history, women, men, equality, difference, the terms of liberal theory itself. Rather than assume to know the meaning of these terms, we need instead to examine them as they have been developed and used in specific historical contexts as the products of culture, politics, and time. We cannot write women into history, for example, unless we are willing to accept the notion that history as a unified story was a fiction about a universal subject whose universality was achieved through implicit processes of differentiation, marginalization, and exclusion. Man was never, in other words, a truly universal figure.

The processes of exclusion that established man's "universality" must be the focus of the new narrative. One aspect of those processes involved the definition of *women* and the attribution of particular characteristics, traits, and roles to women to differentiate them from men. The difference historians have documented in so much of women's history was constructed through processes of exclusion; it did not arise from some essential quality inherent in the female sex. Thus "women's experience" and "women's culture" exist only as expressions of female particularity in contrast to male universality; they are not realms of empirical data but concepts through which a certain vision of social life is realized.

Differentiation also involved constant readjustment in the relationship between equality and difference. Absolute equality has never been achieved, but for particular purposes in some contexts the exclusions enforced against certain differences have been suspended. The relative importance of some differences has varied with time and circumstances. For instance, sex differences did not limit access to the profession of history, but they became a major consideration for the AHA in establishing leadership and allocating power within the association. It is this kind of story that must constitute the focus of new historical narratives.

The presence of difference complicates the story of democratization as a process of access, for many inequities persist even after physical barriers are removed. The problem of difference also indicates that power relationships within presumably homogeneous organizations are related not only to sociological distinctions among practitioners but also to the very conceptions of knowledge produced and protected by a discipline or a profession. This is not to say that access and concepts of difference are distinct issues, for there is clearly a relationship between them: lines of inclusion and exclusion are drawn in terms of difference, as are internal hierarchies. Still, it seems useful to distinguish among kinds of differentiation and not to conflate such issues as access and internal hierarchy even though both involve drawing lines according to sex. These related processes have a history that requires precise recounting. Precision of focus and close analysis permit appreciation of how varied and yet how persistent are the interconnections between gender and the politics of a discipline such as history.

ENDNOTES

I am grateful to Jill Conway and Jacqueline Goggin for their critical readings of the first draft of this paper, and to Goggin for generously providing me with information she has gathered in her own extensive work on the subject of American women historians. Elizabeth Weed provided crucial advice for conceptualizing the argument.

[1]Cited in Arthur S. Link, "The American Historical Association, 1884–1984; Retrospect and Prospect," *American Historical Review* 90 (February 1985), p. 5.

[2]Fewer than 100 scholars held Ph.D.'s in history before 1900; among these were eight women. Many more women, however, held master's degrees or were working on Ph.D.'s. The other women recruited to the AHA in its early years were members of historical societies, archivists, librarians, and (historian) wives of male historians. See William Hesseltine and Louis Kaplan, "Women Doctors of Philosophy in History," *Journal of Higher Education* 14 (1943), pp. 254–59.

[3]Lawrence Veysey, "The Plural Organized Worlds of the Humanities," in Alexandra Oleson and John Voss, eds., *The Organization of Knowledge in Modern America, 1860–1920* (Baltimore: Johns Hopkins University Press, 1976), pp. 51–106, esp. pp. 53–78. On the early history of the AHA see J. Franklin Jameson, "The American Historical Association, 1884–1909," *American Historical Review* 15 (October 1909), pp. 1–20, and "Early Days of the American Historical Association, 1884–1895," *American Historical Review* 40 (October 1934), pp. 1–9. See also John Higham, "Herbert Baxter Adams and the Study of Local History," *American Historical Review* 89 (December 1984), pp. 1225–39, and David D. Van Tassel, "From Learned Society to Professional Organization: The American Historical Association, 1884–1900," *American Historical Review* 89 (October 1984), pp. 929–56.

[4]Nellie Neilson, "A Generation of History at Mount Holyoke," *Mount Holyoke Alumnae Quarterly* (May 1939), cited in Penina M. Glazer and Miriam Slater, *Unequal Colleagues: The Entrance of Women into the Professions, 1890–1940* (New Brunswick, NJ: Rutgers University Press, 1987), p. 53.

[5]Cited in John Higham, *History* (Englewood Cliffs, NJ: Prentice Hall, 1965), p. 6.

[6]Ibid., p. 13.

[7]Herbert Baxter Adams, *The Study of History in American Colleges and Universities* (Washington, DC: Bureau of Education, 1887), Circular #2, pp. 211–12.

[8]Ibid., pp. 213–17. See also his *Methods of History Study* (Baltimore: Johns Hopkins University Press, 1884).

[9]Herbert Baxter Adams, *The Study and Teaching of History* (Richmond, VA: Whittet and Shepperson, 1898), p. 11.

[10]Ibid., p. 10.

[11]Although the focus of much of this work was on formal politics, it sometimes extended to other kinds of institutions—even to things as seemingly remote from politics as domestic service. Lucy Salmon, for example, who had written a master's thesis on the "History of the Appointing Power of the President," made domestic service the subject of a book she wrote as part of her preoccupation with the history of democracy. She saw the institution of service as a remnant of an aristocratic social system that perpetuated dependence and subservience, and she devised ingenious ways to study the history of service and its current practice. She did not conceive of the project as a separate study of the family, the private sphere, or of women. Rather, her argument was that domestic service was an economic and political phenomenon and, as such, within the province of scientific historical

investigation. Lucy Maynard Salmon, *Domestic Service* (1897; reprint, New York: Ayer, 1972).

[12]Adams, *The Study and Teaching of History*, p. 14.

[13]AHA *Records* (1905), cited by Jacqueline Goggin, "Challenging the Historical Establishment: Women in the Historical Profession, 1890–1940," (unpublished paper, Berkshire Conference, June 1987), p. 30.

[14]Cited in Van Tassel, "From Learned Society," p. 953.

[15]Ibid., p. 954. Salmon's perseverance resulted in an increase in female representation on AHA committees; at the end of her council term in 1920, there were four women on various committees. See Goggin, "Challenging the Historical Establishment," p. 37.

[16]Link, "The American Historical Association," p. 5.

[17]Referring to the period 1926–39, one study concluded, "teaching history—or even holding positions in which graduate training in history is of some use—is predominantly a man's occupation. Part of the reason for this situation is the more limited job opportunities for women. No woman teaches history in a man's college, although men may teach in a woman's college. Coeducational institutions employ a far greater percentage of men than women." Hesseltine and Kaplan, "Women Doctors of Philosophy in History," pp. 255–56.

[18]Link, "The American Historical Association," p. 5.

[19]Howard K. Beale, "The Professional Historian: His Theory and His Practice," *Pacific Historical Review* 22 (August 1953), p. 235.

[20]In the early 1960s much of the discussion of women in the professions had assumed that an increase in numbers would end discrimination. Barnaby Keeney, then president of Brown University, wrote in 1962 that "all things being equal, 50 percent of the professors in the total of colleges and universities ought to be women. . . . " in "Women Professors at Brown," *Pembroke Alumna* 27 (October 1962), pp. 8–9. See also Jessie Bernard, *Academic Women* (University Park, PA: Pennsylvania State University Press, 1964), p. xii; and Lucille Addison Pollard, *Women on College and University Faculties: A Historical Survey and a Study of Their Present Academic Status,* (New York: Ayer, 1977).

[21]American Historical Association, *Report of The Committee on The Status of Women,* November 1970, p. i.

[22]Jesse Dunsmore Clarkson, "Escape to the Present," *American Historical Review* 46 (April 1941), pp. 544–48. See also *Proceedings—1940 (Annual Report of the American Historical Association for the Year 1940),* pp. 21, 59. Merle Curti remembers receiving a letter of thanks from the secretary of the Berkshire Conference for the recognition the 1940 program gave to women: "I felt ashamed we hadn't done more and that it had seemed appropriate to thank us for so little." Merle Curti, letter to the author, 25 March 1987.

[23]*Annual Report of the AHA, Proceedings—1939,* p. 58. I am grateful to Noralee Frankel for helping me locate these materials.

[24]"Historical News: The American Historical Association," *American Historical Review* 45 (1939–40), p. 745, cited in Goggin, "Challenging the Historical Establishment," p. 52. The members of the 1940 nominating committee were Howard K. Beale, Paul Buck, Curtis Nettles, and Judith Williams. Beale, its chairman, had long championed the inclusion of blacks in the council and other committees. Although that effort repeatedly failed (indicating the degree of racism in the AHA), he supported the movement to name a representative from another "different" category—women.

[25]Jessie Bernard, *Academic Women;* Patricia Albjerg Graham, "Expansion and Exclusion: A History of Women in Higher Education," *Signs* 3 (Summer 1978), pp. 759–73; Susan Carter, "Academic Women Revisited: An Empirical Study of Changing Patterns in Women's Employment as College and University Faculty, 1890–1963," *Journal of Social History* 14 (Summer 1981), pp. 615–97. For a study of the impact of the G.I. Bill (The Servicemen's Readjustment Act of 1944), which poured government money into universities for the enrollment of returning veterans, see Keith W. Olson, *The G.I. Bill, The Veterans, and the Colleges* (Lexington, KY: University Press of Kentucky, 1974).

[26]Allan Nevins, speech at a history conference at Stanford University, reported in the *New York Times,* 16 August 1951, cited in Beale, "The Professional Historian," p. 246. An example of Cold War ideology and education can be found in *National Defense and Higher Education* (Washington, DC: The American Council on Education, 1951).

[27]Beatrice Hyslop, Mount Holyoke College, "Letters of the Class of 1919" (1969). I am grateful to Ellen Bullington Furlough for this and other information about Hyslop. See her "Beatrice Fry Hyslop: Historian of France," (master's thesis, University of South Carolina, 1978), p. 87.

[28]It would also be interesting, if one had more time, to look at what might be called the uncritical strategies—those that insisted that individual excellence or tact could overcome the disabilities of sex. Thus the authors of a 1953 study on the Radcliffe Ph.D. ended their book by suggesting the best way for women to succeed: "The solution . . . is for women to do work of such high quality that no question of 'competition' arises. It would take a very prejudiced anti-feminist to refuse to employ, on the ground of sex, a woman who has demonstrated ability and achievement clearly superior to that of the men available." *Graduate Education for Women: The Radcliffe Ph.D.* (Cambridge, MA: Harvard University Press, 1956), p. 108. The book also contains reports from women Ph.D.'s on their strategies. One tells how she tries to "hide [her] mind" (p. 36); another does "not attempt to press forward as strenuously as a man would" (p. 39); another simply dismisses as trivial her exclusion from social events "like clubs and stag dinners" (pp. 27–28). For many, any evidence of stridency or feminism constitutes dangerous behavior, to be avoided at all costs (pp. 26, 38). The point seems to be either to be so competent that one's sex is excused or to be so discreet that it goes unnoticed. In either case, the evidence for consciousness of female difference is overwhelmingly clear.

[29]Louise Fargo Brown, *Apostle of Democracy: The Life of Lucy Maynard Salmon* (New York: Harper & Row, 1943), p. 98. See the entry on Salmon by Violet Barbour in J.T. James, ed., *Notable American Women,* vol. III (Cambridge, MA: Harvard University Press, 1971), pp. 223–25. See also Helen Lefkowitz Horowitz, *Alma Mater: Design and Experience in the Women's Colleges from Their Nineteenth-Century Beginnings to the 1930s* (Boston: Beacon Press, 1984), pp. 180, 186–87, 194.

[30]Brown, *Apostle of Democracy,* pp. 101–2.

[31]Ibid., p. 132.

[32]Ibid., p. 136.

[33]Ibid., p. 256.

[34]Cited by A. Underhill in his foreword to the posthumously published book by Lucy Maynard Salmon, *Historical Material* (New York: Oxford University Press, 1933), p. vii.

[35]Higham, *History,* pp. 124, 206, and passim.

[36]Evidence of protest by women historians existed prior to the 1920s in individual expressions of anger and in concerted efforts to include women in the AHA leadership structure. It was not until the 1920s, however, that widespread evidence of collective action appeared.

[37]"U of M gets First Woman History Prof," *Detroit Free Press,* 29 October 1961, p. C-5; letter from University of Michigan history department chair, John Bowditch, to vice-president and dean of faculties, Marvin L. Niehuss, 15 February 1961.

Information about Dr. Robinson and the provisions of her bequest was obtained from the University of Wisconsin (Madison) history department. It took years for bequests such as these to generate enough income to pay the salaries the donors stipulated. Only in the 1960s and 1970s, when alumnae pressure and a new concern with increasing the number of women Ph.D.'s drew attention to the existence of these chairs for women, were they fully funded and permanently filled.

[38]Schlesinger Library, Radcliffe College, Papers of the Berkshire Conference, MC267 (5). Louise R. Loomis, letter, 8 May 1952. See also, Kathryn Kish Sklar, "American Female Historians in Context, 1770–1930," *Feminist Studies* 3 (Fall 1975), pp. 171–84.

[39]Papers of the Berkshire Conference, MC267 (2), 16 March 1931. The influence, however indirect, of labor movement concerns in this period is also evident here.

[40]Papers of the Berkshire Conference, MC267 (3), *Minutes,* 20–22 May 1938.

[41]It would be interesting to know exactly why Nellie Neilson was chosen as the women's nominee. She was, of course, an accomplished historian with an excellent reputation. That she was a medievalist also seems important, especially in light of the fact that medieval history attracted many extraordinary women historians. I speculate that there was a relationship between the skills required of medievalists (facility with esoteric languages and epigraphy) and women's entry into this field. Mastery of these difficult skills were unqualified marks of competence and erudition. To prove one's self in medieval history might be harder but also more sure for a woman than other more accessible areas of the field (for which scholars had only to read English or a modern foreign language). Historian William Roy Smith wrote of Nellie Neilson that she had "an uncanny faculty for inspiring her students with a love for mediaeval history, but she also [taught] them how to use manuscript material and enjoy the game." Cited in Goggin, "Challenging the Historical Establishment," p. 15.

[42]Louise Phelps Kellogg was an archivist at the Wisconsin State Historical Society. She was the first woman president of the Mississippi Valley Historical Association (the forerunner of the current Organization of American Historians), elected in 1930.

[43]Jacqueline Goggin, of the J. Franklin Jameson Papers at the Library of Congress, is at work on this history of women historians from 1884–1940.

[44]Higham, *History,* p. 148.

[45]Mary Beard, *Women as a Force in History* (1946; reprint, New York: Octagon Books, 1985). For examples of women's history see also Mary Sumner Benson, *Women in Eighteenth Century America: A Study of Opinion and Social Usage* (1935; reprint, New York: AMS Press, 1976); Elizabeth W. Dexter, *Colonial Women of Affairs: A Study of Women in Business and The Professions in America before 1776* (1931; reprint, Fairfield, NJ: Augustus Kelley, 1972); and Julia Cherry Spruill, *Women's Life and Work in the Southern Colonies* (New

York: Norton, 1972). For extensive bibliographic treatment see Jill K. Conway, *The Female Experience in Eighteenth and Nineteenth Century America: A Guide to the History of American Women* (Princeton: Princeton University Press, 1985).

[46]Beatrice Hyslop, "Letter to the Editor," *American Historical Review* 62 (October 1956), pp. 288–89, cited in Furlough, "Beatrice Fry," p. 67.

[47]The history of this period is told by Alice Rossi and Ann Calderwood, eds., *Academic Women on the Move* (New York: Russell Sage, 1973). See especially the essays by Alice Rossi, Jo Freeman, and Kay Klotzburger.

[48]Hilda Smith, *CCWHP: The First Decade* (unpublished history of the Coordinating Committee on Women in the Historical Profession, 1979).

[49]American Historical Association, *Report of the Committee on the Status of Women,* 9 November 1970. See also the annual reports of the Committee on Women Historians in the *Proceedings* of the AHA.

[50]Higham, *History,* p. 225.

[51]On women see Joan Kelly-Gadol, "Did Women Have a Renaissance?" in *Women, History and Theory: The Essays of Joan Kelly* (Chicago: Chicago University Press, 1984); Gerda Lerner, *The Majority Finds Its Past: Placing Women in History* (New York: Oxford University Press, 1979); and Joan Hoff Wilson, "The Illusion of Change: Women and The American Revolution," in Alfred Young, ed., *The American Revolution: Explorations in the History of American Radicalism* (DeKalb, IL: Illinois University Press, 1976), pp. 383–446. On Native Americans, see Francis Jennings, *The Invasion of America: Indians, Colonialism and The Cant of Conquest* (New York: Norton, 1976); Michael Paul Rogin, *Fathers and Children: Andrew Jackson and the Subjugation of the American Indian* (New York: Knopf, 1975); Mary Young, *Redskins, Ruffleshirts and Rednecks: Indian Allotments in Alabama and Mississippi* (Norman, OK: University of Oklahoma Press, 1961). On racism see George Fredrickson, *The Black Image in the White Mind: The Debate on Afro-American Character and Destiny, 1817–1914* (New York: Harper & Row, 1971); Winthrop Jordan, *White over Black: American Attitudes Toward the Negro, 1550–1819* (Chapel Hill: University of North Carolina Press, 1968); Edmund Morgan, *American Slavery, American Freedom: The Ordeal of Colonial Virginia* (New York: Norton, 1975). On manifest destiny see Walter LaFeber, *The New Empire: An Interpretation of American Expansion 1860–1890* (Ithaca, NY: Cornell University Press, 1963), and William Appleman Williams, *The Roots of Modern American Empire* (New York: Random House, 1969).

[52]A recent attempt to synthesize the new knowledge about women is Marilyn J. Boxer and Jean H. Quataert, eds., *Connecting Spheres: Women in the Western World, 1500 to the Present* (New York: Oxford University Press, 1987). On "women's culture" see the symposium, "Politics and Culture in Women's History," *Feminist Studies* 6 (Spring 1980), pp. 26–64. On women's writing see the special issue, "Writing and Sexual Difference," of *Critical Inquiry* 8 (Winter 1981); on political consciousness, see Temma Kaplan, "Female Consciousness and Collective Action: The Case of Barcelona, 1910–1918," *Signs* 7 (1982) pp. 545–66.

[53]For a brilliant analysis of the historical variability of the category "woman," see Denise Riley's forthcoming *"Am I That Name?" A History of the Languages of Feminisms* (London: Macmillan, 1988).

[54]Carl Degler, "What the Women's Movement Has Done to American History," *Soundings* 64 (Winter 1981), p. 419.

Miriam Slater and Penina Migdal Glazer

Prescriptions for Professional Survival

I N THE UNITED STATES TODAY professional training has become the goal of most educated women. In 1987 they were one-third of the entering class in the nation's medical schools and half its cadre of aspiring lawyers. Beyond these notable statistics in law and medicine are others equally striking. Since 1967 women have doubled their numbers in pharmacy, quadrupled their ranks in optometry, and increased their representation in veterinary medicine so that they constitute more than half the entering class in many veterinary colleges. Although women are only 24 percent of practicing pharmacists, 8 percent of optometrists, and 13 percent of veterinarians, the impressive increase of women in the professional schools seems to promise an end to discrimination in the professions.[1] Nevertheless, we believe that persistent inequalities remain that must still command our attention.

This is not the first but the second wave of feminism in the twentieth century. The first occurred at the turn of the century; the second, in the 1960s and 1970s. Both were marked by dramatic

Miriam Slater, born in 1931 in Brooklyn, New York, is Harold F. Johnson Professor of History at Hampshire College. Her principal works include "Motherhood and Medicine" (with Penina Glazer, 1983), The Family in the Seventeenth Century: The Verneys of Claydon House *(1984), and* Unequal Colleagues: Women's Entrance into the Professions *(with Penina Glazer, 1987).*

Penina Migdal Glazer, born in 1939 in Roosevelt, New Jersey, is dean of faculty and professor of history at Hampshire College. She is coauthor of Unequal Colleagues: The Entrance of Women into the Professions, 1890–1940 *(with Miriam Slater) and* Sociology: Understanding Society *(with Peter I. Rose and Myron Glazer, 1978).*

This paper is based on a larger work, *Unequal Colleagues: The Entrance of Women into the Professions, 1890–1940* (New Brunswick: Rutgers University Press, 1986).

change in women's access to professional education and careers. The gains made in women's career opportunities seemed permanent in the early 1900s but were lost during the politically conservative twenties and the economic decline of the Depression. These years of contracting opportunities partially account for the sharp decline in the number of professional women in America between 1930 and the resurgence of the women's movement in the late 1960s. Beliefs about gender characteristics and roles also profoundly influenced the decline. These beliefs in turn affected the responses of women who encountered discrimination and resistance to their professional ambitions.

Our purpose in this essay is to analyze the characteristic responses to discrimination of the first generation of women who entered professional life in significant numbers. In our view these responses were only partially successful ways to deal with the problem. Similar strategies have reappeared in the second expansion of women's recruitment into the professions and had similar results. Contemporary society thus faces the same questions about discrimination against women in the professions as in the opening decades of the century.

The first entrants were ideally suited to professional recruitment in all characteristics except their gender. As white, native-born, college-educated women of the middle class, they were similar to the men entering medicine, law, and engineering in increasing numbers between 1900 and 1930. Yet instead of moving easily into secure places in professional hierarchies, they found themselves marginalized in both explicit and subtle ways. Believing they had entered fields of endeavor where new talent was welcome and rewards were earned by merit, early women professionals had to develop a number of strategies to cope with the experience of discrimination. Their analysis of the problem and their responses to it helped to shape the structure of the American professions. Their styles of professional behavior have persisted; indeed, the second generation has replicated them without much critical analysis of the preceding experience. Such critical analysis is badly needed if we are to succeed in integrating and retaining the current influx of professional women. It is an even more pressing requirement if we are to include previously debarred racial and ethnic minorities in advanced education and professional training.

The first wave of women professionals reacted to discrimination by becoming superperformers, subordinates, career innovators, or sep-aratists. These roles were not mutually exclusive; some women used more than one strategy to manage their careers over the course of their lives. Our analysis of these strategies is an effort to trace the responses of women who work in settings where the formally stated requirements are professional merit but the informal experience is one of unstated bias and discrimination.

Today's women on the fast track are not the first group to adhere to the ideal of superperformance. At the turn of the century a group of talented women in fields such as medicine clearly relied on extraordinary achievement to reap what were at best very ordinary rewards. For these women no barrier was too high to surmount, no task too arduous to complete, no client too lowly or dangerous to treat, no personal sacrifice too great to make. Nothing inhibited the desire of this group of middle-class women to serve the needy in the most trying circumstances. These intrepid superperformers overcame barriers by dint of hard work, outstanding ability, and willingness to sacrifice traditional relationships for careers.

The issue of marriage, children, and sustaining emotional bonds is of critical importance to our understanding of this group and our appreciation of its parallels to contemporary professional women. A sizable proportion of the first generation of professional women chose not to marry. Their decision evoked some of the same concerns one finds in today's debate about the later age of marriage and child rearing among young professional women.

For the small minority among the superperformers who did marry, the situation was very complex. They felt impelled to go to great lengths to avoid any intimation that they might be shirking their duty as mothers and wives. When their husbands' careers required it, the wives arranged for necessary moves, smoothed over irregularities in schedules, entertained new associates, and ameliorated the inevitable pressures that arose in their households. These women believed that they had to be superperformers in the home as wives and mothers as well as in the workplace, but they often found their own career ambitions repositioned at the end of a long line of other demands. Sometimes they had to retreat from their highest goals, accept a more subordinate role, or move into a new kind of work that dovetailed more easily with their domestic obligations. But they, their husbands, and the rest of the society viewed the obligations of the home and children as primarily wives' responsibilities, no matter what their professional training and aspirations.

Anne Walter Fearn (1865–1939) is an example of a superperformer who started life in favored circumstances that few women would have the courage or desire to reject in favor of professional work. She was a southern debutante who had her coming-out party in the Mississippi governor's mansion. Her socially prominent family was surprised and horrified when she chose to pursue a medical career in China. She was outspoken in asserting that she was not a missionary, "not even a church member," but "a physician." Nevertheless, she did ultimately meet and marry a missionary-physician and both partners practiced in China.[2]

The marriage suffered from the tensions two careers produce. She tells us in her memoirs that she "honestly endeavored to follow his wishes. . . . one of his obsessions was that the day should begin with prayer and Bible reading, and that the Bible should be read through methodically once or twice a year." None of this was especially surprising for a missionary family. It would certainly not have been unusual for a conventional wife of that period. But it made Anne Fearn late for rounds and interfered with her care of patients. One morning, when the pressure of work seemed particularly acute, she lost control, seized the Bible, threw it to the floor, and rushed from the room screaming "I wish I'd never seen the damned thing." She did succeed in ending the Bible readings, but her husband, she said, "never forgave nor forgot, and I lost forever my taste, if I ever had any, for the Old Testament."[3]

The necessity of following her husband to a new assignment some years later, however, overshadowed this modest victory. There was no comparable work for her in the new situation. She wrote that "after the first excitement of settling a new home had subsided I found that I missed Soochow and my own work with a poignancy that made me restless and dissatisfied."

The alterations World War I made in their married life rescued her from a lifetime of drifting. Her husband served in France and she returned to her hospital work in China. Even an event of such magnitude did not free her from the need to justify her profound engagement with her work. She had known since early in the marriage that "he would much rather have had his wife sit at home and be managed by him." And at the end of his life (1926) it was her husband who forgave her for devoting her life to ameliorating the suffering of the sick.[4] She is a striking example of the professional woman burdened by guilt about whether she has fulfilled her family responsibilities to her own high standards.

Fearn's experiences highlight the difficulty of combining superperformance with marriage. She had few structural or normative supports for her choice of career, marriage, and children. Very few of her contemporaries, even among the superperformers, attempted to "have it all." Such expectations are much more common on the part of educated women today, many of whom expect or need to work. Today's women have few children, and the childbearing years are telescoped into a much smaller segment of an increasingly long life span. They can realistically count on decades of productive work beyond their childbearing years.

Yet young women continue to receive several conflicting messages. We expect our daughters as well as our sons to go to college and to complete the training necessary for entrance to professional life. While families invest increasingly greater resources in their childrens' education, irrespective of gender, we also expect that our adult children will marry and have families of their own.

The two-career family is now seen as a necessity for the maintenance of middle-class life. Any conflicts that this ambitious agenda raises are supposed to be worked out privately by individual families. When we consider that there is no national day-care policy, that women are still too often paid less than men for the same jobs, and that studies of domestic arrangements all tell the same unsettling tale—that wives rather than husbands still bear the major responsibility for child care and household management—we know that even a superperformer will have difficulty managing all fronts.

These givens of modern life ensure that most women compete for professional status and rewards from a condition of inequality. If a woman is married and especially if she has children, society still offers few supports for her efforts to achieve professional parity. The standards of performance and the expectation of accomplishment for women in their public lives are now, as in the past, modeled on male patterns of commitment, attendance, and single-minded devotion to duty. Similarly, women's responsibilities as mothers are modeled on older styles of engagement from an era when mothering was considered a full-time "profession." Certainly, superperformance is required to manage two full-time professions. But as we see from Fearn's life, the effort may be disproportionate to the rewards.

One strategy that allowed women to combine marriage and career with less conflict was what we have called voluntary subordination. It entailed their decision to work as assistants or in other subordinate positions. Often this strategy meant that women accepted positions of lesser rank in a male-dominated field than their abilities and training warranted. For example, in the early part of the century women were hired in astronomy research to record data and do all the tedious measurements and calculations on the understanding that they would never be promoted to faculty rank.[5]

Many women found such positions attractive because they provided professional employment in fields from which women were otherwise excluded. At the same time, their response as subordinates removed the need to compete with men or to justify such competition. While male supervisors welcomed women as research assistants and used many of the discoveries and ideas of their subordinates, they were often resistant to giving women public credit or offering them equal rewards. Director of the Harvard College Observatory, Edward Pickering, justified his employment of a score of female assistants to the Harvard overseers by pointing out that "many of the assistants are skillful only in their own particular work, but are nevertheless capable of doing as much good routine work as astronomers who would receive much larger salaries. Three or four times as many assistants can thus be employed, and the work done correspondingly increased for a given expenditure."[6]

Furthermore, the subordinate route was sometimes even encouraged by female leaders who were eager to create places for the increasingly large pool of college-educated women. Playing on widely held notions of women's special "natural" abilities, Williamina Fleming, curator of astronomical photographs and supervisor of research assistants at Harvard, spoke for many other women of her time when she suggested in 1893 that "while we cannot maintain that in everything woman is man's equal, yet in many things her patience, perseverance, and method make her his superior."[7] Thus we see today the proliferation of college training in the role of "legal assistant," "executive secretary," or "nurse practitioner." These roles are all subordinate ones within large organizations, roles outside the regular structure of promotion, and—most important—roles where compensation is never correlated with experience. Young women who seek this kind of education are never told that they are training for the subordinate option and for a low return on their investment in education. What this education does lead to is a predictable work routine for a woman who expects to invest much of her psychic energy in family life.

The clear selection of a subordinate role still did not mitigate male fears of competition. Thus in female-dominated professions such as nursing, where the competition with men was notably less and where clear lines of subordination to a predominantly male profession should have diminished fears of women's achievement, women were still viewed with suspicion. The bid of male physicians for hegemony over medicine and allied health-care delivery tended to make them extremely sensitive to competition of any kind. Doctors complained about "the aggressiveness of the public health nurse"[8] and stepped up their efforts to convince policymakers of the correctness of their exclusive control of health care and to eliminate the female strongholds of homeopathic medicine and midwifery.

Obviously, the subordinate route did not lead to substantial reward or status. While such positions provided work for many women, the presence of an alternative subordinate role was used to justify women's exclusion from predominantly male professions on the grounds that women preferred careers that would fit better with marriage and career aspirations.[9] This line of reasoning was widely asserted despite the evidence that many of the women in these fields did not marry. Many women, married or not, still take the subordinate route. Witness the nurse practitioner in the physician's office, the hygienist in the dentist's office, the research associate in the laboratory. All of these roles for women are evidence of the hierarchical nature of professional activity as well as its continued gender stratification. Common to both historical periods has been the compatibility between voluntary subordination and a female gender stereotype based on nurturance, self-sacrifice, limited ambition, and lack of concern with financial reward. The low status and low pay of today's helping professions and the predominance of women in those fields are reminders of the enduring consequences of this juxtaposition.

One primary reason for advocating gender segregation was that it provided a cheap source of labor in the helping professions. The creation of an unsegregated work force would require the creation of structural supports—day care, flexible work hours, and an openness to diversity in the workplace. Under these conditions women could compete on equal terms with men. These changes would enhance the possibility of careers open to talent and merit as a standard of entrance, but the creation of such opportunities would also increase competition. While increased competition is acceptable during periods of continued economic expansion, the recent outcry against affirmative action indicates a genuine fear of diminished opportunities on the part of those who have historically benefited from traditional methods of recruitment, especially in times of limited economic growth.

The strategy of innovation worked well where the innovators elected to enter fields that were not directly competitive with the market for the services of male professionals. When a well-trained group of women doctors attempted to develop the new field of public health medicine, they found male doctors resistant to an alternative system of care that might compromise fee-for-service delivery of health care.

In her memoirs Dr. Josephine Baker reported a blunt statement of the conflict between women physicians concerned with public health and male medical practitioners. She describes the testimony of a male physician who was representing a New England medical society before a congressional committee. The committee was considering appropriation of funds "for the newly founded Federal Children's Bureau," an agency organized and run by women physicians who were interested in public health care and preventive medicine. The New England doctor testified that "we oppose this bill because, if you are going to save the lives of all these women and children at public expense, what inducement will there be for young men to study medicine?" The senator who was chairing leaned forward in disbelief and inquired: "Perhaps I didn't understand you correctly, you surely don't mean that you want women and children to die unnecessarily or live in constant danger of sickness so there will be something for young doctors to do?" And this physician unabashedly replied, "Why not, that's the will of God, isn't it?"[10]

Successful innovators sought out or created new occupations for women professionals. In new fields the career patterns were not clear and the rewards were uncertain. Hence the issue of direct competition with men or encroaching on male-defined territory was muted.

Alice Hamilton's medical career is a vivid example of successful innovation in a field that did not compete directly with male physicians. Hamilton left her position as a laboratory bacteriologist in order to investigate health conditions in factories that used poisonous chemicals. When she made her choice, there was practically no research or interest in environmentally caused illness. Hamilton's work involved personal jeopardy as she investigated hazardous work sites. It also involved career risks. Her first surveys were unpaid research efforts, and it was not clear what her career path would be. Her results challenged factory owners' control of the workplace and pinpointed their responsibility for the lead and mercury poisoning affecting their workers. This kind of inquiry removed the researcher from the sanitary and comparatively safe environs of the laboratory and placed her in the rough and tumble labor conflict on the factory floor. This career did not fit the conventional idea of women's work, nor did it appeal to young professional men, whose ideal of professional activity emphasized the objective, scientific aloofness from the contaminating influence of political life, the attraction of the aseptic laboratory, and the solitary glory of making stunning scientific breakthroughs. This ideal was very different from the slow, incremental, statistical inquiries of the fieldwork that Hamilton had chosen. Hamilton wrote to her mother in 1911 about her experiences:

Today, I went over to the West Penn Hospital to look through the records. It is an indescribably dingy place, smoke-begrimed and ugly. One of the great Carnegie Steel Mills is just below it and as I sat by the window I could watch the ambulances crawl up the hill to the accident entrance with a new victim inside. Three came while I was there. So many cases are sent from the mills that evidently the clerk got tired of writing the name of the Company and had a rubber stamp made which, appropriately enough, he uses with red ink. All down the page came these red blotches just like drops of blood.... [11]

Hamilton's reputation as an expert in industrial medicine grew. During World War I, the breakdown of trade relations with Germany spurred the growth of chemical and dye companies in the

United States. As disease rates soared, some universities were prod-
ded into providing new curriculum materials and research in industrial medicine. After the war Harvard decided to make an appointment
in industrial medicine. The field "still had not attracted men," Hamilton wrote, "and I was really the only candidate available."

The Harvard reception of a woman was mixed, and not everyone
agreed with Dean Edsall that this appointment marked "a step
forward." President Abbott Lawrence Lowell wanted it clearly
understood that Hamilton's appointment did not signify opening the
door to women students. In fact, the corporation of the university
was displeased with the medical school's decision to appoint a
woman, and "one member had sworn roundly over it." Those
pressing for the appointment tried to appease the opposition by
promising that Hamilton would never use the faculty club, or request
faculty football tickets, or "embarrass the faculty by marching in the
Commencement procession and sitting on the platform."[12] While
these restrictions seem petty, they also emphasize the medical school's
position that women were not welcome and that even the most
outstanding among them would not receive equal treatment.

Hamilton's hope of opening Harvard to women was not realized
during her tenure there. Harvard Medical School remained closed to
women until 1945, six years after her retirement. She realized that she
had not broken the barriers she had set out to remove and observed
that "in the United States a woman finds it harder to gain entrance to
the medical schools than does a man, much harder to get her
internship in a first-class hospital, and difficult if not impossible to get
on the staff of an important hospital. Yet without such hospital
connections she can never hope to reach the highest ranks in her
profession."[13]

The strategy of pursuing separate careers in female-led institutions,
the fourth response we are considering, brought women supportive
colleagues and the fulfillments of congenial working sociability.
Many women spent their professional lives in predominantly female
communities such as settlement houses and women's colleges because
they saw the special possibilities of female-controlled institutions.
Given the choice between isolated or lesser positions in larger,
male-dominated organizations and paramount positions in smaller
female enclaves, the separatists chose the latter, for there women
could control the decision making and the rewards.

In the first decades of this century Mount Holyoke College, under the leadership of its president, Mary E. Woolley, was such a separatist community for its predominantly female professoriat. Mary Woolley believed that faculty women were unable to pursue professional careers and conventional private lives at the same time. For faculty who chose, like her, not to marry, the college became both workplace and home.[14] The college responded to this unusually large number of single women by serving as a residential institution for the faculty as well as for the students. This was a model that had served single men well at Oxford and Cambridge, so Mount Holyoke adapted it for women.

These arrangements had several consequences. Women were freed from the domestic obligations and chores that traditionally consumed so much time and energy. They enjoyed access to a community of scholars who served both as friends and as a reference group for ambitious professionals who were bucking the tide of received opinion. Communities like Mount Holyoke College became "the world turned upside down."[15] Women assumed positions of leadership and succeeded in developing a crucial redefinition of the public and the private sphere.

The educational reforms these pioneering academics sought depended on their notion that a great part of their energy had to be spent in demonstrating that women's intellectual capacities and potential for achievement were the equal of men's. In many departments they succeeded in earning high scholarly esteem. For example, English historians who were ordinarily reluctant to accept either Americans or women into their ranks acknowledged that under the leadership of Professors Bertha Putnam and Nellie Neilson, "Mount Holyoke became a notable focus of medieval, legal, and economic historical studies."[16] At the time, this commitment to scholarship represented a radical challenge to the status quo and to pervasive beliefs about women's intellectual inferiority. To state boldly, as the educator M. Carey Thomas did, that "most women's lives were spent in clearing things out of one place to put them in another, and we had forsaken that sphere," was quite a departure.[17] Because these women scholars viewed the problem rationally and were firmly committed to the ideals of merit and achievement, they were convinced that the demonstration of women's achievement would win support and provide equal opportunity in the future.

Although these expectations were too optimistic, the women's colleges did play a significant role as the continual employers of professional women scholars. In some fields, such as physics and math, the women's colleges were virtually the only possible employers of female scholars. The most ambitious among the women presidents, Mary Woolley and M. Carey Thomas among others, were fully aware of the need to foster opportunities for the ongoing professional development of their faculties. They ferreted out every possibility; they cajoled, bargained, and pleaded to obtain adequate financial resources to fund postgraduate work, sabbaticals, and attendance at professional meetings and to build endowments that would secure the future of their institutions. Even in the less overtly feminist colleges for women, where the presidents were men and the faculties were made up of both men and women, there were greater opportunities for women's advancement than in any coeducational institution.

The development of separatism as a strategy for women went well beyond the women's colleges. The late nineteenth century saw the flowering of women's clubs, the suffrage movement, the settlement houses, and a variety of other separatist women's organizations. These offered women opportunities to articulate and defend their own interests and to build female networks. These institutions also offered leadership opportunities to the most committed and talented. For women who used this strategy, the question of marriage was not so much a problem to be resolved as a choice to be rejected.

In the 1920s, when the "new" woman sought opportunities in male institutions, the winning of the suffrage and the new concern with women's sexual liberation meant that separatism became less popular as a strategy. The contraction of employment opportunities during the Depression accelerated the competition for scarce jobs. In the 1930s women were excluded from many professional opportunities so that they would not take employment away from men. In the postwar period of the 1940s the G.I. Bill gave male veterans greater opportunities than women to enter advanced education and the professions. Thus, just as the separatist option became less psychologically attractive, opportunities for women in mixed-sex institutions were also declining.

Women's colleges began to retreat from earlier demands for equal opportunity for women, in part because of the deeply held convictions of the majority of Americans that both nature and culture required that the single breadwinner of the family be a male head. The question of women's employment was presented as though participation in paid work was in conflict with family responsibilities. Since the family was seen in the United States as the major guarantor of social and cultural stability, women's work could be seen as a force undermining the very basis of society.

It was not until the Second World War produced a serious shortage of labor that women were actively recruited again for employment outside the home. In 1940 about 13,800,000 women were employed; by 1944 the number rose to 18.5 million—almost a 40 percent increase.[18] The 1941–45 expansion was brief, however, because returning veterans demanded that they receive preferential consideration for places in education and the professions. The national agreement to give preference to veterans encouraged a major exodus of young families to the suburbs, where the child-centered family occupied center stage. Because more and more women in this era saw homemaking as their major career, women college graduates in the 1950s normally did not contest the reduced quotas for the admission of women to medical and other high-status professional training schools.[19] The second wave of feminist sentiment in the late 1960s and early 1970s reversed this preference for homemaking and suburban life. The women's movement began a major protest about the exclusion of women from professional work. As they gained political experience through their participation in civil rights and peace activities, women broadened the base of their movement and gained significant male support for a feminist agenda. For professional women the research and writing of feminist scholars brought fresh awareness of the lives of the pioneering women professionals of the 1900–20 era and their remarkable achievements.

As a result of this new wave of feminist sentiment and its accompanying political expression, both legal and popular pressure led to the abandonment of quotas based on sex for admission to law, medical, dental, and engineering schools. However encouraging the figures for women's entry to the professions may be, we should remember that the professions continue their traditional hierarchical organization and that the small core of powerful positions at the top of the hierarchy remain male preserves. Very few women are deans of medical, law, or business schools, and the small number of tenured women on the faculties of major research universities has remained remarkably stable since the 1960s. Of the 127 medical schools in the United States, for example, only the University of Puerto Rico School of Medicine has a woman as dean. About a dozen medical colleges have associate deans who are women. Thirteen of the 185 law schools in the Association of American Law Schools have deans who are women.[20] In the universities and colleges the pattern is similar. Women constitute about 20 percent of the faculties at four-year institutions but less than 10 percent of their full professors. At Harvard University only 5 percent of tenured faculty members are women. In 1975, 5.4 percent of the presidents of four-year colleges were women. By 1982 the number had risen to only 7.7 percent despite the efforts of several educational groups to promote women as candidates. Even among this small select group almost 50 percent headed women's colleges.[21] Only one major private and one major public research university are headed by women. The average American college has only 1.1 women in senior administrative positions.

The small number of women in upper-echelon positions is not limited to graduate and professional schools. In the federal judiciary, the court of appeals had 154 circuit judges as of May 1987, and only seventeen of them were women. Of the 529 judges sitting in the district courts, only forty-eight were women.[22] In business, women compose 33 percent of corporate middle management, but in the Fortune 500 companies women represent a mere 1.7 percent of the corporate officers. A recent study found that male and female executives have similar profiles, but women in management positions are paid less and given smaller budgets, less access to high-status conferences, and fewer perks. This is true when the men and women hold comparable positions and Harvard MBAs.[23]

None of the career strategies that the first or second wave of women professionals have adopted will alter this prevailing pattern, in which men hold leadership positions and women work at the entry level or in the middle ranks. We have now been able to observe superperformance, voluntary subordination, career innovation, and separate institutional career paths for some eight decades. All offer some opportunities for women during periods of economic expansion or shortage in highly educated labor. These gains are lost, however, in periods of low economic growth.

To make more permanent gains and consolidate the expanded opportunities of economic booms, women professionals and their male supporters must develop new psychological and political perspectives on the experience of professional life. At the psychological level, we must recognize that for able men the ideology of meritorious professional performance has produced prestige and professional rewards. For women, no matter how stellar their performance, the ideology of merit has frequently been evoked to limit their access to professional rewards and status. Superperformance has not, and likely will not, change this experience. Similarly, voluntary subordination is unlikely to disappear and will continue to be used to justify women's lesser professional rewards. As long as women remain the primary source of care and nurturance for children and the aged or carry a disproportionate share of responsibility for the home, many women will find such employment more compatible with the competing demands on their time. Innovation remains a career path alternative that usually does not lead to the same rewards as the established professions. The strategy of separation, essentially a political strategy, has gained renewed strength from the vitality of contemporary women's organizations, such as women's professional networks, caucuses, watchdog committees, schools, and colleges. On their own, however, these institutions cannot change the structure of existing hierarchies any more effectively than superperformance can.

Fortunately, the research of feminist scholars has given an overtly political focus to the study of professionalization in modern societies. This research has shifted the focus of attention from an emphasis on defining the characteristics of professional activity (lengthy training, objectivity, and devotion to public service rather than the profit motive) to the process of recruitment, the monopolization of markets for highly salable services, and the exclusion of likely competitors via the mechanism of highly selective entrance to training programs. If women are to cross the boundaries excluding them from leadership and the highest rewards of their professions, they must gain greater psychological insight into the nature of the boundaries and a clearer political sense of the nature of today's professions.

ENDNOTES

[1]G.G. Kapontais, National Center for Health Statistics, *Decennial Census Data for Selected Health Occupations, United States, 1980,* Vital and Health Statistics,

series 14, no. 3 (Public Health Service, Washington, DC: U.S. Government Printing Office, December 1985), p. 18.

[2]Anne Walter Fearn, *My Days of Strength: An American Woman Doctor's Forty Years in China* (New York: Macmillan, 1939), pp. 6, 18.

[3]Ibid., p. 96.

[4]Ibid., pp. 216, 261.

[5]Deborah J. Warner, "Women Astronomers," *Natural History* (May 1979), pp. 12–20.

[6]Ibid., p. 14.

[7]Ibid.

[8]Barbara Melosh, *The Physician's Hand: Work, Culture, and Conflict in American Nursing* (Philadelphia: Temple University Press, 1982), p. 129.

[9]A modern variant of this paradox is found in the reasoning behind the Equal Employment Opportunity Commission's recent court action against Sears, Roebuck and Co. The EEOC filed a discrimination suit against Sears in the 1980s, charging that the company discriminated against women employees on two counts: (1) women were not offered equal opportunity for commissioned sales jobs in the appliance, plumbing, and automotive departments but were instead relegated to the lower-paid sales positions in fashion areas, and (2) there were substantial wage differences between women and men in Sears's management.

The Sears defense argued that women preferred to work in familiar areas and resisted assignments selling tires, stereos, or carpets. The company's hiring patterns mirrored cultural values about gender and work, the defense continued, because women preferred nurturing and support roles to competition. The case received wide publicity when feminist historians were brought in as expert witnesses for both sides and attempted to clarify whether the historical record supported EEOC's charges of discrimination or Sears's argument about cultural preference. In 1986 the judge ruled that EEOC had not proven its charges against the company. For a fuller description, see "Women's History Goes to Trial: EEOC and Sears, Roebuck and Company," *Signs* 11 (Summer 1986), pp. 751–79; also Ruth Milkman, "Women's History and the Sears Case," *Feminist Studies* 12 (Summer 1986), pp. 375–400.

[10]Baker, *Fighting for Life*, p. 138.

[11]Alice Hamilton, *Exploring Dangerous Trades* (Boston: Little, Brown, 1943), pp. 132–33.

[12]Ibid., pp. 252–53.

[13]Ibid., p. 268.

[14]Viola Barnes, *Mount Holyoke in the Twentieth Century*, Oral History Interviews, Mount Holyoke College Library Archives, 1971–72.

[15]Christopher Hill, *The World Turned Upside Down: Radical Ideas During the English Revolution* (New York: Penguin, 1984).

[16]*London Times*, February 1960. Faculty biographical files, Mount Holyoke College Library Archives.

[17]Edith Finch, *Carey Thomas of Bryn Mawr* (New York: Harper, 1947), p. 92.

[18]U.S. Department of Commerce, *U.S. Historical Statistics* (Washington, DC: Bureau of the Census, 1975), p. 133.

[19]The numbers of women in the work force never dropped to the 1930s levels, but women were relegated back to traditional female work. See Maureen Honey, *Creating Rosie the Riveter* (Amherst, MA: University of Massachusetts Press, 1984), pp. 20–25.

[20]*Medical School Admission Requirements 1988–89,* Association of American Medical Colleges, Washington, DC.

[21]American Council on Education, *Fact Book on Higher Education 1984–85* (New York: Macmillan, 1984), tables 121, 130; also, "Women Gain Degrees but Not Tenure," *New York Times,* 4 January 1987.

[22]Personnel Office, Administrative Offices of the U.S. Courts.

[23]Ann M. Morrison, Randall P. White, Ellen van Velsor, and The Center for Creative Leadership, *Breaking the Glass Ceiling* (Reading, MA: Addison-Wesley, 1982), pp. 5–6. Also by the same authors, "Executive Women: Substance Plus Style," *Psychology Today* (August 1987), pp. 18–26.

Jill K. Conway

Politics, Pedagogy, and Gender

I N THE MID-NINETEENTH CENTURY the public education system of the United States drew its corps of teachers from the nation's population of young women. In contrast, European public education remained a male-dominated enterprise until well into the twentieth century. Traditionally, the United States' early and extensive recruitment of female teachers has been interpreted as a sign of enlightened attitudes about women and their place in society. Horace Mann's innovative Massachusetts normal schools, which trained young women to be teachers, are customarily cited as examples of feminism in action. So, until recently, was the career of Catherine Beecher, the archetypal proselytizer for the female teaching profession. The development of a public elementary school system before the Civil War and the extension of that system through the establishment of secondary schools in the last quarter of the nineteenth century provide a happy ending to the traditional story of the establishment of the first "women's" profession.[1]

Underlying this popular history of women in teaching is the assumption that access to new work opportunities has the same meaning for everyone. If we stop to ask what gender meant for the

Jill K. Conway, born in 1934 in Hillston, New South Wales, Australia, is a visiting scholar in the Program in Science, Technology and Society at the Massachusetts Institute of Technology. She is the author of numerous books and articles, including biographical works in Notable American Women *(1971),* The Female Experience in Eighteenth and Nineteenth Century America: A Guide to the History of American Women *(1982), "Women Reformers and American Culture, 1870–1930" (1971–72), and "Utopian Dream or Dystopian Nightmare? Nineteenth Century Feminist Ideas about Equality" (1987). Professor Conway has held teaching appointments at several academic institutions, and has served as vice president of the University of Toronto (1973–1975) and president of Smith College (1975–1985).*

137

nineteenth-century founders of American public education, however, the story takes on new levels of meaning. Some of its themes speak directly to our educational dilemmas today. Its interest lies not in the sex of the teachers who staffed America's one-room schools but in the political and psychological images that men and women held regarding the gender of those teachers. The story of women's opportunities to enter teaching as a respectable occupation for single women outside the home is a case study in the meaning of access. Examination of the case of women teachers' recruitment in the mid-nineteenth century should make us rethink the incremental model of change that is presumed to characterize the liberal state.

The number of women involved in this recruitment is certainly striking. By 1848 women greatly outnumbered men as annual entrants to the teaching profession; in absolute numbers their predominance was established. In that year 2,424 men taught in the public (or common) schools of America beside 5,510 women.[2] During the 1850s the same pattern was replicated in the Midwest. After 1864 one of the impositions of the victorious North on the southern states during Reconstruction was the establishment of a predominantly female cadre of elementary school teachers. In the last three decades of the nineteenth century the same pattern emerged in the public high schools. By 1890, 65 percent of all teachers in the United States were women. Members of the new female profession were remarkably youthful, averaging from twenty-one to twenty-five years of age in different regions of the country.

Popular attitudes encouraged single women to become teachers but discouraged their presence in the schools once they married. The country's teachers were predominantly daughters of the native-born, from rural families. In comparison with European teachers, American teachers were not well educated. As late as the 1930s only 12 percent of elementary teachers in the United States had earned bachelor's degrees.[3] In the nineteenth century many entrants to the profession had not even completed high school. Because so many teachers were drawn from rural farm families, most had not traveled more than 100 miles from their place of birth. Their experience of high culture was minimal. Surveys carried out at the turn of the century recorded that most teachers had never seen reproductions of works of art during their own schooling. As adults their only reading was an occasional novel and the standard popular magazines of the day. To compensate for these deficiencies, the normal schools offered teaching programs that were largely remedial.[4]

The woman teacher, whether rural or urban, earned about 60 percent of the salary paid to men in the same school system. Around 1900 the average woman teacher's salary was $350.00 per year. Higher earnings were available to women in the textile industry and in most other industrial settings. In some states mechanics and clerks earned twice the annual wages of male teachers, whose earnings were more than a third higher than those of their female counterparts. The universal custom of "boarding out" was a major factor in depressing the level of teachers' earnings: nineteenth-century school districts held down the cost of elementary schools by housing teachers in rotation with families whose children were currently school pupils. This dubious hospitality was motivated partly by economic considerations and partly by the prevailing sentiment that young single women should not be allowed to live outside a family setting. The school district's room and board carried with it a censorious social control that young single women could resist only at their peril. In short, the young teacher's social status was marginal.[5]

This marginality was not borne for long; rates of turnover were very high. Most women elementary teachers taught for only three or four years. Although 90 percent of the elementary instructors by the 1920s were women, their rapid turnover meant that they did not develop as school leaders or as curriculum planners.[6] Men did not remain teachers for long either; they did not form strong bonds to the occupation of teacher as they did to the professions of medicine and engineering. Yet male teachers were seven times more likely to become school administrators than their female colleagues. Despite the social changes that have raised women's work aspirations in recent decades, these early trends have continued unaltered. Today men hold 99.4 percent of all school superintendencies. The only area of school administration in which women predominate is librarianship. Clearly gender shapes one's status within the teaching profession, even though teaching has traditionally been singled out for its supposed hospitality to women. What, then, are we to make of women's early access to teaching in the United States? What values shaped the establishment of the common schools in America, and what was the operative significance of ideas about gender in that process? To paraphrase William James, what was the meaning of the ideas being translated into action when people like Horace Mann began to recruit women for teacher training?

If we look at the political debates that preceded the establishment of the public education system in the 1830s and 1840s, we see that political forces divided over the level of intellectual aspiration desired as an outcome of state-supported education and over the place of elites of education and talent within the young republic. One thing that united Jefferson and his Federalist opponents was the value they saw in an educated elite drawn from the best talent of their new society. Jefferson wanted his elite to be democratically recruited, its education publicly supported; he expected the result to be the highest intellectual achievement.

One of the major shifts of value in the Jacksonian era was the rejection of the idea of a socially valuable elite formed by education and high culture. Instead, Americans of that era favored a popular education that was broadly accessible and limited in its intellectual goals. As Michael Katz has shown in his study of the development of public education in Massachusetts, some of the old Federalist elites found popular education attractive not so much as a means of training the mind but as a way of providing instruction in behavior.[7] Many New England moralists who sought to control the excesses of frontier behavior thought that this goal might be achieved through the common schools. Their intellectual aspirations for the students who were expected to attend these schools were minimal.

We know from recent studies of the legislative decisions approving the establishment of the common schools that Federalists and Jacksonians alike sought to develop public education as inexpensively as possible. The compromise that led to agreement on tax-supported public education combined the older Jeffersonian ideal of wide access to public education with Federalist and Jacksonian concerns for limited education at minimal cost to the taxpayer. The goal of cost containment made the recruitment of women completely logical because all parties to the educational debate agreed that women lacked acquisitive drives and would serve at subsistence salaries. The potentially explosive conflict over the intellectual goals of public education could also be avoided by choosing women as teachers. Their access to education was slight, so that male control over the normal schools that trained teachers insured control over the content

of the curriculum. Furthermore, beliefs about the female temperament promised that the pedagogical style of women teachers would
be emotional and value-oriented rather than rational and critical.
Thus neither Jacksonians nor Federalists needed to make resolution
of their conflicts over the goals of education an explicit part of their
political agenda.[8] The resolution of fundamental contradictions
about a strategic institution for the evolving society could safely be
postponed as long as women teachers presented no threat to the
objectives of low cost and strictly utilitarian public education.

The following three quotations demonstrate gender stereotyping at
work in the public-education policy discussions of late nineteenth-
century legislators and public officials. Each of the speakers favored
the recruitment of women teachers. These passages illustrate the
important components of the gender ideology accepted by all parties
to the dispute over the goals of education.

[Women] manifest a livelier interest, more contentment in the work, have
altogether superior success in managing and instructing young children, and
I know of instances, where by the silken cord of affection, have led many a
stubborn will, and wild ungoverned impulse, into habits of obedience and
study even in the large winter schools (Henry Barnard, *Second Annual
Report* [Connecticut School, 1840], pp. 27–28).

[Women] are endowed by nature with stronger parental impulses, and this
makes the society of children delightful, and turns duty into a pleasure.
Their minds are less withdrawn from their employment, by the active scenes
of life; and they are less intent and scheming for future honors and
emoluments. As a class, they never look forward, as young men almost
invariably do, to a period of legal emancipation from parental control. . . .
They are also of purer morals (*Fourth Annual Report* [Boston Board of
Education, 1841], pp. 45–46).

In childhood the intellectual faculties are but partially developed—the
affections much more fully. At that early age the affections are the key of the
whole being. The female teacher readily possesses herself of that key, and
thus having access to the heart, the mind is soon reached and operated upon
(Assemblyman Hurlburd, *New York State Education Exhibit* [World's
Columbian Exposition, Chicago, 1893], pp. 45–46).

At the center of the cluster of ideas that made up each writer's
picture of women we see a belief in women's capacity to influence
children's behavior through the emotions. Barnard's "silken cord of

affection" and Hurlburd's "access to the heart" were characteristic themes in discourse about women as teachers. The writer of the Boston Board of Education's annual report associated women's ability to establish emotional links with children with women's lack of acquisitiveness and acceptance of dependence. These presumed qualities made women ideal candidates to teach in elementary schools, the purpose of which was to instill principles of behavior and convey basic literacy at a minimum cost to the public purse. Women were favored and actively recruited as elementary teachers because their presence in the schools satisfied a larger political agenda. Their perceived gender characteristics and their lack of academic preparation were positive advantages in the eyes of early public education officials; with a corps of women teachers there was no danger that investment in public education might foster the creation of new elites.

What, then, were the consequences of this congruence of ideology and economic concerns that served to give women preferred access to the teaching profession in the United States? The first consequence, extensively commented on by foreign visitors, was that discipline in American schools was very different from any known in European classrooms. As women were not thought suited to administering corporal punishment, the rod was virtually absent from America's schools. Maintaining discipline and conveying knowledge became more a matter of persuasion than an exercise of power based on authority. One learned because one liked the teacher, not out of respect for the learning that the teacher represented, as was the case in the French lycée or the German gymnasium. The climate in the American schoolroom was wholly different; the classroom was considered an extension of the home.

This should not be taken to mean that the stereotype of the steely-eyed New England schoolmarm was incorrect; there were many such outstanding women. What it did mean, however, was that maleness involved rebellion against the values for which the schoolmarm stood. Many celebrations of maleness in American culture have retained overtones of adolescent rebellion against a female cultural presence that ostensibly cannot be easily incorporated into a strong adult male identity.

We may speculate about the consequences of subsuming school and home within a maternal, domestic culture rather than having the school serve as an impersonal agent of cultural authority, much·like the church or the army. How would *Huckleberry Finn* read if the journey on the raft were an escape from male institutions? Huckleberry Finn's journey raises many profound questions about American culture. One critical question is whether the overrepresentation of one gender in the early stages of schooling permits either boys or girls to develop the balanced identities we associate with creativity. For the purpose of understanding American educational institutions, another question that requires answering is this: If the school exists in opposition to male values and frontier life, how are we to understand higher education? In what ways is there a cultural imperative to redress the balance between maternal and masculine values at different levels of the system? What has that cultural requirement meant for American intellectual life?

Teaching through love made the school a setting in which many ideas about child development were played out; it was never an agency for strenuous effort to discipline and develop young intellectual talents. Thus, the traditional twelve years of schooling did not bring the young American student to the levels of learning aimed at by the lycée or the gymnasium. Instead, and increasingly, American education came to require a further four years of intellectual exploration at the college level before the young person was considered to be in a position to make adult career commitments. Moreover, because of American public schools' identification with maternal functions, colleges and universities have distanced themselves from schools and stressed the "masculine" tough-mindedness of American scholarship. This difference remains an enduring puzzle to Europeans, who see both schools and universities in a continuum of intellectual endeavor, and who value intellectual playfulness.

We may interpret this impulse to distance higher learning from schools as a natural response to some of the major nineteenth-century curricular debates. Because the schools operated as agents of maternal values, school curricula were organized along the lines of accepted models of child development. G. Stanley Hall's celebrated theories of child development, which held that the child recapitulated the various stages of human evolutionary development, required that the teacher act as a helpful director as the pupil traversed these stages. It is unlikely that Hall would have designed so unintellectual a teaching role had he assumed that most elementary school teachers would be men. His ideas about child development were revolutionary in their largely successful redefinition of childhood as a series of developmental stages rather than as a time when the "imp of Satan" had to be disciplined; however, his view of the teacher was based on earlier nineteenth-century assumptions about the female temperament.

John Dewey's Progressive schools discarded the notion of a fixed body of intellectual skills to be acquired entirely in school. Progressive pedagogy asked that the teacher help the young to discover the world through their innate intelligence. It took individuals with an almost superhuman capacity for nurturing to manage this kind of schoolroom. Few teachers could completely repress the desire to instruct, as Dewey's theories required. Many rueful survivors of Progressive schools testified to the demoralizing nature of such self-abnegation. It is reasonable to ask whether educational theorists would have designed teaching roles of such preternatural maternal patience had they expected their male colleagues to take principal responsibility for such instruction. Had the standard levels of education required for elementary school teachers been higher, educational reformers of the Progressive variety might have found earlier curricular ideals less easy to disregard. It was because the minds of young teachers were seen as tabulae rasae that older notions of learning could be easily ignored. Certainly if one assesses Dewey's pedagogy from the standpoint of the gender stereotypes enshrined within it, its conservatism is striking. Dewey advanced a new theory of learning and stated new political goals for American schools, but his assumptions about the temperamental and intellectual characteristics of teachers differed little from the assumptions made by Henry Barnard and his colleagues in the 1840s.[9]

While many of the goals of Progressive education were admirable, the fact that the overwhelming majority of teachers in the American elementary school system were young women was a substantial influence on the way reformers thought about the role of teacher. Because of the persistence of the idea that women related to children primarily through the emotions, reformers prescribed intellectually demeaning roles for teachers—roles that often ignored the teacher's intellectual capacity in relation to the child's.

Similarly, the fact that most teachers did not have the right to vote affected the dynamics of the political relationship between the common schools and the larger society. From its inception the public education system operated at the center of a vortex of political forces, many of which were intrinsically unrelated to pedagogical issues. The schools were affected by political battles over such issues as patronage rights, appointments to teaching staffs and desirable jobs on maintenance staffs, which districts would be granted the economic benefits of building contracts, and which merchants should benefit from the purchasing power of students and their families. Moreover, it was taken for granted that parents, who had an abiding interest in the curriculum and its relationship to employment opportunities, and whose taxes paid teachers' salaries, had a democratic right to influence what was and was not taught to their children. These interests found expression in city and state politics, but women teachers were disfranchised until 1919 and consequently were unable to directly participate in the political process that shaped and established priorities for public education. Fathers and men teachers could mobilize voter support for school policies through their lodges or friendly societies, or later through Rotary, Kiwanis, or Lions Clubs; women could not. This situation affected women's status as teachers and indirectly affected the political importance of schools: an important component of professionalization in all modern societies is the degree to which would-be professionals are able to persuade economically or politically powerful elites that their services are important enough to command special rewards. Women teachers, unable to undertake this effort effectively, found their logical political allies in the ranks of organized labor.

The history that produced this logic is vividly illustrated in the disputes affecting the Chicago school system in the 1880s and 1890s. The city's total population was 500,000 and there were 59,000 pupils in the public schools, which expended a budget of over $1,000,000. The school system was the biggest employer in the city. The school board was appointed by the mayor, and it controlled or influenced three sets of resources critical to Chicago's economic future: land voted to support the public schools, contracts for school buildings, and tax abatements for corporations occupying land within the city. The major issues of concern to teachers were security of tenure, pension rights, and professional evaluation for promotion.[10] Women teachers felt considerable social distance from the exclusively male school superintendents in the city, who were themselves political appointees. In the campaign to secure teachers' pension rights, the female-led Chicago Federation of Teachers found that it carried no weight with the municipal government, so it waged battle in the courts. In her autobiography, Margaret A. Haley, the founder of the federation, records the process by which she came to conclude that, because of women's limited voting rights, her union's predominantly female membership would gain political leverage by affiliating with a strong political organization—the Chicago Federation of Labor. She recognized that laws were only enacted in response to the political pressure of voters. "Except in a few western states," she wrote, "the women of the nation had practically no voting power."[11]

The early choice of unionization was a natural one for nonvoting workers; its consequences were profound. As early as the Chicago Federation of Teachers' 1902 decision to affiliate with the Chicago Federation of Labor, the city's elementary teachers were in a confrontational relationship with political and social elites. The male school principals and superintendents, who identified with management in the labor-versus-management model of the school and the teacher's role within it, were even more distanced from teachers. The working peers of the school administrators were the political actors who had selected and appointed them. The place of the school in political priorities reflected the fact that most of its constituency could not vote and that its spokesmen were distant from the classroom. Decisions about educational policy were usually based entirely on the budgetary priorities of individual districts and regions. Economic considerations favored the selection of women teachers and, by the late nineteenth century, women principals; womens' salaries in such positions did not reflect high esteem for their professional achievements. Jessie May Short, an assistant professor of mathematics at Reed College in Portland, Oregon, described her experience in an Oregon high school in the 1920s.

A personal experience will illustrate the discriminations that are considered normal in the smaller schools. . . . For five years I was principal of a high school in a delightful county-seat town. During the five years the high school enrollment doubled, a new building was erected, I had salary increases each year. I resigned for graduate study although I was offered a small salary increase if I would remain. The man who took my place was freely given a salary fifty percent higher than I had received. Before his first year had closed he was literally taken from the school and thrown into a snow bank. The school board asked me to return and made me what they considered a generous offer, a ten percent increase over my former salary. I suggested that I might consider the appointment at the fifty percent increase the board had willingly given the man who could not handle the situation. The idea of compensating the service without regard to the sex of the one rendering the service was, as I had anticipated, beyond their comprehension.[12]

Short's experience strikingly illustrates that the public's view of the worth of the predominantly female teaching profession and of the predominantly male management of the public schools was fundamentally shaped by the gender of those who served in the system. Because there was little popular respect for the function of the teacher, most important professional prerogatives were gained only after protracted battle. The early decades of unionizing and struggling against low social esteem focused teachers' concerns on job security to the neglect of curricular issues. The cherished right of tenure, sought since the 1880s, was not achieved until the 1950s, when the postwar baby boom and the Cold-War mentality of the Sputnik era gave schools and teachers national importance.

The public's low esteem of the profession was also related to the youthfulness of women teachers. As most of them remained teachers for no more than three or four years, it was easy for local school boards to disregard their opinions. The assumption that young women need protection gave school boards and committees ample justification to scrutinize teachers' conduct and to represent such activity to be in the teachers' best interest. The small minority of men teachers acquired the status of their women colleagues by association. Because society accorded such scant respect to the role of teacher, it was considered perfectly appropriate to pay teachers wages equivalent to those of unskilled labor. By 1900 teacher turnover was as high as 10 percent a year; every year 40,000 new recruits had to be brought into the common school system.[13] The high annual rates of change in teaching personnel throughout the first century of the profession made teachers seem much more like transient workers than career professionals (teaching was not accepted as a lifetime career for women until the Second World War). School reformers even today struggle with the consequences of Margaret Haley's accurate perception that to bargain successfully, women teachers had to unionize like industrial laborers.

If we compare the public esteem accorded to teaching in the late nineteenth century with that held for other emerging professions, we begin to see that the difference lies in the fact that most of the people recruited into public education were women. Consider, for instance, attitudes toward the engineer—the male professional who emerged to meet national needs in transportation, communication, and industrial technology over the same one hundred years that saw the establishment of public education. In the United States the social origins of engineers were almost identical to those of teachers. Engineers too came from rural and blue-collar families. Initially, their training was not highly theoretical and their tasks were strictly utilitarian. Yet engineers were held in high public esteem.

Clearly, gender categories and cultural values had a tremendous influence on the process of professionalization. We have only to read Henry Adams's assessment of the new technology in his commentaries on *The Virgin and the Dynamo,* or Thorstein Veblen's description of the engineer in *The Engineers and the Price System* (1919), to see what a difference gender made. "These technological specialists," Veblen wrote, "whose constant supervision is indispensable to the due working of the industrial system, constitute the general staff of industry, whose work is to control the strategy of production at large and keep an oversight of the tactics of production in detail."[14] During the Depression, when married women teachers were dismissed by school systems to create openings for unemployed men, Lewis Mumford wrote, "The establishment of the class of engineers in its proper characteristics is the more important because this class will, without doubt, constitute the direct and necessary instrument of coalition between men of science and industrialists, by which alone the new social order can commence."[15] No one thought to exclaim on how much the new social order might depend on the labors of "the class of teachers." Engineers, of course, pursued their training at the college level and developed a professional culture of aggressive masculinity. Their skills were of critical and immediate importance to the business elites of American society—but then so were the skills of teachers, although no one recognized their value.

Gender stereotypes helped to account for the differences in social mobility experienced by women and men drawn from the same social background. If we look at the gender composition of the teaching profession cross-culturally, we see that the American pattern established at the time of the creation of the public school system was unique. In 1930–31, a national survey of American teachers showed that women outnumbered men by 19 to 1 in elementary education and by 3 to 1 in secondary education. In contrast, men held 65 percent of the elementary teaching posts in Norway and 69 percent of the secondary teaching positions there. In Germany 75 percent of the primary school teachers and 71 percent of the secondary school teachers were men; the ratios for France were similar.[16] These figures reflect the conditions that existed in societies that had had relatively stable populations when the public system of elementary and secondary education was being established, and that made strongly centralized educational planning a high national priority.

In these European countries, lifetime careers of steady progression through the different levels of the public school system were established; entry-level positions based on long and strict academic preparation were accepted as the norm. In France, for instance, completion of the baccalaureate was required to become a lycée teacher; further progress in the system required an advanced degree. Besides contributing substantially to the intellectual level of the schools, this pattern of recruitment defined the teacher as an agent of the nation's culture, not simply a representative of its maternal values.

When the possibility of recruiting more men to the profession or requiring teachers to undergo more rigorous academic preparation was broached in the United States, it was generally discarded as prohibitively costly. In 1906–7, for instance, the New York City school superintendent acknowledged the desirability of having a cadre of teachers more balanced in gender composition. In a report, he commented that the achievement of this goal would require equalizing the pay scales of the gender groups and raising all salary levels. This, he calculated, was politically impossible. It would add between $8 million and $11 million to the annual school system budget. To propose such a budget increase in the absence of popular demand would be political suicide, and there was not the slightest popular sentiment for such action.[17]

Gender was a highly significant factor in the way American society mobilized its resources to develop its public education system. Assumptions about female temperament and motivation dovetailed with the often contradictory ideals and values of the public school system's creators. Stereotypes about women coincided neatly with the economic priorities that dictated how much money was appropriated for public education, and reinforced popular preferences regarding the purpose of public schooling. Assumptions about the gender and intellectual level of the typical teacher influenced successive waves of curricular reform. Culturally, these gender stereotypes had a tremendous impact on everyone involved in the schools— teachers, pupils, principals, superintendents, school board members. These assumptions played a part in what it meant to grow up male or female in America. Their enduring power explains the continued inability of our affluent society to muster either the will or the resources to create and maintain schools that are intellectually demanding and that accord the profession of teaching sufficient dignity to engender high teacher morale.

Much has been made of the degree to which teaching offered American women the opportunity to move out of family subordination and into an independent existence. The memoirs of some of America's greatest women reformers tell us that this new life outside the family was a heady experience. Frances Willard, for example, wrote of learning to live without reliance on her parents as a very young teacher. Through her struggles with unruly children in rural one-room schools, she came to see herself as an agent for improving society. Dozens of other young women documented similar experiences. Service as teachers inspired many young women to seek other active careers. Both as individuals and as a group, women proved themselves capable of creating and sustaining demanding intellectual tasks when they were given adequate preparation and appropriate renumeration. It was not the sex of women teachers that created problems in the school system and made the status of teachers so lowly; it was the gender identity that women carried into the schools with them. It is the terms on which women enter occupations that govern their opportunities. The mere fact of entry does not create opportunities. Horace Mann and Henry Barnard, two of America's greatest educational reformers, actively admired women and thought that by employing them as teachers they could secure both a better society and important advantages for women. They bore women no ill will whatsoever. Their assumptions about women, however, established the terms on which women entered the teaching profession, and those terms were far more consequential than the great numbers of women who were invited to teach in the public schools. Those terms still matter today. So too does our ambivalence about the goals of public education. This piece of unfinished business from the politics of the Jacksonian era matters as much today as it did in the 1840s. We cannot conclude it satisfactorily without taking into account the unintended consequences of our assumptions about the gender of teachers. They matter not only to women but to our whole society.

ENDNOTES

[1] Horace Mann, *Eleventh Annual Report* (Massachusetts Normal Schools, 1845), p. 24.

[2] Redding R. Sugg, Jr., *Motherteacher: The Feminization of American Education* (Charlottesville, VA: University Press of Virginia, 1978), p. 37.

[3] Lindley J. Stiles, ed., *The Teacher's Role in American Society* (New York: Harper & Row, 1957), p. 279.

[4] Lotus D. Coffman, *The Social Composition of the Teaching Population* (New York: Bureau of Publications, Teacher's College, Columbia University, 1911), p. 550.

[5] Ibid., p. 550. See also Myra H. Strober and Audri Gordon Lanford, "The Feminization of Public School Teaching: A Cross-Sectional Analysis, 1850–1880," Signs 11 (2) (1986), pp. 212–35, and Willard S. Ellsbree, *The American Teacher: Evolution of a Profession in a Democracy* (New York: American Book Company, 1933), p. 281.

[6] Ellsbree, *The American Teacher*, p. 206.

[7] Michael Katz, *The Irony of Early School Reform* (Cambridge, MA: Harvard University Press, 1968).

[8] Sugg, *Motherteacher*, pp. 4–25.

[9] On G. Stanley Hall's educational theories, see Dorothy Ross, *G. Stanley Hall, The Psychologist as Prophet* (Chicago: University of Chicago Press, 1972). On Dewey and Progressive education, see John Dewey On Education (New York: The Modern Library, 1964).

[10] Robert J. Braun, *Teachers and Power: The Story of the American Federation of Teachers* (New York: Simon and Schuster, 1972), pp. 21–27. See also Robert I. Reid, ed., *Battleground: The Autobiography of Margaret A. Haley* (Urbana, IL: University of Illinois Press, 1982).

[11] Reid, *Battleground*, p. 90.

[12] Jessie May Short, *Women in the Teaching Profession: Or Running as Fast as You Can to Stay in the Same Place* (Portland, OR: Reed College, June 1939), p. 10.

[13] B.A. Hinsdale, "The Training of Teachers," *Education in the United States: A Series of Monographs Prepared for the United States Exhibit at the Paris Exposition, 1900,* ed. Nicholas Murray Butler (Albany: J. Lyon, 1900), p. 16.

[14]Thorstein Veblen, *The Engineers and the Price System* (New York: Heubsch, 1921), pp. 52–53.

[15]Lewis Mumford, *Technics and Civilization* (New York: Harcourt Brace, 1934), pp. 219–20.

[16]Edward S. Evenden, Guy C. Gamble, and Harold G. Blue, "Teacher Personnel in the United States," U.S. Department of the Interior Bulletin no. 10 (1931), in vol. 11, *National Survey of the Education of Teachers,* p. 20.

[17]Sugg, *Motherteacher,* p. 122.

Robert Fox and Anna Guagnini

Classical Values and Useful Knowledge: The Problem of Access to Technical Careers in Modern Europe

D URING THE SECOND HALF of the nineteenth century, the educational systems of both Britain and France were attacked on the grounds that they were unresponsive to change in modern society. The change critics had in mind was the rise of industry, but along with it came a second development to which they gave less attention—the first involvement of women in scientific and technical fields. In each country, ·the debate centered on the shortcomings of higher scientific and technical education. Assessments of the state of the economy were gloomy, and critics worried about the lead that Germany was taking. The world of education had let industry down in Britain and France, they said, whereas Germany was benefiting from a long period of reform that had culminated in fruitful cooperation between scientists and manufacturers. German industry had the advantage of being able to draw on academic

Robert Fox, born in 1938 in Bradford, England, is professor of the history of science, University of Lancaster, U.K., and director of the Centre de recherche en histoire des sciences et des techniques, Cité des sciences et de l'industrie, Paris, France. He is the author of The Caloric Theory of Gases from Lavoisier to Regnault *(1971) and* Sadi Carnot: Réflexions sur la puissance motrice du feu *(1978; English translation 1986), and editor (with George Weisz) of* The Organization of Science and Technology in France, 1808–1914 *(1980).*

Anna Guagnini, born in 1952 in Milan, Italy, is a research fellow in the department of history, University of Lancaster, U.K. She is the author of Scienzia e Filosofia nella cina Contemporanea *(1982).*

153

research and an abundant supply of well-trained graduates, notably in engineering and chemistry.[1]

This nineteenth-century interpretation is still with us, nowhere more so than in Britain. There, anxiety about the country's industrial decline has provoked a resurgence of concern about the persisting influence of traditional cultural values, which today's critics believe undermine the entrepreneurial spirit, and about the educational system, which they say perpetuates these values.[2] The government has played its part by advancing educational reform as a remedy for British industry's lack of competitiveness and by inviting debate on this remedy in academic, industrial, and lay circles. Yet discussion of "the British disease" has done little more than perpetuate the same judgment passed on education in Britain a hundred years ago.[3]

The frequency with which observers in our own day invoke this diagnosis is striking. Even the much-discussed work of Martin Wiener, *English Culture and the Decline of the Industrial Spirit, 1850–1980,* is not original in its assertion that conservative culture is a direct cause of industrial sluggishness.[4] Although the relation between education and industry is not one that Wiener addresses in detail, he sees education as a channel through which traditional cultural values influence industry and speaks of our slowness in overcoming the bias against practical studies as a mark of a wider immobility in the industrial community.[5]

The assumptions behind arguments of this kind (regarding England or any other country), must be treated with care. One is that a high level of provision for scientific (especially technical) education can be taken as an indication of a strong "industrial spirit" and that any increase in this provision will lead naturally to an improvement in performance. A second assumption is that educational systems are intrinsically passive contexts in which dominant cultural values are preserved and transmitted but in which any reaction to economic and social change can, at best, be slow and muted.[6] Difficulties also surround the related assumption that despite their head start in industrialization, Britain and France were in due course hampered by the conservatism of their national cultures.[7]

A wider canvas embracing a consideration of Europe as a whole in the nineteenth and early twentieth centuries reveals a surprisingly uniform pattern: everywhere, it seems, the dialectic between traditional and modern tendencies in culture was similar.[8] This finding is important, for it calls into question the direct link between conservative cultural values and poor industrial performance.

*   *   *

To what extent have educational institutions since the mid-nineteenth century resisted change? Is it possible to unravel the complex factors in the conflict between traditional and modern cultural values? Did this conflict narrow opportunities for women? These questions outline our discussion.

We certainly believe that traditional values in national cultures have been powerful and enduring. But we also argue that emphasizing their perpetuation can obscure other elements in educational systems that may limit industrial competitiveness.

It is now some years since Fritz Ringer published his *Decline of the German Mandarins*[9] and his pioneering comparative study, *Education and Society in Modern Europe*. These books, along with a number of other works, confirm that nineteenth-century Germany moved ahead of her European rivals in reorganizing and expanding her educational system at all levels, giving special attention to the scientific disciplines.[10] Germany made these changes, Ringer and the others say, in a context in which pure knowledge was regarded as the noblest objective and in which, initially, applied studies had to dwell on the margins of learned respectability. Only toward the end of the nineteenth century were the new, technologically oriented disciplines fully accepted in German higher education. The result was a more plentiful provision than other European countries possessed, but it was secured in the face of staunch academic conservatism and specific opposition to the wish of the technische hochschulen to award doctorates.[11] Even if science was acceptable, there were many in the government and the universities for whom technology, with its industrial connotations, was not. Germany, in other words, was not so very different from her rivals: there, as throughout Europe, tradition was a tenacious survivor, and technical careers in industry seem to have had a status that was not conspicuously higher than elsewhere. Even in the technische hochschulen at the beginning of this century, the strongest pupils had usually passed through the classical curriculum of the gymnasium and gone on to administrative careers.[12]

The case of France is revealing by contrast. From the time of the Revolution on, mathematical studies had the lion's share of prestige in French education, with the attitudes and aspirations of the ablest students being formed in large measure by the dominating influence of the Ecole polytechnique.[13] France was unusual in having what was ostensibly an engineering school at the top of its educational hierarchy. But we should not be misled by the Polytechnique's stated purpose. Until well into the twentieth century, its curriculum rested solidly on mathematics and relegated experimental science to a subsidiary position. Industrial studies were almost totally disregarded. The institution's imperviousness to decades of criticism of its purist cast can be easily explained by the ambitions of the *polytechniciens*, who were primarily interested in employment in one of the great technical *corps d'état*. With this end in view, students were willing to engage in intensive study of mathematics, but that study left them with approaches to career making that were as conservative as those of any classically trained student from an English public school. *Polytechniciens* who failed to be appointed to a state service tended to prefer the army and regarded industry as only a last resort.[14]

No doubt this attitude encouraged a high level of mathematical competence among the French professional classes, who went through the lycées, and resulted in a host of well-prepared candidates for the scientific and technical institutions that began to proliferate within and outside the French university system.[15] In status, though, the newer institutions never rivaled the Polytechnique, and the professions for which they trained people remained far less coveted than the civil and military services of the state.

Both in the leading industrial nations and in those that followed their example, higher scientific and technical education made headway in a cultural context that was favorable to mathematics and pure science but indifferent to manufacturing. If we consider the standing of the new institutions that were committed to teaching applied science and technology as an indication of attitudes toward industry and the industrial professions, we have to conclude that Britain, France, and Germany were very similar in this respect. Against this unpropitious background, however, the range of industrially oriented courses increased dramatically in virtually every European country with even the remotest aspiration to economic advancement.[16] In countries as disparate as Britain, the "first industrial nation," and Italy, an industrial latecomer, the decades of the 1880s and 1890s saw a burgeoning of technical education, extending even to the older institutions, which began at last to stop resisting the new subjects.[17] The simultaneity of this movement shows that national economic circumstances did not determine the nature and pace of educational reform. We concede, of course, that the needs of industry, especially those of the science-based sector, influenced the process. But a far more important influence came from the competitiveness inherent in motives such as national pride and intellectual aspiration, which fired scientific communities everywhere.[18]

Traditional educational values persisted at the time of this widespread change, although we must not underestimate the impact of the new departures that were on the cultural periphery. In our view, Ringer's *Education and Society in Modern Europe* overemphasizes the recalcitrance of conservatism in education at the time. A proper understanding of this point can only be achieved by fragmenting the analysis so as to focus on the more complex but significant context of the local communities in which the modern alternatives were established. Although this approach lends itself most naturally to work on a decentralized system such as that of Britain, it can also be successfully applied to countries such as France and Italy, where national administration was by tradition more centralized.

*   *   *

Before now, attempts to adopt a systematically local perspective in analyzing the interaction between education and industry have been few. A number of works that highlight the ferment of cultural initiatives in provincial towns in France and England, however, have stressed the importance that almost all these initiatives accorded to science.[19] In the late nineteenth century, it was in the industrial areas above all that science and other forms of modern culture benefited from a powerful combination of academic, political, and economic support. The movement grew from dissatisfaction with a policy that recognized neither the importance of the expanding industrial communities nor their aspiration for an education geared to something other than the traditional learned professions and the civil service. The alliance of academic and nonacademic interests spawned a new breed of institutions with programs as well as public statements infused with the rhetoric of industrial utility. The new alternative curricula represented the values of modern society.

In England, as in France and Italy, the alliance of these interests was fraught with conflict. In all three countries, teachers of science were with few exceptions sincerely committed to providing instruction appropriate to the engineering professions and to the advancement of industrial research and development. They perceived the new departures as a way of affirming their determination to serve the local economy and thereby of enhancing their status both as scientists and as members of the community. To this end, they had to cultivate manufacturers, regional authorities, and other sources of funds and provide courses that would attract large audiences. As academic scientists, however, they were also concerned about the pursuit of the pure as well as the applied aspects of their disciplines, and they continued to insist that a grounding in science was a necessary foundation for technical studies.[20]

In these attitudes lay the seeds of conflict, for even institutions that were committed to training for the emerging industrial professions found restricting their promotional activities to industrial and local connections impossible. If they were to assert themselves as a recognized part of the national structure of higher education and to assume responsibility for forming the new breed of scientifically competent engineers, these institutions had to adjust their goal of modernizing to the existing criteria for academic quality. This meant that they had to steer a middle course between providing a broad scientific foundation for technology and orienting their teaching to specialization and industrial vocations. The persistence with which the academic world accorded dignity primarily to those engaged in pure learning made holding to this course especially difficult.

The purist drift that resulted from this tension began to affect advanced technical institutions throughout Europe from the last years of the nineteenth century on. As a consequence, these institutions distanced themselves from industry and heightened their commitment to research modeled on that of the pure sciences. Even in Germany in the early years of the twentieth century, the refurbished technische hochschulen had to face a chorus of criticism from industrialists concerned with the growing irrelevance of the schools' teaching.[21] In this respect, these hochschulen were nearly in the same position as the departments of science and engineering in the red-brick universities of England and of the institutes of applied science in the provincial French universities.[22]

Although so far we have stressed the similarities among the various countries of Europe, we do not wish to underemphasize the differences that plainly existed. While these countries were expanding scientific and technical education, the provision each country made for this new learning varied. Moreover, and far more important, each varied in the capacity of its industry to profit from this education. Although the availability of students trained in the applied sciences and technology favored industrial progress, the growth of educational opportunities in these subjects does not seem to have triggered either progress in general or specific advances in science-based production. What really distinguished Germany in this regard were the unusual economic and political conditions that surrounded her industrialization and enabled her manufacturers to make good use of the previous education, both general and vocational, of their employees. As recent studies have suggested, the reputation of German higher education as a finely tuned support system for industry cannot be explained entirely by the curricula of the technische hochschulen.[23] Rather, the explanation lies in the circumstances that led to the highly effective absorption of graduates in Germany's dynamic and innovative industrial structure.

*   *   *

We have suggested that a conservatism in the cultures of the main European countries did not impede the development of modern, industrially oriented education. We have also argued that although these modernization attempts transcended national boundaries, they were made in very different social and industrial contexts, which determined the reforms the countries made. Although both observations are abundantly documented, historians do not easily reconcile them.

It is tempting but misleading to explain the interaction between the development of higher education and the progress of industry by according an exclusive role either to education or to industry. The interaction was never direct.[24] A multiplicity of attitudes and practices was at work in each country. Certainly, the forces of both supply and demand played a part, but the objectives of educators did not necessarily coincide with those of the manufacturers. In our view, therefore, educational reform and industrial advancement have to be seen as following paths that were parallel and related but not systematically convergent.

To explore these paths, we must consider the influence of two groups. One is the societies of professional engineers, which helped to mold the career patterns of their members and to fashion their role in industry and society. Another is the government policymakers who determined the goals of education. Germany again stands out: it was her Ministry of Education that redoubled its already notable effort to resist the prejudice of the academic world by expanding technical education and industrial research. This effort did not occur in Britain or even in the predominantly centralized educational system of France, where from about 1880 on the Ministry of Public Instruction pushed education toward a close link with industry and a diminished reliance on ministry support.[25]

*   *   *

The analysis of the relations between education and industry calls for a model that is anything but straightforward. Its complexity is evident in the entry of women to scientific and technical courses, a process of integration that was slow and cautious throughout Europe.

Despite the expansion of scientific and technical education, women embarking on courses in the applied sciences in the forty years or so before the First World War were scarce. Were they deliberately excluded? Or did the style of teaching in some way discourage women from engaging in scientific disciplines and technical careers?

Our own tentative view follows neither of these interpretations. We believe that science-based industry simply did not offer openings that would encourage well-qualified women to engage in studies directed toward industrial employment. In this respect, the position of able women was not so very different from that of men, who, at the higher levels, also faced a shortage of well-paid, attractive openings in industry, especially from about 1900 on. The proportion of Cambridge graduates going on from the mathematical and natural sciences triposes into engineering was negligible, and their preference for teaching was overwhelming.[26] The perspectives of both men and women on scientific education and employment were essentially the same.

Why did some women opt for science in higher education? We can offer only preliminary suggestions, based on our belief that around 1900 in England and France, the cause of higher education for women drew strength in both the humanities and the sciences from two sources. The first was a sense of indignation at the male exclusiveness of intellectual and cultural life. The second was an expansion of secondary education for girls, which created a new demand for women teachers and an atmosphere that brought many women into the universities for the first time. Neither the prejudice of male scientists nor a supposedly female antiscientific mentality seems to have had much influence, for signs that women rejected the sciences and the modern humanities subjects were remarkably few.

With respect to England, Tables 1 and 2 suggest that the choices women made reflected and reinforced contemporary trends in the modernization of education.[27] Although our figures are based on a small number of women and on evidence drawn from Oxford and Cambridge alone, they point unmistakably to women's readiness to engage in the newer disciplines and, in Cambridge, to prepare for the more traditional mathematical tripos. Of the main degrees, only the traditionally supreme trial of literae humaniores at Oxford was conspicuously not favored by women. Our conclusion is that in Cambridge, women perceived mathematics as a discipline in which they could compete directly with men at the highest level while also displaying their commitment to modernity, whereas in Oxford their previous schooling, in particular an insufficient exposure to the years of grammatical grind that literae humaniores demanded, colored their choice. Oxford women showed a marked preference for the schools of English (which they virtually made their exclusive preserve) and modern history. In the sciences, both at Oxford and Cambridge, women may have had some preference for the "soft" disciplines of botany and zoology; even so, when the figures are adjusted to take the small numbers of women in universities into account, they do not seem to have neglected physics and chemistry.[28]

TABLE 1. Men and Women Undergraduates at Cambridge University, 1882–1914 (Average Number of Undergraduates Passing Per Year in Each Examination)

Period		Mathematical Tripos		Classical Tripos		Historical Tripos		Natural Sciences Tripos		Mechanical Sciences Tripos
		Part I	Part II	Part I	Part II	Part I	Part II	Part I	Part II	
1882–84	Women	5		9	2	3		6	2	
	Men	110	12	94	15	14		46	17	
1885–89	Women	12		11	2	6		9	3	
	Men	111	13	101	15	27		77	22	
1890–94	Women	15	1	14	1	10		9	4	
	Men	103	9	104	11	23		90	17	
1895–99	Women	16	1	13	2	19		11	2	
	Men	88	7	106	13	32		100	21	15
1900–04	Women	21	1	14	4	12	14	11	3	
	Men	68	6	112	7	67	36	115	24	23
1905–09	Women	20		15	3	15	13	15	3	
	Men	104	6	102	12	88	74	142	29	28
1910–14	Women	20	12	16	3	18	20	13	4	
	Men	106	49	90	8	119	73	161	40	39

NOTE: Figures are given only for those triposes (apart from the mechanical sciences tripos) in which women were significantly represented.
SOURCES: *The Historical Register of the University of Cambridge to the Year 1910* (Cambridge, England: Cambridge University Press, 1910); *Supplement to the Historical Register of the University of Cambridge, 1911–1920* (Cambridge, England: Cambridge University Press, 1921).

TABLE 2. Men and Women Undergraduates at Oxford University, 1893–1914
(Average Number of Undergraduates Passing Per Year in Each Examination)

Period		Literae Humaniores		Mathematics		Modern History	Natural Sciences	English
		Honour Moderations	Greats	Honour Moderations	Final			
1893–94	Women	8	1	4	1	14	2	
	Men	208	143	24	15	100	44	
1895–99	Women	7	2	8	2	18	2	12
	Men	202	137	35	22	133	45	
1900–04	Women	8	2	3	7	22	3	15
	Men	193	140	34	23	159	50	
1905–09	Women	8	3	3	1	21	4	17
	Men	186	112	39	16	149	69	9
1910–14	Women	8	4	2		24	4	22
	Men	163	141	38	16	160	82	12

NOTE: Figures are given only for examinations in which women were significantly represented.
SOURCES: *The Historical Register of the University of Oxford, 1220–1900* (Oxford: Clarendon Press, 1900); *Supplement to the Historical Register of the University of Oxford* (Oxford: Clarendon Press, 1919).

In France, women's access to advanced scientific and technical education was limited by the power of the technical *grandes écoles,* admission to which was restricted until recently to men. This exclusion meant that women could not even compete for the most prestigious technical careers in the state corps of engineers and the army. They could still, of course, train for technical careers in lesser schools and the technical institutes that became a prominent part of the French faculties of science after 1890 or so. But in France as in Britain, very few women chose this option, almost certainly because of their assessment of the career opportunities that awaited them after graduation.

Despite men's domination of higher technical education before the First World War, there is little evidence that women spurned the sciences in the institutions that were truly open to them. In France, the pattern of student enrollment in the largest faculty of science, at Paris, reveals growth in the proportion of women, especially in the decade before the war (see Table 3). Between 1903 and 1913, the proportion of French women among the students enrolling in science rose from just over 2 percent to well over 11 percent. After 1905 their choice of science remained consistently higher than their choice of medicine, though their choices of both were a good deal lower than their enrollment in the faculty of letters, which by 1913 was almost 30 percent.[29] Only in the obdurately male preserve of the faculty of law was the proportion of women negligible, barely topping half a percent.

Going beyond these figures is no easy matter. But there can be little doubt that in the early years of this century women occupied a significant, if minor, place in the classes of at least the Paris faculty of science. When the many women students from abroad (most of them from Russia) are included, the ratio of women to men enrolled in this faculty is remarkably high: it rose to a peak of almost one to five in 1909.

We can still only speculate on the careers of the French women we have just discussed. As in England, there is little evidence that many of them applied their scientific knowledge in industry. Apart from interest in the subject matter, the main lure for women with mathematical or scientific leanings was a career in teaching. It was the Third Republic's encouragement of secondary education for girls that

TABLE 3. Students in the Faculty of Science, University of Paris, 1904–13

Year	Men			Women			Total Men and Women Enrolled in Science Faculty	Percentage of Women Enrolled in Science Faculty (French Students Only)	Percentage of Women Enrolled in Science Faculty (French and Foreign Students)	Percentage of Women in University (French Students Only)	Percentage of Women in University (French and Foreign Students)
	French	Foreign	Total	French	Foreign	Total					
1904	1,333	170	1,503	43	93	136	1,639	3.1%	8.3%	3.2%	6.1%
1905	1,313	173	1,486	36	88	124	1,610	2.7	7.7	3.7	6.7
1906	1,405	231	1,636	48	115	163	1,799	3.3	9.1	4.1	8.4
1907	1,575	330	1,905	89	159	242	2,147	5.3	11.3	3.8	9.1
1908	1,430	386	1,816	85	151	236	2,052	5.6	11.5	4.9	10.8
1909	1,390	372	1,762	138	188	326	2,088	9.0	15.6	6.0	12.0
1910	1,451	502	1,953	104	137	241	2,194	6.7	11.0	6.2	11.2
1911	1,197	377	1,574	111	95	206	1,780	8.5	11.6	7.0	12.5
1912	1,236	403	1,639	146	117	263	1,902	10.6	13.8	7.6	13.8
1913	1,195	366	1,561	152	80	232	1,793	11.3	12.9	7.6	12.9

SOURCES: The numbers are taken from the annual reports of the University of Paris, published with the reports on all the French universities by the Ministère de l'instruction publique in the series *Enquêtes et documents relatifs à l'enseignement supérieur.*

stimulated the foundation of the Ecole normale supérieure d'enseignement de jeunes filles at Sèvres in 1881. And it was in the science section at Sèvres that a select group of gifted women was exposed each year to some of the most distinguished scientists of the day, among them Paul Langevin and Marie Curie. Curie's rise to prominence was itself evidence that women were not disadvantaged in the provision made for them in science and that they should not see science as an inappropriate, male culture.

*   *   *

Our first look at the problem of gender and scientific education in late nineteenth-century Europe in the period up to the First World War gives us no grounds for believing that women avoided mathematics and the physical sciences because they found something intrinsically alien about these disciplines. Swayed by two very positive considerations—the challenge of competing with men in the newer modern subjects and the unprecedented availability of teaching posts—women were more than ready to enter the ivory tower of science, including the "hard" sciences. But they responded judiciously and selectively, preferring the protected career opportunities that awaited them in education and seeing few reasons to enter industry, still less to embark on curricula aimed explicitly at industrial employment. It was not so much that traditional cultural values made the technical industrial subjects distasteful as that through these educational and career choices, women could avoid some of the keenest areas of competition with men. Only after the First World War did women begin to look seriously at industry as a likely source of employment and to recognize, to their cost, how difficult it was to turn an academic qualification into an industrial career, indeed into any professional occupation other than teaching.

ENDNOTES

This paper was written in the context of a four-year program of research financed by the Joint Committee of the Science and Engineering Research Council and the Economic and Social Research Council. The program, entitled "The Relations Between Scientific Education and Research and Industrial Performance in Europe Since c. 1850," was launched in October 1982 and conducted in the department of history at the University of Lancaster. We would like to thank the Joint Committee for its generous financial support. Robert Fox is also grateful to the British Academy for the Readership in the Humanities, during the tenure of which this paper was written.

[1]As a typical example of the many comments in this vein, see Lyon Playfair's letter to Lord Taunton, 15 May 1867, published in the *Journal of the Society of Arts* 15 (1867), pp. 447–48, and reprinted in Eric Ashby, *Technology and the Academics. An Essay on Universities and the Scientific Revolution* (London: Macmillan, 1958), pp. 111–13. Views similar to Playfair's were frequently expressed in parliamentary reports on education in the late nineteenth century. See, for example, *Report from the Select Committee on Scientific Instruction* (the Samuelson Report), Parliamentary Papers 1867–68, vol. 15; *Reports (and Minutes of Evidence) of the Royal Commission on Scientific Instruction and the Advancement of Science* (the Devonshire Commission), a series of nine command papers published in Parliamentary Papers between 1872 and 1875; *Reports of the Royal Commissioners on Technical Education* (the Samuelson Report), 5 vols. in Parliamentary Papers published between 1882 and 1884. For the view of an enlightened industrialist see Ludwig Mond, address delivered at the opening of the Schorlemmer Laboratory of Organic Chemistry at Manchester, 3 May 1895 (paper published by request of the Council of Owens College, Manchester, 1895). English attempts to follow the German model in reforming scientific and technical education are described in George Haines IV, *Essays on German Influence upon English Education and Science, 1850–1919* (Hamden, CT: Archon Books, 1969).

The equally vast French literature reflecting a sense of inferiority to Germany in the field of education and research includes: Charles Lauth, *Ministère de l'agriculture et du commerce. Exposition universelle internationale de 1878 à Paris. Groupe V, Classe 47. Rapport sur les produits chimiques et pharmaceutiques* (Paris: Imprimerie Nationale, 1881); Albin Haller, "L'industrie chimique à l'Exposition de Chicago," in *Ministère du commerce, de l'industrie, des postes et des télégraphes. Exposition internationale de Chicago en 1893. Rapports publiés sous la direction de M. Camille Krantz. Comité 19. Produits chimiques et pharmaceutiques, matériel de la peinture, parfumerie, savonnerie* (Paris: Imprimerie Nationale, 1894), pp. 1–31, esp. pp. 10–15; and Victor Cambon, *L'Allemagne au travail* (Paris: P. Rogier, 1908), chapter 2.

[2]This interpretation of the malaise of British industry has been voiced time and again in this decade. A typical comment is that of Sir Geoffrey Chandler, formerly director of the National Economic Development Office and more recently director of Industry Year 1986, a venture jointly promoted by the British government and the Royal Society of Arts. In a BBC program entitled "The Politics of Innovation" (Radio Three, 28 September 1984), Sir Geoffrey described Britain as "an industrial country with an anti-industrial culture." This phrase encapsulates a view shared by economists, industrialists, and journalists across the whole spectrum of political opinion.

[3]A typical "official" document that bears on the theme of this essay is the British government's Green Paper, *The Development of Higher Education into the 1990s* (London: Her Majesty's Stationery Office, 1985). For a comment on that Green Paper, see Robert Fox and Anna Guagnini, "The Flexible University: Some Historical Reflexions on the Analysis of Education and the Modern British Economy," *Social Studies of Science* 16 (1986), pp. 515–27.

[4]Martin J. Wiener, *English Culture and the Decline of the Industrial Spirit, 1850–1980* (Cambridge, England: Cambridge University Press, 1981).

[5]See in particular Wiener, *English Culture and the Decline of the Industrial Spirit,* chapter 7. An alternative interpretation is given in Michael Sanderson, *The Universities and British Industry 1850–1970* (London: Routledge & Kegan Paul, 1972).

[6]This assumption underlies Fritz Ringer's volume, *Education and Society in Modern Europe* (Bloomington, IN: Indiana University Press, 1979). For a critical view of Ringer's book, see Robert Fox, "Technological and Scientific Studies and the Democratization of Higher Education," *Minerva* 18 (1980), pp. 164–70.

[7]This point has been made repeatedly by historians concerned with the failure of the British and French economies to respond to the challenge of other industrial nations (most notably Germany and the United States) in the period 1870–1914; see, for example, David S. Landes's comments in his classic work *The Unbound Prometheus: Technological Change and Industrial Development in Western Europe from 1750 to the Present* (Cambridge, England: Cambridge University Press, 1969). Deficiencies in scientific and technical education and British entrepreneurs' failure to fully appreciate the importance of science and technology are highlighted in Derek H. Aldcroft, "The Entrepreneur and the British Economy, 1870–1914," *The Economic History Review,* 2nd series, 17 (1964), pp. 113–34. A contrasting evaluation of the attitude of British industrialists toward technical innovation (based on a rejection of the idea that inadequate scientific and technical education and the shortage of technical expertise had a crucially damaging effect on industry) is offered in Roderick C. Floud, "Britain 1860–1914: A Survey," and Lars Sandberg, "The Entrepreneur and Technological Change," both in *The Economic History of Britain Since c. 1700,* vol. 2: *1860 to the 1970s* (Cambridge, England: Cambridge University Press, 1981). Bernard Elbaum and William Lazonick provide an interpretation of the impact of cultural conservatism on British industrial performance that breaks with both of the approaches just mentioned and closely resembles our own point of view, in their study "The Decline of the British Economy. An Institutional Perspective," *Journal of Economic History* 64 (1984), pp. 567–83. For a strong contemporary comment on attitudes in France, see Placide Astier and I. Cuminal, *L'enseignement technique industriel et commercial en France et à l'étranger* (Paris: G. Roustan, 1908), pp. 348–93.

[8]Robert Fox and Anna Guagnini, "Britain in Perspective: The European Context of Industrial Innovation, 1880–1914," *History and Technology* 2 (1985), pp. 133–150.

[9]Fritz K. Ringer, *The Decline of the German Mandarins: The German Academic Community, 1890–1933* (Cambridge, MA: Harvard University Press, 1969).

[10]At the two chronological extremes of a long tradition of historical studies, see Friederich Paulsen, *Die deutschen Universitäten und das Universitätsstudium* (Berlin: A. Asher, 1902), and Charles McClelland, *State, Society, and University in Germany, 1700–1914* (Cambridge, England: Cambridge University Press, 1980).

[11]This opposition is treated fully in Karl-Heinz Manegold, *Universität, Technische Hochschule und Industrie. Ein Beitrag zur Emanzipation der Technik im 19.Jahrhundert unter besonderer Berucksichtigung der Bestrebungen Felix Kleins* (Berlin: Duncker & Humblot, 1970). See also, by the same author, "Technology Academised. Education and Training of the Engineer in the Nineteenth Century,"

in Wolfgang Krohn, Edwin T. Layton, Jr., and Peter Weingart, eds., *The Dynamics of Science and Technology* (Dordrecht and Boston: Reidel Publishing Co., 1978).

[12]The point was made at the time by an attentive foreign observer, Frederick Rose, the British Consul at Stuttgart, in his survey *Chemical Instruction in Germany and the Growth and Present Condition of the German Chemical Industries* (London: Diplomatic and Consular Reports, 1901), misc. series no. 56, pp. 33–36.

[13]For a critical view of the powerful influence of the Ecole polytechnique, see Haller, "L'industrie chimique à l'Exposition de Chicago," pp. 27–31. A recent account that reinforces Haller's view is in Terry Shinn, *Savoir scientifique & pouvoir social. L'Ecole polytechnique, 1794–1914* (Paris: Presses de la Fondation Nationale des Sciences Politiques, 1980).

[14]Shinn, *Savoir scientifique & pouvoir social*, pp. 80–99, 158–72.

[15]On this proliferation see Terry Shinn, "The French Science Faculty System, 1808–1914: Institutional Change and Research Potential," *Historical Studies in the Physical Sciences* 10 (1979), pp. 271–332; C.R. Day, "Education for the Industrial World: Technical and Modern Instruction in France Under the Third Republic, 1870–1914"; and Harry W. Paul, "Apollo Courts the Vulcans: The Applied Science Institutes in Nineteenth-Century French Science Faculties," both in Robert Fox and George Weisz, eds., *The Organization of Science and Technology in France, 1808–1914* (Cambridge, England: Cambridge University Press, and Paris: Editions de la Maison des sciences de l'homme, 1980), pp. 127–53, 155–81; George Weisz, *The Emergence of Modern Universities in France, 1863–1914* (Princeton, NJ: Princeton University Press, 1983), chapter 5; Mary Jo Nye, *Science in the Provinces. Scientific Communities and Provincial Leadership in France, 1860–1930* (Berkeley, CA: University of California Press, 1986).

[16]This point can be gleaned from virtually any of the standard histories of education and scientific institutions in the countries we have examined. For England, see Michael Argles, *South Kensington to Robbins. An Account of English Technical and Scientific Education Since 1851* (London: Longmans, Green & Co., 1964); W.H.G. Armytage, *Civic Universities. Aspects of a British Tradition* (London: Ernest Benn Ltd., 1955); and Donald Cardwell's masterly book, *The Organisation of Science in England* (London: Heinemann Educational Books, 1972). On France, see the sources in endnote 15.

[17]The reform of the educational system, launched by the Italian government in 1859 in the immediate aftermath of unification, led to the reorganization of the existing school of engineering of Turin and to the opening of a new one in Milan. These measures reflected the concern of the Ministry of Public Instruction with the improvement and modernization of the educational curriculum for the traditional engineering profession (i.e., for engineers engaged chiefly in public works and in the construction of railways and private houses). But over the next few years the concern of the local communities to foster the very different type of technological education that they regarded as essential for industrialization, and their attempt to do so by emulating foreign models, prompted the opening of sections of industrial engineering in both Turin and Milan.

A general survey of the problem of education in the industrialization of Italy is to be found in Carlo G. Lacaita, *Istruzione e sviluppo industriale in Italia, 1859–1914* (Florence: Giunti Barbera, 1973).

[18]It is hardly necessary to point out that this international rivalry assumed a very visible form in the universal exhibitions that were mounted with increasing panache in the major cities of the world, beginning in the late nineteenth century. These exhibitions are of special interest for our present work because important sections were almost invariably devoted to reviews of the state of scientific and technical education.

[19]On France, see the works cited in endnote 15, especially those of Shinn, Paul, Weisz, and Nye. A recent, very pertinent source on Britain is *The Steam Intellect Societies. Essays on Culture, Education and Industry, Circa 1820–1914*, ed. Ian Inkster (Nottingham: University of Nottingham, 1985).

[20]For a particularly good illustration of this commitment to science as the basis of a modern education that was at once liberal and professionally oriented, see the report by Henry E. Roscoe, professor of chemistry at Owens College (later the University of Manchester): *Record of the Work Done in the Chemical Department of the Owens College, 1857–1887* (London: Macmillan, 1887).

[21]See the comment in Rose, *Chemical Instruction in Germany*, pp. 33–35.

[22]For a critical comment on the French institutes of applied science, see Henri Le Chatelier's preface to Leon Guillet, *L'enseignement technique supérieur à l'après-guerre* (Paris: Payot, 1918), pp. 19–27.

[23]The effectiveness with which the German chemical industry took advantage of the graduates prepared by the universities and the higher technical schools was brought out well a quarter of a century ago in John Joseph Beer, *The Emergence of the German Dye Industry* (Urbana, IL: University of Illinois Press, 1959), vol. 44, esp. chapters 7 and 8. The point is developed more explicitly in Georg Meyer-Thurow, "The Industrialization of Invention: A Case Study from the German Chemical Industry," *Isis* 73 (1982), pp. 363–81. A more general reexamination that questions the impact of education on economic growth and industrial development in Germany is found in Peter Lundgreen, *Bildung und Wirtschaftswachtstum im Industrialisierungsprozess des 19.Jahrhunderts* (Berlin: Colloquium-Verlag, 1973); see also Peter Lundgreen, "The Organization of Science and Technology in France: A German Perspective," in Fox and Weisz, *The Organization of Science and Technology in France.*

[24]Our thinking on this point has been greatly influenced by a discussion with Terry Shinn following his presentation of the paper "Industry, Knowledge, and Education" at the Economic and Social Research Council workshop "The Relations Between Scientific Education and Research and Industrial Performance in Europe Since c. 1850" (University of Lancaster, 11–13 July 1985).

[25]Shinn, "The French Science Faculty System," pp. 310–26, and Weisz, *The Emergence of Modern Universities in France*, chapter 3.

[26]David B. Wilson, "Experimentalists Among the Mathematicians: Physics in the Cambridge Natural Sciences Tripos, 1851–1900," *Historical Studies in the Physical Sciences* 12 (1982), pp. 325–71, esp. pp. 353, 358–61.

[27]Brief accounts of the opening of the English universities to women can be obtained from the standard histories of individual institutions, such as Hugh Hale Bellot, *University College, London, 1826–1926* (London: University of London Press, 1929), chapter 10; and Edward Fiddes, *Chapters in the History of Owens College and Manchester University, 1851–1914* (Manchester: Manchester University Press, 1937), pp. 38–39, 110–11, and Appendix VII. For more specific studies of this process see Vera Brittain, *The Women at Oxford. A Fragmentary History*

(London: Harrap, 1960); Mabel Tylecote, *The Education of Women at Manchester University, 1883 to 1933* (Manchester: Manchester University Press, 1941); and, more recently, Rita McWilliams-Tullberg, *Women at Cambridge. A Men's University though of a Mixed Type* (London: Victor Gollanctz Ltd., 1975). However, none of these works addresses the problem of women and science or women and technology in detail. On the employment of women graduates (though chiefly in the interwar period) see Sanderson, *The Universities and British Industry,* chapter 11.

[28]This point is brought out, with respect to the Cambridge natural sciences tripos, in Roy MacLeod and Russell Moseley, "Fathers and Daughters: Reflections on Women, Science, and Victorian Cambridge," *History of Education* 8 (1979), pp. 321–33.

[29]*Ministère de l'instruction publique. Enquêtes et documents relatifs à l'enseignement supérieur.*

Susan C. Bourque and Kay B. Warren

Technology, Gender, and Development

INCORPORATING GENDER IN THE STUDY OF DEVELOPMENT

FAITH IN THE POSITIVE IMPACT of technology has been part of Western liberal thought since Locke. Questioning his belief that man's improvement of nature is the key to human progress has also been part of the West's intellectual tradition. Contemporary evaluations of the commercialization and diffusion of technology from the industrialized nations to the developing world reflect both lines of thought. For the optimists, technology is a primary mechanism for promoting economic modernization and enhancing standards of living. For those who are disenchanted with technology, its transfer from the industrialized nations has been a mistake, for it has led the developing nations to misdirect their limited resources to the adoption of Western patterns that are inappropriate to their needs.[1]

Early analysts of technology dissemination assumed that the process was positive and unproblematic, beneficent and full of promise. It was an integral element in the pursuit of modernization.

Susan C. Bourque, born in 1943 in Detroit, Michigan, is professor of government at Smith College. She is coauthor, with Kay B. Warren, of Women of the Andes: Patriarchy and Social Change in Two Peruvian Towns *(1981) and coeditor, with Donna R. Divine, of* Women Living Change *(1985). Professor Bourque is currently director of the Project on Women and Social Change at Smith College.*

Kay B. Warren, born in 1947 in Stanford, California, is associate professor of anthropology at Princeton University. Her books include The Symbolism of Subordination: Indian Identity in a Guatemalan Town *(1978) and* Women of the Andes: Patriarchy and Social Change in Two Peruvian Towns *(1981), the latter coauthored with Susan C. Bourque. Professor Warren is the founding director of the Program in Women's Studies at Princeton University.*

173

Development was unquestionably the goal, and using the technologies of the industrialized nations the most efficient avenue. Development, however, was to come under closer scrutiny. In the late 1960s and early 1970s, critics pointed out that industrialization and modernization policies were not producing the expected social and economic improvements. They argued that conditions in the Third World were deteriorating because of these economies' dependency on the capital, credits, technology, training, and markets of the developed nations. This troubled dependency led many scholars to conclude that the wide-ranging adoption of Western models and technologies might not be the solution to the problems of developing nations.[2]

Questions raised by scholars exploring women's experience have further complicated this debate. Consideration of gender has added a new dimension to the discussion. Social scientists now pursue questions such as these: How has the dissemination of technology from industrial to developing countries affected women's lives, sexual divisions of labor, and gender relationships at home and at work? To what extent have newer technologies improved women's lives, lessened their work loads, increased employment opportunities, and enhanced their authority? How might women gain greater access to contemporary technologies and play a greater role in their development and dissemination? In the course of addressing these questions, the standard formulation of the issues surrounding the development and dissemination of technology has been widened to include the cultural and economic complexity of gender relations.

Initial attempts to explore gender and development policies showed that women's status in many Third World countries had declined and that part of the problem was the change accompanying technology's transfer to new social contexts. While men had also been affected, crucial differences in the experience of the sexes resulted in more erosion of women's status. Women were denied their customary rights to land, excluded from agricultural development projects, and deprived of access to new tools, techniques, and training on the same terms as men.[3]

The mix of these factors varies somewhat by region. Scholars record that many African women lost their rights to land during the commercialization of agriculture. European colonial administrators, applying their own notions of appropriate gender roles, gave land titles to men. Contemporary development advisors from the industrialized nations have reinforced the same pattern when they have made men the preferred recipients of new seeds, tools, training, and credit, even in areas where women are the primary agriculturalists.

Nor is the problem necessarily obviated when development schemes are directed by the governments of the developing society. Local cultural values, reflecting male dominance in community affairs rather than female involvement in productive activities, often transfer to the new tools and crops. Men, as the political leaders of communities, were invited to attend sessions where new tools and techniques were introduced. Rural Latin American women without title to land could not qualify as members of agricultural cooperatives or as beneficiaries of agrarian reforms. In India and Southeast Asia, new machinery displaced women from wage labor and adversely affected the poorest households. In each instance the difference in access each sex had to new technology led to a decline in women's status.

In these initial analyses unequal access was defined as the major issue, and therefore the logical solution seemed to be to equalize it. Women needed the ability to use tools and machines as well as literacy and education. The message was explicitly protechnology: women had lost ground because of restricted access. The solution to inequity was to open the restricted channels of education and training.

The call to widen access for women has rekindled the debate about technology's desirability. Scholars in both industrialized and developing nations have spoken from four different perspectives. We shall call them the feminization-of-technology, the appropriate-technology, the global-economy, and the cultural-political-integration approaches. Each has a social critique and proposals to enhance women's position. The reassessment of technology has been an arena in which the international nature of the new scholarship on women's experience has been apparent. Not only do many of the issues crosscut the experience of women in the industrialized and developing worlds, but the dialogue among scholars has helped shape how the issues have been perceived and analyzed.[4]

In some ways these perspectives parallel familiar lines of argument in the Western philosophical tradition, but the consideration of gender has added to them a call for clarification of the links among family, cultural values, and access to the polity and the economy. By enhancing our understanding of social change, gender also raises new questions about how equity is to be achieved in modern social systems.

The Feminization of Technology

The feminization-of-technology perspective has intellectual roots in eighteenth-century romanticism and twentieth-century Freudian thought. Those who hold this perspective have serious doubts about technology and argue that women have a nature quite distinct from that of men, two ideas derived from Rousseau. Rousseau believed that women's nature disqualifies them from participation in political life; in contrast, those who advocate the feminization of technology argue that women's distinct values, developed through their familial roles, must become part of the public realm if technology is to serve the common good and promote human welfare. Proponents of this view include Hilda Scott, Elise Boulding, and Maria Bergom-Larsson.

As technological innovation is now organized, they say, a masculine world view determines its development and application. The result is continual reinforcement of hierarchy, competition, immediate measurable results, material accumulation, depersonalization, and economic and political expansion. It is not that bearers of masculinist views are ignorant of values other than these; it is just that the economic order has forced them to suppress their "needs for subjectivity, feelings, intimacy, and humanity" and to "project them onto the private life and women."[5] In response to this situation, the feminization-of-technology proponents advocate a radical restructuring of the economic and political orders.

Those who hold this view postulate a distinct women's culture and see it as a critical tool for orienting society toward more humanistic, egalitarian ends so that it becomes concerned with relationships and welfare rather than individual success and profit. The primary source of this utopian vision is women's involvement in the family, where these critics hold that hierarchy is successfully deemphasized, nonviolent persuasion is stressed, and investment is directed toward the nurturance of future generations. From their familial vantage point, women learn that hierarchy, whatever its form, inevitably subordinates and exploits the weaker.[6]

Proponents of this position dangerously romanticize women's values, the family, and the nature of Third World societies. While important feminist frameworks, particularly psychoanalytic perspectives, ascribe universal characteristics to women's nature, little empirical evidence for transcultural and transhistorical female values exists. Thus it would be a serious mistake to conclude that distinctly feminine values (in opposition to masculine values) should play a central role in international development. One has only to look at the rich and various constructions of gender in contemporary societies to see that the same images of masculinity and femininity do not always apply.[7] Furthermore, by distancing men from the "natural" concerns of women, this perspective limits, by definition, those with whom women might ally themselves, those whose vested interests are to question current arrangements, to articulate options, and to promote change.

A common theme in the literature of this perspective is the connection between technological innovation and military objectives. Those arguing for the feminization of technology say that women are less violent than men and will offer an alternative to what many of these writers feel is the imminent danger of war. This view of women has a long history in feminism. It is neither new nor singularly evoked by the issue of technology. While it is often used to argue for women's expanded access or participation, little evidence suggests that women would behave differently than men in such a case.[8]

Nevertheless, those who argue for the feminization of technology maintain that women's values are currently imprisoned by the separation of home and work. Effective change requires an expansion of women's sphere, they say, and a new political procedure for evaluating technology, one that involves women in policymaking roles and includes questions about the impact of new technologies on women and women's culture. As female values successfully inform the public world, the hope is that hierarchical distinctions between "productive, paid" work and "nonproductive, unpaid" work will be questioned, women and men will share a personal commitment to responding to the needs of the community, and unnecessary divisions of labor will be rejected.[9]

The feminization-of-technology perspective is best seen as a contribution to our understanding of the intersection of capitalism and patriarchy in the West. From its critique emerges a utopian quest, though not much elaboration of strategies to achieve political goals.

In contrast to this utopianism, the appropriate-technology perspective focuses on concrete development problems and strategies for change.

Appropriate Technology

Those who say that technology is desirable if appropriate to a country's needs share Locke's view that in appropriating the goods of the earth, man must leave much of the same wealth behind for others. Unlike Locke, however, they do not assume that the world has infinite wealth but see instead a world of shrinking, irreplaceable resources. They identify the adoption of inappropriate technologies as a major factor in the destruction of the environment and a mistaken route to change.

Proponents of appropriate technology prefer to attack Third World poverty and underdevelopment by increasing production in each country without reinforcing the pattern of dependency on the industrialized world. Their strategy is to move away from capital-intensive solutions toward a less costly intermediate technology emphasizing local resources.

Advocates of appropriate technology are loath to see women in developing societies caught in the same technological trap that, they argue, has engulfed women in the industrialized world. Marilyn Carr has laid this line of thought out as a field of study and, along with others, argued that appropriate technology would increase women's productivity and give them more time for other obligations and community development. In rural societies, for example, where women spend hours every day gathering fuel for their kitchen fires, women and development planners have designed new low-tech mud-brick stoves that cut fuel consumption. Where rodents, insects, or rot destroy more than a third of family harvests during the early months of storage, design projects have concentrated on low-cost storage practices that would increase the availability of food. Hand-operated grinding machines for corn, wheat, and millet as well as rice hullers and palm-oil presses can free women from hours of daily drudgery without displacing workers. Solar energy, wind power, and biogas are forms of energy that lower dependence on expensive commercial fuels and make use of self-renewing resources.[10]

While in conception appropriate technology makes sense, in practice it has brought new dilemmas. Foremost is the fear that unemployment will rise as new technologies mechanize formerly labor-intensive agricultural tasks. The fear is particularly high for women, who often find themselves caught in a circle of limited resources, which restrict their use of the very technologies that might increase their productivity and give them access to credit, education, and land.[11] Furthermore, their economically marginal position makes it very difficult for women to experiment with their families' welfare. They cannot afford to learn new skills unless they receive compensation for the time they take from other work to experiment with new technologies and unless those technologies increase women's productivity enough to make the new investment pay off.[12] Women's access to credit and low-interest loans may be just as critical as their access to tools, instruction, and economic exchange.

This perspective has a Rousseauian cast in the legitimacy it accords the voice of the community. Criticizing top-down decision making in the development of new technologies, leading exponents of appropriate technology point out that what may appear appropriate to engineers and development workers may not be at all appropriate to the people expected to use the new techniques. For instance, African women found serious drawbacks in solar cookers, which were designed to be an appropriate fuel-saving technology. These stoves required women to cook during the heat of the day and to continually move the stoves to collect the sun's rays. Since they also could not support family-size pots, the stoves were roundly rejected. Such examples show the need to ask what would make it possible for women to create their own technological innovations.[13]

Even if full consultation with the so-called "end users" takes place and designs are consistent with local needs and use patterns, the concept of appropriate technology to lighten women's work may fail. It certainly fails if development projects end up creating a sexual division of technology in which women gain appropriate technology for domestic work while men become the focus for technology training that generates new employment opportunities. This issue is especially important in societies where women are expected to be the financiers of the traditional domestic economy with their own earnings and where social change has multiplied the number of households headed by women.

Surely the concept fails if development policymakers focus their concerns about women exclusively on the household and the family.

Men are seldom viewed as members of households unless they are seen as "heads" or "breadwinners." The concentration on women's domestic and reproductive roles tends to limit policymakers' concerns to those roles. Of course the family and household are central elements in both men's and women's lives, and reproduction and child-care responsibilities affect women's labor force and political participation. However, the history of policy in this area has shown that if concern is directed to reproduction and domestic roles, those issues are likely to set limits to national policies on women.[14] As a result, women become the targets of population programs and welfare projects, or they are integrated into the lowest levels of production as part-time workers. Little thought is given to providing women access to the full range of skills that would allow them to control and direct development activities.[15] As long as women are primarily conceived of as members of households, there may be a tendency to leave unquestioned their absence from society's significant political, social, and economic institutions.

Feminist advocates of appropriate technology call for women to become involved in policy planning in order to influence the use of technology, the agenda for research priorities, the choice of government subsidies, and the discussion of needs. They conclude it is not the form of technology that determines which gender uses it, but rather who controls its development, dissemination, and products. Nevertheless, adherents of this perspective leave a more fundamental question unaddressed: What would give women access to the realms where such decisions are made? The Rousseauian community of direct democratic participation excluded women from its eighteenth-century formulation. Today's call for community control over technology has not resolved the issue of women's political subordination either. No advocate of appropriate technology has yet found a way to redress this inequality.

Moreover, the appropriate-technology approach seems out of touch with the worldwide changes that technology has brought, and somewhat slow to explore ways to enhance women's control of these changes.[16] Scholars who take a global approach to technology address some of these issues in their attempt to integrate an examination of the household with their wider concern about the state and the international division of labor.

The Global Economy

Proponents of this perspective begin from a neo-Marxist position similar to that of Immanuel Wallerstein's world systems, in which capitalism limits the developing countries' capacity to compete in international markets. In this view the capitalist economies have shaped the international division of labor so that the developing countries become sources of cheap labor and raw materials for technologically sophisticated industrialized countries, where capital is accumulated.[17] People who take the global-economy approach question using *technology* in its narrow sense of focusing investigation and argue that the primary issues in today's world of interdependence are economic exploitation and political domination. One cannot consider technology, they assert, without studying the issues of its production and consumption in the context of changing class relations, state policy, and international economics.

The global-economy perspective underscores what is neglected in many analyses of technology—the interplay between national governments and international markets in shaping national planning, policy development, and resource allocation. Of particular concern is the state's creation of labor policy in areas such as employment, migration, education, housing, agriculture, and industrial development. How does the state formulate priorities for its own development? For the agrarian sector, how can the state balance the need to produce food crops for domestic consumption with the need to encourage the production of commodities for export? How does the state deal with the oversupply of commodities and unstable national currencies? What alternatives does it see for increasing domestic production, for dealing with shifts in subsistence agriculture and wage labor, and for reducing dependency on the international market for food supplies?

Feminist scholars who begin from this position have stressed the interdependence of national economies in the world economic system, the scope and power of multinational corporations, and the electronic communication and information-processing revolutions as the major dimensions in the debate over technology development and commercialization. These analysts link a critique of capitalism and imperialism with the stratification of gender. Major figures in this field include June C. Nash, María Patricia Fernández-Kelly, Lourdes

Bené ría, Gita Sen, Kate Young, Heleieth Saffioti, Carmen Diana Deere, Zenebeworke Tadesse, and Verena Stolcke.[18]

These scholars have called for major revision of the approaches to political economy by demonstrating how much is missing from class analysis when scholars fail to examine gender relations within and between classes. They focus on changing divisions of labor and the reproduction of the labor force in the household. They argue that the international system of capital accumulation reinforces existing gender inequities to keep wages at the lowest possible level. Thus the question of women's subordinate position can never be resolved simply by increasing their access and participation, for they will always be integrated at the lowest level, where they will remain a secondary, low-paid, and potentially expendable work force.

Some of the most important work on the global economy has focused on women and multinational employment. Studies from societies and economies as distinct as the Mexican border zone and the Chinese communities of Hong Kong demonstrate the centrality of cultural values in mediating the significance of women's employment and the primacy of family-based strategies in the allocation and investment of earnings.[19] These insights challenge the Lockean notion of the freely contracting individual and call for the addition of a fuller cultural analysis to neo-Marxist approaches.

Those who work from the perspective of the global economy call into question the tendency to treat women as individuals without other competing identities, or to see women as a category with uniform interests and concerns. To overcome these conceptual simplifications, advocates of the global-economy view argue that we must examine household units by their class position in mixed-subsistence, cash-crop, and urban economies. Women's domestic responsibilities, varying by class and involving intricate balances of monetized and nonmonetized activities, rapidly respond to changing market conditions.[20] However socially valued or devalued, women's private household roles are critical for the physical and social reproduction of the labor force. The central analytic project for these scholars is to study women's reproductive and productive roles as they are mediated by their class position in the wider economy. The perspective of the global economy helps restore concrete social contexts to women's work and perceptions. This concreteness overcomes a serious shortcoming in the approach based on the feminization of technology.

Socialists who seek redistributive alternatives to free market economies and nationalists who reject Western influence in their politics and economics find this perspective useful. While liberal researchers do not share the socialists' vision, it is clear that neo-Marxist analyses have influenced their thinking about the importance of an international perspective that sees various forms of inequality as interactive and central to explanations for current patterns of development. Furthermore, the attention to state-level planning and influence sets this viewpoint apart from those of appropriate technology and the feminization of technology.

In identifying the dimensions of gender in the global economy, proponents of this perspective have rewritten the neo-Marxist position. Yet they have left several vital questions incompletely addressed. When they use the household as the unit of analysis, they downplay the conflicting and competitive interests in the family. As a result, they assume that internal tensions and compromises result from new patterns of employment and fail to scrutinize the impact of local culture and power relations on women's access to technology, training, income, and education. Similarly, to the extent that economic change is expected to direct cultural and political changes, the issues of how to increase women's access to advanced training and leadership are deemphasized in favor of their concern with the decentralized, grass-roots mobilization of women workers.

Cultural-Political Integration: A Systems Analysis

Those who argue from the perspective of the global economy see little hope for significant structural change within the confines of the world capitalist system. For those who do not expect that socialist governments will end the gender inequities of capitalism or who do not believe in the feminization of technology, the avenue to change lies in rethinking the present structures of access. They would integrate cultural and political analysis by using the insights of recent feminist scholarship to identify the limits of access and show the degree to which gender permeates institutions and expectations. Analysts who take this perspective are in the field of development and are concerned with science and education. They include Shirley Malcom,

Amartya Sen, Nelly Stromquist, Ann Briscoe, Sheila Pfafflin, Mary Anderson, Krishna Ahooja-Patel, and Rounaq Jahan.

Those who advocate the cultural-political integration approach move well beyond the liberal formulation of equal access to ask what must happen to institutional cultures, power relations, social values, and stereotypes beyond lifting official or legal barriers to women's entry. Proponents of this perspective use the insights of systems theory and its emphasis on the interactive nature of phenomena to account for women's low enrollment in fields directly related to technology, to identify obstacles to women's educational and employment achievements, and to devise programs to reverse gender asymmetries.[21]

Advocates of this approach start from the assumption that no single causal explanation or linear approach has adequately dealt with the issues of gender in access to technology or the consequences of the transfer of technology from one society to another. Rather, they argue that the only way to widen women's access to technology is to understand the elements of gender in the social and political systems that impinge on participation. What happens in the school and the workplace that limits women's technological competence, and how can that be changed?

Proponents of this position focus on the ideologies that surround the acquisition of technical competence and the structural arrangements that reinforce stereotypes marking scientific fields and expertise as male. Not surprisingly, they see the key to change in the culture and politics of education and the workplace. In order to change gender stereotypes and opportunities, they argue, we must understand the processes that reproduce existing patterns.[22]

Fundamental to this perspective is an understanding of how institutions shape meaning and values as well as how individuals can both internalize and challenge social norms.[23] In this perspective the school and the workplace become cultural and political environments where rules and norms are perpetuated and legitimated by contemporary ideologies of gender-based exclusion, segregation, and avoidance. With respect to technology, the challenge is to examine the fields in science and engineering in which women have been poorly represented and explore ways to increase women's enrollment in those fields. That may entail developing methods to deal with mathematics anxiety or the stereotypes of women that place them in the category of nonscientists.[24]

Advocates of this view neither assume that individuals are autonomous decision makers who choose whether or not to participate in technological development, nor reduce years of education to the status of a variable that mechanically accounts for higher rates of technology adoption. Instead these analysts see education as a process of structural and ideological tracking. As a result they readdress the question of widening access as a solution to gender inequality and see institutional change as necessary to alter the structures that constrain choice and equity.

The challenge for the cultural-political systems perspective is to transform the arenas that have resisted change. Reform in education and the workplace requires the intervention of political forces. They must be convinced that there is good reason for pursuing reform and that it will bring reward. They must seek transformation from the reaches of the national political system down to the political relations within each household. Not only ministers of education and labor but also parents, teachers, coworkers, and employers will effect meaningful change.

Exponents of this approach emphasize the perceptual biases surrounding women's contributions to the household. They note people's reluctance to face the powerful conflicts of interest within households—especially those between men and women, which are often hidden by the efforts of households to emphasize their common concerns. Inequality in the treatment of women is widely perceived as legitimate because women's contributions are perceived as marginal or subsidiary and, consequently, their lesser "entitlements" as justified.[25]

In addition to family-level perceptual and political issues, the reforms proposed by the cultural-political integrationists have staggering difficulties at the national level. In many developing countries it is becoming harder and harder to convince government authorities that they should expand educational opportunity, let alone to plead the special case of women and the need to restructure basic institutions. The experience of the past twenty years has demonstrated that the rapid expansion of education does not solve and may not even lessen development problems. While most leaders must publicly declare themselves in favor of greater educational opportunity, they may privately fear that expanded education puts new pressure on overtaxed systems. Since policymakers in the developing world already find themselves unable to meet educated workers' demands for jobs, they find expanding the number of educated workers by giving special attention to women—particularly in the face of potential opposition, limited funds, and overwhelming debt burdens—an unattractive option.[26]

Further complicating the issue are employment opportunities, which are shrinking in both the industrialized and the developing world, partly because of the mechanization of labor-intensive processes. Constructing a political agenda to expand women's employment opportunities will be even more difficult where employment opportunities are limited. Proponents of the cultural-political integration approach are alarmed by such trends and have focused their research on both the educational and the employment dilemmas facing women in the developing world. It is from such material that a political agenda supporting change must be constructed.

CONSTRUCTING AN AGENDA FOR CHANGE

Our review of current perspectives on women and technology persuades us that there are several arenas in which to formulate agendas for change. This would mean using insights from both the global-economy and the cultural-political integration perspectives. The main issues are how to develop policies that provide adequate education and employment for women in today's world of interdependence and how to build political support for expanding opportunity for women, given the economic and cultural obstacles to their education. In sum, how can public resources be redirected to meet the needs of women as well as men in national development?

This is a formidable task, but both the global-economy and the cultural-political integration perspectives help identify an agenda for change. Advocates of the global-economy perspective, for example, claim that schools perpetuate gender inequality and class difference by regulating access to knowledge and by teaching world views that justify the status quo. The political and cultural integrationists are quick to point out that the expansion of educational opportunity for women in the developed world has not eroded unemployment or closed the earning gap between men and women.

Nor have expanded educational opportunities ended the underrepresentation of women in science and technology, though these fields have had important changes.[27] As women have entered the science-based professions, the less prestigious and less remunerated positions have taken on the highest proportion of women. This pattern is reported in both capitalist and socialist societies.

These critiques have led some scholars to conclude that conventional education is a mistaken focus for changing women's relation to technology. Educational systems, they assert, are bound to reflect the cultural biases and elite class interests of the societies that establish and support them. Consequently, the schools are unlikely to be the locus of a radical restructuring of gender roles or power relations.

While we see considerable validity in these critiques, it is clear to us that women will have very little impact on national development priorities, political ideologies, and development planning until they are literate and have the basic arithmetic skills with which to analyze political and economic systems. It is hard to imagine women playing a role in a technological world without educational equity. Thus we believe that the issue is how to improve the educational environment for girls so that technology is not defined as something outside their realm. This means not only getting girls into schools but changing what is taught formally and informally in those institutions.

What are the chances of altering educational systems and women's education in particular? Certainly, educational equity remains an elusive goal. A substantial educational gap persists between men and women throughout the developing world. Studies continue to find marked differences in school attendance between boys and girls at all levels. Girls have much higher dropout rates and much greater illiteracy.[28] These gender disparities will persist and become greater if programs do not focus on women's educational needs.

As we see it, a prime difficulty is that schooling does not necessarily offer the same direct economic payoff for women as it does for men. Parents decide whether to educate their daughters largely on the basis of how education seems to affect women's roles and behavior. That governments tend to put more financial resources into secondary and higher education than into primary instruction exacerbates the problem and leaves the initial imbalance between men and women unaddressed. Moreover, while women show considerable interest in literacy programs if they are linked to income-producing activities, governments have made little effort to orient programs to these activities.[29]

Once girls enter a school system, they face another series of obstacles. In nations where girls and boys attend school at the same rate (including the Philippines, Western Europe, Eastern Europe, Chile, and the United States), sexual segregation in tracking and curricula creates different educational experiences for boys and girls. Streaming at the lower secondary stage filters most young women into terminal courses that prepare them for the traditionally female vocations.[30]

This "hidden" curriculum is very much a part of the experience of both the industrialized and the developing nations. Authority patterns in administration and staffing as well as expectations communicated to girls determine the outcome of their schooling. Girls may see academic achievement as "masculine" and receive little reinforcement for superior performance.[31]

The kind of policy that would remedy this situation would relate issues of the workplace and education to household dynamics, for income and perception are core issues. If women's time invested in education leads to remuneration in the cash economy, and if that contribution is perceived as important to the family's welfare, then it appears to affect the family's decisions about who is "entitled" to investments in such resources as education and nutrition.[32] In this, as in so many areas, the issues of education and employment are linked to one another and to the larger questions of how gender hierarchies are constructed and perceived within a society. We emphasize that these are arenas that are open to change.[33] Private voluntary organizations have successfully worked with the urban poor to provide access to credit and to match learning to women's needs and schedules. Such programs set a good example of how to allocate educational funds. Where such opportunities present themselves, women take them up with enthusiasm.

Technological development may help solve the problems of learning environments, the hidden curriculum, and gender tracking. Advances may expand instruction where too few teachers, schools, and texts are available. New strategies become possible with videos and television. These technologies could decentralize and diversify the production of educational materials and make advanced technical materials available in places that are far apart. Who controls the production and the content is the issue.

In addition to rethinking education and its relationship to employment, new findings on fertility, child welfare, and infant mortality may also provide grounds to capture the attention of national development experts. The impact of women's education on fertility has been examined in a variety of contexts, and the research findings appear mixed and at times contradictory. Some researchers conclude from their review of this literature that increased female education is associated with low fertility and that maternal education is related to children's health and survival.[34] While these results are encouraging and should serve as the basis for additional research and policy planning, using the traditional sexual division of child care and nurturance to mobilize political support for change is problematic. Reliance on this strategy, while politically appealing, could ultimately limit women's opportunities in other areas where their work is just as important for family welfare.

To build support among policymakers, we suggest that political agendas be based on careful assessment of the changing relationship between educational investment and its perceived return, the link among education, increased child welfare, and low fertility, and the cost of failing to introduce women to technological innovations in agriculture and other areas of the economy. To our minds, the most hopeful route lies in demonstrating the costs and benefits of addressing women's educational issues in terms of reduced health care costs and increased productivity. For instance, emphasizing the consequences of failing to train women in the areas of a developing country's economy in which they have traditional productive responsibilities may prove persuasive. Some researchers argue that sex stereotyping in India has resulted in an absence of women from agriculture and forestry schools and left the country with no female extension agents to take new technologies to village women, whose traditional responsibilities included gathering fuel and fodder. As a result, "development programs in critical areas of women's work . . . are designed, directed and evaluated by male experts who, because of customary practice in most of India, have no direct access to village women."[35]

If reformers can convince development planners that scarce training resources are being squandered on the wrong populations or that investment in training women would better the returns, one essential component of the agenda would be secure. But policymakers would accept such propositions only if they became convinced that women are technologically capable and educable, so renewing attention to learning environments is essential.

*   *   *

Technology and its transfer have elicited not just one feminist voice but a range of positions, politics, and policies. Each perspective complicates our understanding of change by adding gender to the issues surrounding technology, and poses important questions to political and social theories. A consideration of gender forces us to rethink the household and its relationship to politics, the economy, and professional life and to question our assumptions about the organization of political life. This rethinking has brought the internal dynamics of household structure under scrutiny. No longer do we accept the Lockean assumption that the male head of household adequately represents the conflicting interests of its members. Similarly, Rousseau's disqualification of women from citizenship because of their nature has been recast as an argument for a distinctly female voice in the development and control of technology.

Those who argue for the feminization of technology, while limited by their utopian vision of women's values, lead us to question the consequences of separating the home and the family from political consideration. One need not agree with their assumption of distinctly female values or their idealization of the family to recognize that they do us a theoretical service by asking how these realms of human experience should be related to political life. We may in the end decide that these realms should be separate, but it should no longer be an a priori assumption. Moreover, advocates of this perspective are certainly correct to question the values surrounding technological choice and political life. One must be wary, however, of looking to the household for an alternative formulation of what those values might be. Most research shows that households tend to reflect the values of the cultural and political systems in which they are located.

Those who advocate appropriate technology have emphasized the power relations operating in the transfer of tools and skills to solve development problems. By adding gender to their considerations, they remind us that consigning women to low-technology solutions would perpetuate inequity by institutionalizing a hierarchy of technology. The sexual division of technology does not seem a hopeful route to parity. Furthermore, their analysis underscores the reality that securing control for the end user is only meaningful if it is insured by a role in decision making that includes the capacity to develop new technology.

Advocates of the global-economy framework have moved neo-Marxist analysis beyond economic reductionism with their attempts to integrate cultural and ideological constructs into materialist analysis. They have demonstrated the inadequacy of class analyses that do not include gender relations and they have advanced discussion of the politics of the household demonstrating the ties between it and the wider economy and polity. Their analysis demonstrates the limits of assuming a unitary set of interests within the household. For a position so clear about international divisions of power and authority, however, it is remarkably quiet about redistributing domestic power and duties.

When we turn to the cultural and political integration advocates, we can appreciate the complex picture of gender and technology they bring us. The household, to which the neo-Marxists have given new significance, can be examined anew to appreciate the conflicting interests within it. Just as the global-economy advocates demonstrate that a simple economic model of "the rational man" cannot adequately explain women's behavior, so the cultural-political integrationists identify the perceptual issues that link the evaluations of household members' contributions to the channels of access. By taking seriously the obstacles that block access and their relation to gender, they outline a political agenda that could open up opportunity. Since advocates of this perspective must think of the policy implications of their analyses, they have been able to demonstrate the greater cost of ignoring gender in national development programs.

For us, a combination of insights from the cultural-political systems analysis and the global-economy perspectives is the most promising avenue for change. The cultural-political integration view underscores the importance of developing a female technological and educational leadership that can speak effectively to policymakers. The global-economy perspective stresses the importance of empowering women on a grass-roots level to articulate demands that may be muted by existing institutional arrangements. These two groups of women are very likely to have important class differences, yet feminist groups in many developing nations have shown the potential for significant cross-class development projects in health, income generation, and informal education. The alliance between these groups may be a catalyst for clarifying women's development priorities in the Third World.

Clearly, access to technology, education, and employment are not independent solutions to the problems of equity, underdevelopment, and women's continued marginalization. Rather, all are better understood as clusters of economic, institutional, and ideological relations that shape and are shaped by power relations in national and international spheres. Technology does not offer answers to women's equity independent of the political and economic contexts in which it operates. As attention is paid to the context of the production of ideas, skills, tools, and commodities, one realizes how much each factor is a bearer of social relations marked by gender. Just as the schools have a hidden curriculum, so production in technology has a hidden organization. Giving access to education, technology, and employment is not enough to change gender inequality. Contemporary feminists have made it clear that family structures, the decisions taken within them, and women's access to technology are all linked in an interdependent global economy. Understanding the political, economic, and cultural context of access is the real key to equalizing opportunity.

ENDNOTES

Our analysis has been sharpened by extended discussions with Jill Conway and Stephen Graubard, and with the participants at the Bellagio Conference on Gender, Technology, and Education—in particular, Penina Glazer, Joan Scott, and Fiona Wilson. Vanessa Schwartz, Anna Vigh, and Elissa Adair assisted us with the endnotes and Kathleen Thayer handled the word processing. We would like to add that, as always, this joint project has been a thoroughly collaborative effort at all stages, from conception to computer disks.

[1]Frances Stewart, *Technology and Underdevelopment* (New York: Macmillan, 1977). This analysis uses the anthropological definition of *technology* as the systems of knowledge, tools, and skills for production viewed in their social and economic contexts. This usage contrasts with the conventional first definition of the term as the application of science for industrial or commercial objectives.

There is little consensus about what *development* actually means. Thus, at the heart of many disagreements over research methodologies and policy initiatives are strikingly different perspectives on change. Critiques of Western models and measurements of change as appropriate standards for Third World societies have been central to scholarship on gender and development. See Kay B. Warren and Susan C. Bourque, "Women, Technology, and Education: Conceptual Insights from the U.N. Decade, 1975–1985" (unpublished ms., 1986).

For some scholars *development* simply refers to the patterns of change that countries are undergoing. For others the concept involves state intervention and planning to achieve higher gross domestic product or other macro-level changes measurable with aggregate statistics that reflect changes in standards of living. For many scholars, the issue is both improving standard of living and widening poor households' active participation in agendas for change. In this case, development is not fully measured by conventional statistical indicators but rather by structural changes to broaden equity, widen women's economic and political participation, recognize women as agents rather than as targets of change, and empower local groups to engage in grass-roots development focusing on their perceived needs. The measurement of successful development—that is, increased productivity and efficiency—may be different for these alternative perspectives on change.

[2]For a fuller discussion of the relation between the critique of development and the reconsideration of development's impact on women, see Susan C. Bourque and Kay B. Warren, *Women of the Andes: Patriarchy and Social Change in Two Peruvian Towns* (Ann Arbor: Michigan University Press, 1981), chapter 8. Also, Krishna Ahooja-Patel makes the point that the mid-1970s marked an important historical conjunction, "when almost simultaneously women and the developing countries made new demands for restructuring economies and societies. Both the Declaration and the Plans of Action of the New International Economic Order and the Mexico Conference emphasized somewhat similar goals, the core of which was the urgent need to create new equitable relationships between the industrialised and the developing countries in international economic relationships and between men and women in internal relationships." Ahooja-Patel, "Women, Technology and Development," *Economic and Political Weekly* 14 (36) (1979), p. 1550.

[3]Ester Boserup's formulation of this process as a matter of class in *Women's Role in Economic Development* (New York: St. Martin's Press, 1970) has been critiqued by Lourdes Benería and Gita Sen in "Accumulation, Reproduction, and Women's Roles in Economic Development: Boserup Revisited," in Eleanor Leacock and Helen I. Safa, eds., *Women's Work: Development and the Divison of Labor by Gender* (South Hadley, MA: Bergin and Garvey, 1982), pp. 141–57, and in Sue Ellen Huntington, "Issues in Woman's Role in Economic Development: Critique and Alternatives," *Journal of Marriage and the Family* 37 (4) (1974), pp. 1001–12. Important comparative formulations include: June C. Nash and Helen I. Safa, eds., *Sex and Class in Latin America* (South Hadley, MA: Bergin and Garvey, 1985); Barbara Rogers, *The Domestication of Women: Discrimination in Developing Societies* (New York: St. Martin's Press, 1980); Mona Etienne and Eleanor Leacock, eds., *Women and Colonization* (New York: Praeger, 1980); Iftikhar Ahmed, ed., *Technology and Rural Women: Conceptual and Empirical Issues* (London: Allen & Unwin, 1985); Naomi Black and Ann Baker Cottrell, eds., *Women and World Change: Equity Issues in Development* (Beverly Hills: Sage, 1981); and Irene Tinker and Michele Bo Bramsen, eds., *Women and World*

Development (New York: American Association for the Advancement of Science [AAAS], 1976).

⁴See Gita Sen with Caren Grown, *Development, Crisis, and Alternative Visions: Third World Women's Perspectives* (Development Alternatives for Women for a New Era [DAWN]), (Stavanger, Norway: Verbum, 1985); Pamela M. d'Onofrio-Flores and Sheila M. Pfafflin, eds., *Scientific-Technological Change and the Role of Women in Development* (Boulder: Westview Press, 1982); Roslyn Dauber and Melinda L. Cain, eds., *Women and Technological Change in Developing Countries*, AAAS Selected Symposium 53 (Boulder: Westview Press, 1981); and June C. Nash and María Patricia Fernández-Kelly, eds., *Women, Men and the International Division of Labor* (Albany: State University of New York Press, 1983).

⁵See Maria Bergom-Larsson, "Women and Technology in the Industrialized Countries," in D'Onofrio-Flores and Pfafflin, *Scientific-Technological Change*, p. 35.

⁶See Elise Boulding, "Integration into What? Reflections on Development Planning for Women," in Dauber and Cain, *Women and Technological Change*, and Bergom-Larsson, "Women and Technology in the Industrialized Countries," pp. 29–75.

Much of this discussion stems from psychoanalytic claims that women engage in a gender-distinct form of maternal thinking. See Dorothy Dinnerstein, *The Mermaid and the Minotaur* (New York: Harper & Row, 1976); Nancy Chodorow, *The Reproduction of Mothering* (Berkeley: University of California Press, 1978); and Carol Gilligan, *In a Different Voice* (Cambridge, MA: Harvard University Press, 1982).

⁷See Carol MacCormack and Marilyn Strathern, eds., *Nature, Culture and Gender* (Cambridge, England: Cambridge University Press, 1980); and Sherry B. Ortner and Harriet Whitehead, eds., *Sexual Meanings: The Cultural Construction of Gender and Sexuality* (Cambridge, England: Cambridge University Press, 1981).

⁸See Jill K. Conway, "The Women's Peace Party and the First World War," Canadian Association for American Studies, in *War and Society in North America*, ed. J.L. Granatstein and R.D. Curr (Toronto: Thomas Nelson and Sons, 1971); and Jill K. Conway, "The First Generation of American Women Graduates" (Ph.D. diss., Harvard University, 1968).

⁹See Hilda Scott, *Working Your Way to the Bottom: The Feminization of Poverty* (Boston: Pandora Press, 1984), and Bergom-Larsson, "Women and Technology in the Industrialized Countries," pp. 141–57.

¹⁰See Irene Tinker, "New Technologies for Food-Related Activities: An Equity Strategy," and Marilyn Carr, "Technologies Appropriate for Women: Theory, Practice and Policy," both in Dauber and Cain, *Women and Technological Change*, pp. 51–88, 193–203.

¹¹See Iftikar Ahmed, ed., *Technology and Rural Women* (London: Allen & Unwin, 1985).

¹²See Tinker, "New Technologies for Food-Related Activities," p. 58.

¹³See Carr, "Technologies Appropriate for Women," p. 193; and also Marilyn Carr, *Blacksmith, Baker, Roofing-Sheetmaker* (London: Intermediate Technology Publications, 1984).

¹⁴See Jane Jaquette and Kathleen Staudt, "Women 'At Risk' Reproducers: Biology, Science, and Population in U.S. Foreign Policy," in *Women, Biology and Public Policy*, ed. Virginia Sapiro (Beverly Hills: Sage, 1985); Lourdes Benería and Gita

Sen, "Class and Gender Inequalities and Women's Role in Economic Development—Theoretical and Practical Implications," *Feminist Studies* 8 (1) (1982), pp. 157–76; Mayra Buvinić, "Women's Issues in Third World Poverty: A Policy Analysis," in Mayra Buvinić et al., eds., *Women and Poverty in the Third World* (Baltimore: Johns Hopkins University Press, 1983), pp. 14–31; Mayra Buvinić, "Projects for Women in the Third World: Explaining Their Misbehavior" (Washington, DC: International Center for Research on Women, 1984); and Judith Evans, with Robert G. Myers, "Improving Program Actions to Meet the Intersecting Needs of Women and Children in Developing Countries: A Policy and Program Review," ms. prepared for the Carnegie Foundation, New York, 1985.

[15]In "Projects for Women in the Third World," Buvinić provides an illuminating discussion of the practical consequences of this process in development projects directed to women. See also the wide-ranging discussion in Gita Sen, with Caren Grown, *Development, Crisis, and Alternative Visions: Third World Women's Perspectives* (DAWN) (Stavanger, Norway: Verbum, 1985).

[16]For instance, advanced electronics, important for decentralized data processing and media, have not been addressed as a possible next generation of technology for rural populations by those who take the appropriate-technology perspective.

[17]See Immanuel Wallerstein, *The Modern World System: Capitalist Agriculture & the Origins of the European World Economy in the 16th Century* (New York: Academic Press, 1974). For a summary of those interrelations, see Lourdes Benería and Gita Sen, "Accumulation, Reproduction and Women's Roles," p. 157.

[18]See Lourdes Benería and Martha Roldan, *The Crossroads of Class and Gender* (Chicago: University of Chicago Press, 1987); Heleieth Saffioti, *Women in Class Society* (New York: Monthly Review Press, 1969); Carmen Diana Deere and Magdalena León de Leal, *Women in Andean Agriculture* (Geneva: International Labor Organization [ILO], 1982). See also Kate Young, Carol Wolkowitz, and Roslyn McCullagh, eds., *Of Marriage and the Market: Women's Subordination in International Perspective* (London: CSE Books, 1981); Lourdes Benería, ed., *Women and Development: The Sexual Division of Labor in Rural Societies* (New York: Praeger, 1982); Annette Kuhn and Ann Marie Wolpe, eds., *Feminism and Maternalism* (London: Routledge & Kegan Paul, 1978); as well as the works by Leacock, Safa, Nash, and Etienne cited in endnote 3.

[19]In our paper "Women, Technology, and Education" (see endnote 1), we characterized the various schools of thought that have emerged around this issue. For one perspective see June C. Nash, "The Impact of the Changing International Division of Labor on Different Sectors of the Labor Force," in Nash and Fernández-Kelly, *Women, Men, and the International Division of Labor*, pp. 3–38; and María Patricia Fernández-Kelly, *For We Are Sold, I and My People: Women and Industry in Mexico's Frontier* (Albany: State University of New York Press, 1983); for another point of view see Linda Y.C. Lim, *Women Workers in Multinational Enterprises in Developing Countries* (Geneva: ILO, 1985), and Janet Salaff, *Working Daughters of Hong Kong: Filial Piety or Power in the Family?* (New York: Cambridge University Press, 1981).

[20]See Bina Agarwal, "Women and Technological Change in Agriculture: The Asian and African Experience," in Ahmed, *Technology and Rural Women*, pp. 67–114; Deborah A. Bryceson, *Women and Technology in Developing Countries: Technological Change and Women's Capabilities and Bargaining Positions* (Santo

Domingo: United Nations International Research and Training Institute for the Advancement of Women [UN/INSTRAW], 1985); Bourque and Warren, *Women of the Andes;* and Susan C. Bourque and Kay B. Warren, "Rural Women and Development Planning in Peru," in Naomi Black and Ann Cottrell, eds., *Women and World Change: Equity Issues in Development* (Beverly Hills: Sage, 1981).

[21]See the essays in the volume edited by Anne Briscoe and Sheila Pfafflin, *Expanding the Role of Women in the Sciences,* vol. 323 of *Annals of the New York Academy of Sciences* (1979); Shirley Malcom, "The Participation of Women in Policy and Decision-Making Regarding the Use and Development of Technology," in Malcom et al., eds., *Science, Technology and Women: A World Perspective* (Washington, DC: AAAS and Centre for Science and Technology for Development, United Nations, 1985), pp. 61–66; and Mary B. Anderson, "Technology Transfer: Implications for Women," in Catherine Overholt, et al., eds., *Gender Roles in Development Projects* (West Hartford, CT: Kumarian Press, 1985), pp. 57–78.

[22]This statement implies that we must (1) understand sexual hierarchy as a product of culturally created social ideologies and the material conditions of women's and men's lives and (2) appreciate that sexual divisions of learning and work are not immutable behavioral specializations to be justified as functional or as vestiges of early human evolution.

[23]See Bourque and Warren, *Women of the Andes,* and Evelyn Fox Keller, *Reflections on Gender and Science* (New Haven: Yale University Press, 1985).

[24]See the essays in the volume edited by Anne Briscoe and Sheila Pfafflin, *Expanding the Role of Women in the Sciences.*

[25]See Amartya Sen, *Women, Technology and Sexual Divisions* (Santo Domingo: UN/INSTRAW, 1985).

[26]See Rounaq Jahan, "Participation of Women Scientists and Engineers in Endogenous Research and Development," in Shirley Malcom, Hiroko Morita-Lou, Patricia Boulware, and Sandra Burns, eds., *Science, Technology and Women: A World Perspective* (Washington, DC: AAAS and Centre for Science and Technology for Development, United Nations, 1985), pp. 44–52.

[27]See Andrew Hacker, "Women and Work," *The New York Review of Books,* 14 August 1986, pp. 26–32.

[28]Even in Latin America, where there has been some improvement, a recent Comisión Económica para América Latina (CEPAL) study found that women continue to have higher rates of illiteracy and are less likely than men to complete primary school. This gender difference is greatest in the rural areas and most notable in Peru, Mexico, Paraguay, El Salvador, Guatemala, Bolivia, and Ecuador—all countries in which gender intersects with marked class and ethnic disparities.

[29]See Nelly Stromquist, "Empowering Women through Knowledge: Politics and Practices in International Cooperation in Basic Education" (ms. submitted to UNICEF, 1985).

[30]See Audrey Smock, *Women's Education in Developing Countries* (New York: Praeger, 1981).

Differential return on educational investment is found in both industrialized and developing countries. Even in nations with roughly comparable numbers of male and female undergraduates, rates of professional employment and achievement vary markedly. Professions in which women predominate, such as teaching and nursing, require substantial educational investments and yet are poorly paid.

Persistent patterns of occupational segregation lead to the seeming paradox that the difference between men's and women's wages increases at the higher levels of education.

[31]See Carolyn Elliot and Gail P. Kelly, "New Directions for Research," and Jeremy Finn, Janet Reis, and Loretta Dulberg, "Sex Differences in Educational Attainment: The Process," both in Carolyn Elliot and Gail P. Kelly, eds., *Women's Education in the Third World* (Albany: State University of New York Press, 1982), pp. 331–43, 107–26.

[32]See Fernández-Kelly, *For We Are Sold, I and My People,* and Salaff, *Working Daughters of Hong Kong.*

[33]For instance, multinationals in high-technology fields seek young women employees and may cause families to invest resources in daughters who need higher levels of education to qualify for assembly-line work. Thus, girls living along the border in Mexico have a much higher educational attainment than the national average. These girls, however, do not necessarily use their education on the job, where repetitive manual work is the norm and promotion is unlikely. Rather, multinationals see educational level as a way to adjust the size of labor pools to fit the demand and as a proxy for the ability of workers to successfully function in a disciplined environment. Therefore, when explaining increasing rates of female education, it is important to examine changing labor-force requirements, sexual divisions of labor, and the latent functions of education. See Fernández-Kelly, *For We Are Sold, I and My People,* and Nash and Fernández-Kelly, "The Impact of the Changing International Division of Labor on Different Sectors of the Labor Force," pp. 3–38.

[34]According to one report: "Research done in the late 1970s in developing countries found a surprisingly consistent positive effect of maternal education on infant and child mortality rates and on child nutritional status in all regions.... Although higher levels of maternal education are usually associated with both higher levels of paternal education and higher levels of household income, most research has found a positive effect of maternal education on child survival and health separate from its association with other socioeconomic variables." Joanne Leslie, Margaret Lycette, and Mayra Buvinić, "Weathering Economic Crises: The Crucial Role of Women in Health," paper prepared for the Second Takemi Symposium on International Health, Harvard University School of Public Health, 1986, p. 8.

[35]See Elliot and Kelly, "New Directions for Research," p. 342.

Carl N. Degler

On Rereading "The Woman in America"

M UCH INEVITABLY DATES A VOLUME like "The Woman in America," the Spring issue of *Dædalus* published almost a quarter of a century ago in 1964. Yet the essays it includes merit attention, for they represent the very beginning of the new history of women in America. The conference out of which the book emerged convened before the publication of Betty Friedan's *The Feminine Mystique*,[1] arguably the catalyst of what would become "the gender revolution." So it is not surprising that some of the essayists referred to "girls" and "spokesmen" and described black families as being "matriarchal" when today they would automatically write "women" and "spokesperson" and avoid characterizations that isolate one group from another. If such early usages seem dated, it is worth recalling that the *New York Times* accepted "Ms." as a title for women only in 1986.

The 1964 *Dædalus* issue was far ahead of its time in that its authors confronted a number of issues that are still central to the question of woman's place in America. Undoubtedly the most discussed in the volume, and today still the most persistent, is how a woman could combine career or job with marriage and family. When the conference met, the Civil Rights Act of 1964 was barely out of the legislative hopper, yet the question of equality of job opportunity was

Carl N. Degler, born in 1921 in Orange, New Jersey, is Margaret Byrne Professor of American History at Stanford University. His principal books include Place Over Time: The Continuity of Southern Distinctiveness *(1977),* At Odds: Women and the Family from the Revolution to the Present *(1980), and* Out of Our Past *(3rd edition, 1984). Professor Degler is currently writing a book on the role of biological ideas in social science from 1890 to the present.*

199

pressed not only by Esther Peterson in her essay "Working Women" but also by Alice Rossi in her strongly feminist piece "Equality Between the Sexes: An Immodest Proposal." Rossi's essay would now probably be described as a moderate call for women's rights; at the time it was hailed by some and greeted with head shaking by many others.

On the whole, though, the 1964 issue did not emphasize the social roles or activities of women so much as their identity. As psychologist Robert J. Lifton, the editor of the expanded, hardcover edition published by Houghton Mifflin in 1965, observed in his introduction, five questions shaped the essays: "What in woman may be said to be enduring, and what is subject to social and historical modification? To what extent is woman's psychological life determined by her anatomy and biology, and to what extent can we speak of a specific feminine psychology? What opportunities does American society hold out to its women, and are these appropriate to their needs? What are the special problems and potentials of highly educated women? Are there ways in which women can make special contributions toward the particularly grave dilemmas which now confront the world?"

In their essays in that edition, David McClelland, Erik Erikson, and David Riesman referred not only to psychological and biological differences between men and women but also to "boundaries" between the sexes, a term that comes close to the vocabulary and concepts of Carol Gilligan and other recent writers on female identity and character. Gilligan, for example, in her book *In a Different Voice*, writes of the "hard" boundaries of men and the "permeable" boundaries of women,[2] concepts that both Erikson and McClelland adumbrated. But neither Gilligan nor others like her, who have recently identified differences in the psychological makeup of men and women, have followed Erikson and McClelland in ascribing the roots of those differences to divergences in the biological makeup of the two sexes. Today, socialization theory dominates. Thus, when Alice Rossi, in a famous article in *Dædalus* in 1977—"A Biosocial Perspective on Parenting"—partly repudiated some of the socialization arguments in her 1964 article by identifying biological sources for women's parenting behavior,[3] most of her sister feminists would have none of it. Socialization, they contended, could explain everything that Rossi ascribed to biology; there was no need to look to biological sources of behavior.

The work of Carol Gilligan and others, however, suggests that the search for a peculiarly female influence in society is still with us, as it was in the 1964 essay on Jane Addams by Jill Conway, who wondered what the "feminine" contribution to the making of the social order was. The need, if you will, for identifying a peculiarly female influence is also reflected in some of the more recent literature on woman's character that stresses the peaceful nature of women in contrast to the aggressive and combative nature of men. The spread of sociobiological ideas among social scientists, especially anthropologists, has also intensified the search for a female identity. At the same time, the search for sociobiological bases for differences between men and women has driven some feminist writers to press for a virtual denial of any identifiable biological basis for female (or human) behavior. The debate, in short, goes on.

That it does suggests another novel development: the explosion in scholarship by and about women. Before 1960 the scholarly literature on women in history, for example, was largely biographical, depicting the lives of important and sometimes fairly obscure women. Only an occasional woman historian, such as Mary Beard, Eileen Power, or Eleanor Flexner, wrote about women as a social group. Since then, however, scholars in a variety of fields in the humanities and social sciences have been turning out studies about women, many of which are reshaping the fields or moving them in new directions. No longer can the American Revolution or the growth and organization of the industrial labor force, for example, be discussed without including the part taken by women. Even the history of the American frontier, once a male arena according to Frederick Jackson Turner, now includes references to women, whose lives, we have learned, bore little similarity to those of men. One measure of the impact scholarship on women has had on history is that men as well as women are engaged in the quest for how women have shaped the past.

The new scholarship on women has been nowhere so influential as in literature. Women as literary figures have been freshly and forthrightly reexamined, while some long-forgotten writers—like the "female scribblers" of Hawthorne's day—have been placed in new and highly informative perspectives.

In the social sciences, scholarship on women has proliferated. In anthropology, for example, new questions are being asked of old research, particularly in regard to male-female relations, child rearing, and familial life. In psychology and sociology, the old, almost abandoned field of sexual differences has revived with the outpouring of scholarship on women by both women and men, research that is frequently catalyzed and informed by the women's movement. Political science and the law have begun to respond with studies that explore women's impact on political behavior and reshape the conceptualizations at the foundation of jurisprudence. Even natural science, often thought to be outside or beyond ideology, has not escaped reassessment from the standpoint of women. Women scientists and historians of science have adroitly exposed its masculine origins and assumptions.

None of the 1964 essayists in "The Woman in America" anticipated the role that ideology would play in stimulating scholarship about women or in altering their position in society during the next quarter of a century. Of no essay was this underestimation truer than my own, which I heedlessly entitled "Revolution Without Ideology: The Changing Place of Women in America." The concluding point of my historical survey was that the dramatic changes in women's public place described in the essay had come about without any coherent ideology or social theory to guide them.

The history of American women since then, it now seems clear to me, is a radically different story. Ideology has actually stood at the heart of the changes that have transformed women's place since 1964. Equal rights has been the ideological principle, a concept picked up from the broadly influential black revolution of the times, which in 1964 was just mustering strength. The idea is, of course, old and peculiarly American, yet the history of the last two decades suggests that equal rights may no longer be adequate for maximizing equality for women.

The ideology of equal rights worked its influence primarily through the law, an agency of change that, again, was not anticipated in the 1964 essays. In that very year, though, the law entered the national discussion on women's rights with the almost accidental inclusion of the word *sex* in the 1964 Civil Rights Act, which had originally been formulated to outlaw racial discrimination alone. The use of the law to enhance women's equality continued with the concept of affirmative action and reached its culmination in the campaign to ratify the Equal Rights Amendment.

No one writing in the 1964 issue of *Dædalus* foresaw that the Equal Rights Amendment would revive the feminist movement. After all, the ERA had been around ever since 1923, and few women leaders in the mid-sixties were prepared to press it upon legislators or the public. (In her 1964 essay, Alice Rossi did just that, but her advocacy accurately measured the essay's "radicalism" at the time.) The Women's Bureau and the Department of Labor did not endorse the ERA until the early 1970s, principally because its ratification would render illegal the so-called protective legislation on behalf of working women that had been enacted in the states in the course of the preceding seventy-five years. That legislation had regulated wages, hours, and conditions of labor for women and was considered a major achievement of women's rights activists. But if the principle of equal rights was to be the legal and ideological basis of woman's equality, then such legislation would have to be abandoned since men were not included within its protections. And though in the end the Equal Rights Amendment was not ratified, its principle nevertheless prevailed through the Civil Rights Act and through the courts' application to women of an equal rights interpretation of the Fourteenth Amendment.

The legal application of an ideology of equal rights to women's status went far beyond the elimination of protective legislation for women. Occupations that had never been open to women before were now unlocked—police work, firefighting, coal mining, and that most masculine of activities, training for war. Thanks to the across-the-board application of the principle, women not only serve in all branches of the armed services, but they are admitted into the regular courses at West Point, Annapolis, and the Air Force Academy. Only Canada matches that degree of acceptance for women.

At the same time, a problem that Esther Peterson addressed in her 1964 article has barely been affected by the equal rights principle: the difference in average pay for women and for men. The validity of the various explanations that have been offered for this difference, which exceeds 35 percent, need not be examined here. The relevant point is that the persistent disparity between women's and men's average

compensation has sparked a novel legal concept to deal with it—
"comparable pay for comparable work," or for short, "comparable
worth." One explanation frequently offered to justify the relatively
lower wages of women is that women tend to be disproportionately
employed in low-wage industries. The concept of comparable worth
was developed to refute this justification for women's lower wages
and to provide a way of eliminating the disparity.

The essential argument behind comparable worth is that the low
wages in industries in which women workers are concentrated result
not from market forces, as the justification contends, but from a
general unwillingness to pay women workers what they are worth.
Worth is measured by the amount or degree of responsibility,
training, and skills required for a given job. The worth of a woman's
job can then be compared with that of a man's job of similar kind. If
the man's job brings a higher wage, then that is the equitable wage for
the woman's job. The principle was expected to be applied and
enforced in a court of law if employers did not comply, but it has also
been put into practice through collective bargaining.

To date, the principle has not had major impact and is unlikely to
be a source of large economic change since its implementation on a
broad scale would put the courts in the position of shaping the
national labor market. Yet it is worth noting that the concept of
comparable worth bears some similarity to the idea behind protective
legislation. In both cases the law is meant to do for women what they
cannot do for themselves as individuals. According to the advocates
of protective legislation, men improved their working conditions
through unions and collective bargaining, but women were not generally admitted to unions or did not join them, and so they needed
protection through law.

From the standpoint of ideology, comparable worth can fit into the
American principle of equal rights, just as affirmative action can.
Both are assumed to be temporary devices to overcome the unspec-
ified, if long-standing, denial of equality of opportunity to women.
But since both define that denial in general, unspecific terms, the
remedy is similarly general rather than individual.

At the same time, neither principle assumes that women differ in
any socially significant way from men. The assumption is that in time
the discrimination the law seeks to eliminate will disappear and so
will the need for a general protection of women through law. That

assumption, of course, separates affirmative action and comparable worth from protective legislation, which frankly defined women as people in need of legal protection because they are different from men. In short, the principle of equal rights remains at the center of the gender revolution even if the principle in the cases of affirmative action and comparable worth has been pushed hard against its philosophical limits.

The reason the equal rights principle is pressed to its limits is that men and women do of course differ in an important way: only women bear children. Today the typical working woman is married and likely to become a mother. Most children are reared by their mother. In that situation the protection of her job and the provision of financial support during maternity are of broad social importance. Neither in the 1964 issue of *Dædalus* nor more recently has the United States shown much interest in addressing the matter. In most European countries pregnant working women enjoy not only jobs guaranteed upon their return to work after childbirth but also financial support for twenty to thirty-five weeks. These benefits are provided in countries as different from the United States as Spain and Italy and as advanced as Sweden and the Federal Republic of Germany. No more than two-fifths of working women in the United States have any legal right to maternity leave at all, and none of those fortunate enough to have a claim for such leave receives any financial support during the time taken.

Interestingly enough, even when the question of maternity leave has been legislatively acted on, as in California, the ideology of equal rights has proved to be at best ambiguous and at worst divisive. The divisiveness was especially evident in a court case from 1986. A working woman invoked a California statute guaranteeing a woman the right to return to her job after pregnancy. A number of women feminists joined with the woman's employer to challenge the constitutionality of the law on the ground that it violated the equal rights principle since it granted the guarantee to mothers only. Other women feminists supported the law. As the case turned out, the court upheld the validity of the law.

The persistent interest in using equal rights as the legal and constitutional means for advancing women's equality is also apparent in the current effort in Congress to address the question of maternity leaves on the national level. Congress is expected soon to take up a bill that provides for leave for either parent after childbirth. Although the measure falls far short of the range of benefits commonly provided for working mothers in European countries, it has already aroused opposition. Much of the opposition stems from employer groups who dislike the added cost involved and the difficulty entailed in replacing the absent worker. Whether including fathers in the benefits of the bill will be an additional basis for opposition is not yet clear, but since recent surveys indicate that most husbands are reluctant to share child care and house maintenance, opposition on that ground is also likely.

Unlike the women's movement in Europe, the American movement has been slow to address this interest of working-class women. Maternity leaves, unlike abortion, touch the great majority of women who work, especially now that most women no longer interrupt their careers or abandon their jobs by dropping out of the work force when they begin families. The "M curve," which has graphically depicted women's changing participation in the labor force over the female life cycle, has virtually disappeared. Under the circumstances the next step in the equalization of women's opportunities in the United States would seem to be to follow the European policy of support for maternity—at least six months' leave with pay and a guaranteed return to the job.

If it became necessary for practical reasons to follow the European example of confining the benefits to mothers, that would constitute only a short step beyond affirmative action and comparable worth and be entirely consonant with the theory behind protective legislation. This time around, however, the law would not restrict women's opportunities in the way that much early twentieth-century protective legislation did. Its philosophical or constitutional basis would be that equality is not the same as identity. Since all recognize that in some respects women differ from men, what constitutes equality for one may not translate into equality for the other. Moreover, maternity leaves would bring together people of all classes in a cause of significance to all women. The women's movement has been almost entirely middle-class, though its participants want to make connections with working-class women and give them support. Of the four great historical causes of organized women—women's suffrage, temperance, peace, and the Equal Rights Amendment—none has engaged the interest or support of working-class women; maternity leaves on the European pattern certainly would.

Black women in particular would gain from a shift away from exclusive reliance on the principle of equal rights. The situation of black women, together with the class divisions among women in general, went unmentioned in the 1964 volume. Today, black women are almost equally invisible in the organized women's movement, though the single-parent family headed by a mother is among blacks a major social and individual concern. Mother-headed families of all races now constitute 25 percent of U.S. households; among blacks the incidence of such families is double that proportion. Most of these families exist below the poverty line, regardless of their race. The equal rights approach offers no avenue for improvement, though in the recent past it certainly helped many black women get jobs that were once beyond their aspirations. Policy solutions targeted at women who are heads of households are clearly necessary even though inevitably costly.

While no one would deny that the principle of individual rights has done much to open up occupations to women of all classes, it is perhaps time to recognize that certain aspects of women's needs cannot be met through the traditional route of equal rights. In a way, this brings us back to the 1964 essays, a number of which sought a special identity for women. Despite the gender revolution of the 1970s, women still seem to relate to the family in ways that men do not. Betty Friedan has been one of the few leaders of the modern women's movement who have talked about the need to recognize a continuing connection between women and the family. To see the importance of that relation does not mean that women should allow the family to envelop their lives. All that it implies is that if the central question for women is how to reconcile public freedom with private freedom—that is, how to make available the same opportunity for work and family that men have—then the family can no more be ignored in thinking about how to achieve equality for women than can the opportunities for work outside the family. They are two halves of the same problem.

At no time has the special relevance of the family for women been more evident than in the national debate over ratification of the Equal Rights Amendment. Although there are a number of explanations for its ultimate defeat, the fear that ratification of the amendment would somehow threaten the traditional family and the woman's role in it was surely an important one. It is true that many of the egalitarian changes the amendment was intended to bring about had already been accomplished, thanks to decisions of the Supreme Court, executive orders from the president, the Civil Rights Act of 1964, and other legislation. Consequently, by the time the amendment came before the last few states for ratification, a plausible argument could be made that the amendment was no longer as necessary as was once thought. Nonetheless, it is at once strange and revealing that in the very midst of a gender revolution based on equal rights, the capstone could not be placed upon it.

Recent studies by women historians on the defeat of the ERA have pointed out that many women found the proposed amendment, rightly or wrongly, a threat to their familial relations and status. Mary Berry, for example, pointed out in her book on the defeat of the ERA[4] that opponents of the amendment had the support of professionals like Phyllis Schlafly, who nevertheless "managed to remain identified as grassroots housewives and homemakers unmotivated by any broad political purpose. When the first twenty-two states ratified quickly, no debate had taken place or was considered necessary. But as soon as Schlafly and her supporters took the offensive," Berry observed, "ERA backers, unprepared for the onslaught, found themselves having to explain not only to legislators, but to women, why they were trying to undermine women."

The debates, Berry continued, revealed "the essential vulnerability some women felt about their social situation." Many women believed that under the current rules men were constrained to protect women. "Moving to something called equality," Berry concluded, "seemed too threatening to that vulnerability. . . . Better to remain with the known, which at least was clear and understood. Women's rights proponents, in this sense, could be seen as doing women wrong by shattering female solidarity, putting all women at risk."

A similar fear for the traditional familial relation appeared in Elizabeth Pleck's analysis of the defeat of the ERA:[5]

For women against ERA, the amendment became a symbol of secular and sexual change threatening to undermine the traditional family by challenging laws requiring husbands to support the family and giving to women a favored position in divorce settlements. . . . The women's movement, after all, had insisted that the personal is political. The female opponents of the ERA agreed and perceived the amendment as a symbol of changes in women's lives and in sexuality to which they were opposed. These changes represented a threat to their religious beliefs and their views about the proper role of women. The actual change in the constitution, which the ERA would have wrought, became lost in the rhetoric in which the ERA figured as a symbol of undesired social change.

The 1964 issue of *Dædalus* had no references to the so-called sexual revolution, which was then just beginning. That transformation reopened old questions about the nature of women's sexuality and in the process changed women's relations with men inside and outside marriage. In asserting a right to sexual expression and satisfaction, something only a few women—radicals like Victoria Woodhull, Margaret Sanger, and Emma Goldman—had demanded before, the sexual revolution gave fresh support to the view that a woman's body is hers to control. On that principle, expressed as a woman's right to privacy, the Supreme Court in *Roe v. Wade* in 1973 overturned all the nineteenth-century state statutes outlawing or regulating abortion. And though the decision itself and the practices that followed from it aroused intense opposition for a while, the failure of several political efforts to reverse the decision makes it clear that abortion will remain an option for women.

One reason for believing that the change in the public's attitude toward abortion marks a permanent turning point in the expansion of women's rights is that the same alteration has been apparent in a number of other countries, some of which are largely Catholic in religion and historically opposed to public acceptance of abortion. That development in other countries suggests one further difference from the scene in 1964: an upsurge in women's self-consciousness on an international scale. In contrast with 1964, virtually no modern industrial society today is without a women's movement of some significance; in none are women untouched by a new sense of social involvement. While men still dominate the social, economic, and political scene in every modern society, including the United States, some advanced countries and some not so advanced have elected women as heads of government. In this country women fill political and economic roles that were wholly unanticipated twenty-five years ago. The revolution that the ideology of the women's movement has sparked certainly moved well beyond anything that social critics of the early 1960s could have brought about without that ideology. Yet fulfilling the quest for women's equality now may well require moving beyond the traditional definition of equal rights and recognizing that women have needs that men do not.

ENDNOTES

[1]Betty Friedan, *The Feminine Mystique* (New York: Norton, 1963).
[2]Carol Gilligan, *In a Different Voice: Psychological Theory and Women's Development* (Cambridge, MA: Harvard University Press, 1982).
[3]Alice S. Rossi, "A Biosocial Perspective on Parenting," *Daedalus* 106 (2) (1977), p. 1.
[4]Mary Frances Berry, *Why ERA Failed* (Bloomington: Indiana University Press, 1986).
[5]Elizabeth Pleck, "Failed Strategies; Renewed Hope," in Joan Hoff-Wilson, ed., *Rights of Passage; The Past and Future of the ERA* (Bloomington: Indiana University Press, 1986).